THE WELCOME TO COUNTRY HANDBOOK

A Guide to Indigenous Australia

Marcia Langton

Cover artwork by Betty Kuntiwa Pumani, born 1963
Pitjantjatjara people, Anangu Pitjantjatjara Yankunytjatjara Lands,
South Australia
Antara, 2021
Synthetic polymer paint on linen, 200x250cm
Image courtesy the artists, Mimili Maku Arts and Alcaston Gallery.

Aboriginal and Torres Strait Islander people are advised that this book contains the names and images of deceased people. Hardie Grant apologises for any distress this may inadvertently cause.

Hardie Grant
EXPLORE

Contents

Introduction   *1*

1. Pre-colonial history   7
2. Becoming Australia   23
3. On Survival   31
4. A Rightful Place   36
5. Cultural Diversity and Resilience   54
6. Language and Country   65
7. Kinship and Country   77
8. Knowledge   84
9. Art   110
10. Performance   133
11. Storytelling   151
12. Native title   175
13. The Stolen Generations   189
14. Business and Tourism   201
15. Cultural Awareness for Visitors   216
16. Undoing Racist Australia   227
17. Looking to the Future for Indigenous Australia   245

Conclusion   *256*
Glossary   *259*
Endnotes   *269*
Index   *278*
About the Author   *286*

Introduction

Australia is alive with the long history of the First Peoples, our culture and our presence. Nowhere else in the world can you see and experience the oldest living cultures of humankind. This guide to experiencing Aboriginal and Torres Strait Islander places, tourism adventures, art centres and galleries, guided walks and cultural events will help local and international travellers to find their way through our beautiful lands and waters and make a cultural connection with the people who know it best.

There are two distinctive First Peoples cultural groupings in Australia: Aboriginal Peoples on the mainland and most islands; and the Torres Strait Islanders, whose homelands are in the Torres Strait between the northern tip of Queensland and Papua New Guinea. People are believed to have settled on these islands about 20,000 years ago. Aboriginal Peoples have been living on the mainland for at least 65,000 years; archaeologists have uncovered evidence of people living in Arnhem Land in the Northern Territory 65,000 years ago, with ongoing research in other parts of Australia indicating even longer periods.

The footprint of the First Peoples can be found across the Australian continent and its islands, but it is often invisible until it is pointed out. Once you see the evidence of Aboriginal life, a whole new world opens up. You begin to see the country around you differently. Keen to share their cultural riches, hundreds of Aboriginal people have found ways to invite tourists into their lives, even briefly, to enjoy the experience of being in Aboriginal Country with the people who know it best: the Traditional Owners. With a deep knowledge of the natural world, they are the ideal guides to show you the extraordinary range of environments countrywide.

The opportunity for Indigenous Australians to share their experiences and knowledge with tourists opened up when land rights were recognised and Indigenous people became joint managers of large swathes of our Country. Now there are visitors' centres, art and cultural centres, museums and festivals in even the most remote places, showcasing the fascinating

Culture is celebrated with dance and traditional body paint at Laura Dance Festival on Awu-Laya Country where the Quinkan rock-art galleries are located (photo Wayne Quilliam)

history and cultures of Indigenous societies.

When you are travelling around Indigenous Australia, you will find yourself in extraordinary situations with extraordinary people, whether you are exploring by foot, vehicle, boat, horse or camel; in semi-arid areas such as the Central Desert or the Western Desert; savannah country across north Australia with its many dramatic rock outcrops, escarpments and gorges; or the wet rainforests where fast flowing rivers cascade over mountain ranges; the temperate-zone coastal and riverine plains; the forests; the Great Dividing Range in its many forms; on the beaches, islands and reefs; and in the cities and towns.

Across the continent, Indigenous people have established cultural and natural tourism businesses and opened their Country for tourists with great energy, determination and a love of sharing the beauty of their culture and heritage. Also, the benefits of tourism to local Indigenous people are many. In large parts of Indigenous Australia, where there are few other economic opportunities, tourism businesses are a pathway for local families to enjoy the benefits of their unparalleled ancestral heritage.

With their own tourism projects, local people have the opportunity to work on their Country with their family. They can also teach their own young people, as well as tourists, about their culture, history and heritage because Indigenous tourism preserves traditional knowledge and involves the younger generations in its continuation. There are surprises, too, for even the most knowledgeable Traditional Owner. While visiting remote parts of their old estates, where threatened populations were protected from introduced predators and land clearance, Traditional Owners have discovered new species of flora and fauna, and surviving pockets of species thought to be extinct.

The Indigenous domain was reduced to segregated reserves during and after colonisation and the spread of British, Irish, European and other settlers with their land clearing for farming and grazing across the continent. The growth of Indigenous rights over the last fifty years, bolstered by the Mabo ruling by the High Court in 1991 – which rejected the concept of terra nullius wherein the settlers considered the continent an empty land without prior owners – has resulted in the return of land areas to some Traditional Owners and resumption of the Indigenous traditions of management. Free once again to steward the land, they are protecting the biodiversity of Country with a range of strategies. Tourism is one: often it is the Aboriginal rangers who take on the task of conserving the environment as well as working as guides for visitors.

Over the last century, Aboriginal and Torres Strait Islander people, like other Australians, have been attracted to the cities and towns from rural

Sharing of knowledge through cultural dance at Laura Dance Festival, Queensland (photo Wayne Quilliam)

and remote areas. Today, most live in towns and cities. The remainder mainly live in small towns and Aboriginal settlements and communities scattered across the country. Even in the largest cities, Indigenous people have retained their traditional ownership customs and established tourism ventures to guide visitors across their land and waters, and to understand their culture and history.

The best way to see the Sydney Harbour, for example, is aboard the *Mari Nawi*, or Big Canoe, operated by Tribal Warrior Cultural Cruises. The cruise is hosted by local Traditional Owners who tell the stories of the Gadigal, Guringai, Wangal, Gammeraigal and Wallumedegal Peoples of the area as you tour Sydney Harbour. They take visitors ashore at Be-lang-le-wool (Clark Island) to show you their coastal way of life, traditional fishing methods, food gathering techniques, and a cultural performance.

In Melbourne, the Koorie Heritage Trust offers walking tours of the Birrarung Marr (River of Mists / Yarra River) and other sites of cultural significance at Federation Square and in the Melbourne CBD for schools, organisations and the public. I also recommend a walking tour of the city with Wemba Wemba-Wergaia man Dean Stewart and his people, who point out the Aboriginal places that remain despite the growth of this city, and explain their history, names and meanings. Dean's knowledge of Aboriginal Melbourne is encyclopaedic, based in both Aboriginal oral history and the records of the colony and the city. The most popular walks are the Aboriginal Yarra River tour: Walkin' Country, Walkin' Birrarung and Ngargee to Nerm: from Ancient Tree to Ancient Sea cultural tour, which goes from a 600-year-old river red gum in St Kilda to the Albert Park grasslands. Dean has guided thousands of students from high school to university level, as well as tourists, around Aboriginal Melbourne and is a regular contributor to classes at the University of Melbourne.

Many Australians believe that the only 'real' Aboriginal people live in the remote deserts. This is a view based on two centuries of racist ideas that were wrong and should have no place in modern Australia. The official population of Aboriginal and Torres Strait Islander people is approaching one million and is growing at a faster than expected rate (see Appendix E in the colour insert).[1] The Aboriginal and Torres Strait Islander Peoples want their stories, cultures and history to be understood by all Australians, as well as visitors from overseas, and to be respected. When we see visitors learn about and show respect towards our cultures, histories and arts, a connection is made. This is empowering for our young people.

By building the self-esteem of younger generations of Aboriginal and Torres Strait Islander people through culture, they understand how to survive the racism and discrimination – and importantly refuse to accept the ugly stereotypes – instead finding their identities, self-worth and futures in our cultural traditions.

We want an understanding of our peoples based in facts, not myths, and to enjoy all the opportunities on offer to other Australians. Offering the experience of visiting our lands, our Countries and sharing our cultures with visitors is one way of overcoming the many misperceptions about us. Learning about the world's oldest continuous living cultures will help all who come to respect our Country and to learn about our achievements.

Aboriginal and Torres Strait Islander Peoples maintain knowledge traditions with their own philosophies and epistemologies that originated in ancient Australia, tens of thousands of years ago. Many of these knowledge traditions continue today. They have been transmitted from generation to generation by knowledgeable people and taught throughout each person's lifetime through experience living on Country, learning about the world, the sacred origins of people and traditional estates, responsibilities for management of the environment, fauna, flora and to the people of the land, and providing for the material needs of their families. The First Australians conveyed understandings of human nature and the natural world, environmental practices and traditions, medicine and healing, and much more, through their teaching systems and practices, sacred narratives, such as song series or songlines, visual designs, rituals and ceremonies, storytelling and in knowledge used regularly in rich but subtle economic lifeways.[2] These lifeways are both highly localised and also spread regionally according to customs.

Pamagirri Dancers perform at Rainforestation Nature Park, Kuranda, Queensland

For over 200 years, Indigenous Australians have hosted and guided scientists and scientific expeditions seeking to understand the environments, flora, fauna and climate of this continent, as well as the cultures of the First Peoples themselves. While this has resulted in a vast literature on Australian life, until recently much was only read by the experts. A growing number of writers, both Indigenous and other Australians, are now publishing more accessible books to show the wonders of this rich heritage to the world, drawing on the literature, films, audio-visual materials and, increasingly, digital objects about Aboriginal and Torres Strait Islander Peoples. My aim is to introduce you to some of this material so that you will have a well-founded grasp of the important issues for Aboriginal and Torres Strait Islander Peoples and our determination to succeed in keeping our cultures alive and sharing the histories of what happened in Australia in the past.

Our greatest success has been to preserve languages, Indigenous knowledge and land management traditions, and artistic, musical and performance traditions by insisting that we have a right to do so. Now, there is much to share, whereas once, few Australians had access to our Country, our cultures and our own reckoning with history. Most important of all, as we face the challenges of climate change and biodiversity loss, learning how to respect Country and to keep our flora, fauna and other species flourishing is best learnt from the stewards of the places you will be introduced to here. They are the descendants of the first people to come here at least sixty-five millennia ago. The Aboriginal history of continuous occupation of this continent represents a fifth of the total duration of human history and the evidence of this should be regarded as a world cultural and scientific treasure. As I will explain, scientists, ecologists and historians are increasingly recognising this and adding to our knowledge. As researchers and scientists come to terms with these impacts, they have been forced to ask the question, *What do Aboriginal and Torres Strait Islander Peoples know about the places they have inhabited for very long periods and the life forms that they have co-habited with during this unimaginably long period of time?*

The changes to our environments that colonisation, expanding populations and urbanisation have caused cannot be sustained without further extinctions of species and loss of environments and their ability to sustain us. Learning how Aboriginal and Torres Strait Islander people created and managed our environments and biodiversity will inspire you to better care for the natural world we inherited from the ancients and preserve it for the future generations of humanity.

1
Pre-colonial history

Why should we learn about the history of human life and the environment in this country in the time before the British arrived? Because most of the human history on this continent is that of the First Peoples, who lived here for tens of thousands of years. Their descendants – the Aboriginal and Torres Strait Islander Peoples – continue to follow and respect the ancient traditions and customs that make this country unique. It is likely that these are the oldest continuous living cultures surviving anywhere on the planet.

If we only based the history of Australia on what is known about the way people have lived here since the arrival of the First Fleet in 1788, then we would overlook an estimated 65,000 years of human life. Sharing Indigenous knowledge with people beyond the families, clans and language groups that inherited it has given all Australians a rich picture of life in this country before colonisation. It is a very different perspective from the ugly view of Aboriginal and Torres Strait Islander Peoples as 'primitive', 'backward' and 'unchanging' that I was taught in school.

Thanks to many important discoveries, such as those by Chris Clarkson, Associate Professor, and his fellow archaeologists, we know that human history began many thousands of years before the First Fleet landed. This continent 'is the end point of early modern human migration out of Africa and sets the minimum age for the global dispersal of humans', they wrote in *The Conversation*, 20 July 2017. 'This event was remarkable on many fronts, as it represented the largest maritime migration yet undertaken and the settlement of the driest continent on Earth and required adaptation to vastly different flora and fauna.' We should wonder if they were the first seafarers to cross oceans and seas. It must be the case.

Small populations arrived at different times, and their physical attributes were not the same. The historians who studied the small people in the Lake Mungo burials, dated at 35,000 years ago, and the skeletons with large bones discovered at Kow Swamp, in northern Victoria, have documented

This rock art depicts Gwions, described by Wunambal Gaambera Traditional Owner Sylvester Mangolamara: '... Gwion all look different and they dress themselves different for different corroboree and have different job to do like look after trees or special country.' (photo Wunambal Gaambera Aboriginal Corporation/Western Australian Museum)

these physical differences. This diversity is still seen in the many Aboriginal populations across Australia today.

Some archaeologists believe that humans arrived in seagoing vessels on the northern shores of the continent. From there they moved along the coastlines and reached the southern shores about 35,000 years ago. Michael I. Bird from James Cook University and his colleagues wrote an article in 2016 about 'Humans, water, and the colonisation of Australia'. They used satellite imagery and their knowledge of prehistoric waterscapes to show that the migration route most likely followed the 'well-watered routes from northern Australia, through the eastern semiarid and arid zone, to south-eastern Australia and into the rocky arid centre of the continent'.

Given that humans arrived here before the last Ice Age, this was the southernmost human population on the globe. This fascinating history of people living in the world's driest inhabited continent demonstrates great ingenuity.

Modern knowledge about the precolonial history and archaeology of regions around Australia has grown in the last decade. This is partly because of advances in methods and techniques such as radiocarbon and thermoluminescence dating.

In February 2021, scientists announced in *Nature Human Behaviour* that they had dated a 2-metre-long red-ochre painting of a kangaroo on the ceiling of a rock shelter in the Kimberley region of Western Australia at 17,300 years old, the oldest known rock-art date. A new method was used: radiocarbon-dating of ancient mud wasp nests.[3] Scientists have grasped the relevance of the antiquity of Aboriginal culture and have increasingly been bringing their new research findings to the public to great acclaim.

Industry and government have not, however, valued this magnificent cultural heritage. There is a pattern of destruction of sacred sites and important places throughout Australia, first by agriculture, then by mining and other settlements. Even though the rights of Traditional Owners and the importance of Country is now recognised, destruction still occurs.

On Sunday 24 May 2020, at the beginning of Reconciliation Week, under orders at mining giant Rio Tinto's Brockman 4 mining lease in the Pilbara, Western Australia, a blast and drill team destroyed the Juukan Gorge caves, sacred places to the Puutu Kunti Kurrama and Pinikura Peoples. The blast removed the last remaining evidence of the oldest site of continuous human occupation on the continent and possibly in the world; the caves were estimated to have provided shelter for their ancestors for an uninterrupted period of 46,000 years.

The Traditional Owners had settled an Indigenous Land Use Agreement under the *Native Title Act* in 2012 agreeing to the terms and conditions

Traditional dwellings at Budj Bim, Victoria (photo Wayne Quilliam)

of mining on their land with their newly won native title rights. Their intention was that the agreement also include mine exclusion zones for the protection of significant sites, as well as waterholes and ecologically sensitive areas, due to the fundamental religious significance of these places to the Traditional Owners. This expectation was not respected.

The destruction of their caves, and with them the loss of places of religious significance, is a tragedy for the relevant Aboriginal people, for whom these places constitute a part of their identity and a central place in their social fabric. Their loss is a particular travesty because they held significant evidence for further understanding of deep human history and evidence of the astonishing antiquity of human occupation of this continent. The laws to protect such places had failed in this and thousands of other cases of destruction of sacred places. A federal parliamentary inquiry was established to investigate this particular case and tabled an interim report entitled *Never Again*.[4]

Archaeological methods used to explore the past of the First Peoples include historical studies and field studies. These studies can use landscape surveys, excavation, identification of human tools, materials and food waste, as well as weighing, categorising and analysing materials found in trenches dug by the archaeologists.

Prehistorians and archaeologists also work with local Aboriginal groups to locate the sites where their ancestors lived. Together, they interpret the rock art, and they discover facts about daily life thousands of years ago. For example, it was discovered that grooves in some rock surfaces were made by women grinding seed to make flour for bread. Archaeologists and Traditional Owners see the vast array of archaeological finds – wood, stone and bone tools, implements and objects – as evidence of a very different way of life before the impact of colonisation. Through gathering this knowledge, they are changing the conventional – and often mistaken, unfounded and biased – history of Aboriginal people that has been taught for generations in universities and schools.

The ancient peoples left traces of their lives on the rock faces and in the land everywhere they went. Perhaps their greatest legacy is found in the country's vegetation patterns and in their management of the land. Bill Gammage, a historian and adjunct professor in the Humanities Research Centre at the Australian National University, writes about this in his book *The Biggest Estate on Earth: How Aborigines Made Australia*, and the country before the British colonisers arrived.

Gammage read hundreds of historical records, examined decades of scientific research and studied paintings to write this extraordinary history of the continent and its islands. In his book he explains the role of Aboriginal land management practices across the entire country. These practices formed the landscapes and vegetation communities that the Europeans saw when they first arrived.

Gammage sounds a note of sadness for what was: 'People made the land beautiful, but settlers took it because it was useful ... The more carefully they made the land, the more likely the settlers were to take it.' He wrote, 'In 1788 [Aboriginal] people used almost every plant in some way.'[5]

Bruce Pascoe, a Yuin, Bunurong and Tasmanian man, in his book *Dark Emu* also writes about the ways the Indigenous people managed the land and water. He reveals the impact that the hundreds of generations of the First Peoples who lived here before British colonisation had on the places where Australians live today.

Through their research, Pascoe and Gammage give us insights into what life on the continent and its islands was like before 1788. We know from their writing, based on a range of evidence, that Aboriginal and Torres Strait Islander people produced food using unique agricultural and aquacultural methods. They created homes, structures and tools that were ingenious and appropriate to their lifestyles and environments. They managed the land during changes in climate and geography, including an ice age and significant sea-level changes. They developed artistic and design traditions, and followed legal, religious and social practices.

We also now know that there were extensive trade routes that crisscrossed the country, and some are still used as major roads and highways.

Indigenous knowledge and traditions were essential for survival in this continent's changing environments. Creating the conditions for sustainable human societies meant having a broad and deep understanding of the past and the present, geography and potential sources of food, water and other material needs, travel routes, and much more. Geographer Patrick Nunn and linguist Nicholas Reid put it this way:

> In Aboriginal society, great store is still placed on the learning of traditional knowledge while the geography of the land is taught systematically to new generations, locally through stories about country and totems held within patrilines, and on a larger scale through songs that describe songlines – records of ancestral beings crossing the land performing creative acts that placed totemic sites and language and people into the landscape.[6]

Evidence of traditional Indigenous knowledge is all around us today, and many traditions and practices are preserved, still followed and are now better understood. Books, films, documentaries, art exhibitions, cultural festivals, music, theatre, dance and ceremonial and ritual activities have made this knowledge available to a global audience.

Today, Aboriginal and Torres Strait Islander Peoples tell stories that were handed down to them from their ancestors. These stories help us to understand the past.

Aboriginal knowledge and science have contributed greatly to our understanding of the shape of Australia and the remarkable changes that occurred when the seas rose following the last Ice Age, 7000 years ago. Such collaborations between Aboriginal people and scientists have produced many rich and detailed pictures of the ancient past. Patrick Nunn and Nicholas Reid examined stories belonging to some Aboriginal groups that tell of a time when 'the former coastline of mainland Australia was inundated by rising sea level'. Recording stories from twenty-one locations around Australia's coastline, they found that 'In most instances it is plausible to assume that these stories refer to events that occurred more than about 7000 years ago, the approximate time at which the sea level reached its present level around Australia'.

Nunn and Reid concluded that these individually dateable Aboriginal stories 'appear to have endured since 7250–13,070 calendar years BP [Before the Present]'.[7]

In other words, by comparing the details in the stories with scientific investigations, the geographers show that the Traditional Owners have told these stories for more than 7000 years. There are many experiences from different parts of the continent which are becoming more widely known as Traditional Owners work with researchers to reveal more of the past.

Budj Bim, an Aboriginal cultural heritage landscape in south-west Victoria

Budj Bim is an excellent example of an ancient habitat that has been rescued by the Traditional Owners today from environmental destruction. This famous cultural heritage landscape in south-west Victoria is the home of the Gunditjmara People. They have managed this remarkable environment for thousands of years. Their land management agency, Gunditj Mirring, headquartered at Lake Condah north of Portland, has developed a Master Plan for the Budj Bim National Heritage Landscape, and in 2019 also successfully nominated a highly valued part of their Country to the UNESCO World Heritage Listing, citing the cultural values of Budj Bim. The stringent assessment process is based on 'the three serial components of the property' which contains 'one of the world's most extensive and oldest aquaculture systems'. The Gunditjmara People are the only Indigenous people in the world to have been recognised in this way.

> *The Budj Bim lava flows, which connect the three components, provides the basis for this complex aquaculture system developed by the Gunditjmara, based on deliberate redirection, modification and management of waterways and wetlands.*
>
> *Over a period of at least 6,600 years the Gunditjmara created, manipulated and modified these local hydrological regimes and ecological systems. They utilised the abundant local volcanic rock to construct channels, weirs and dams and manage water flows in order to systematically trap, store and harvest kooyang (short-finned eel – Anguilla australis) and support enhancement of other food resources.*
>
> *The highly productive aquaculture system provided a six millennia-long economic and social base for Gunditjmara society. This deep time interrelationship of Gunditjmara cultural and environmental systems is documented through present-day Gunditjmara cultural knowledge, practices, material culture, scientific research and historical documents. It is evidenced in the aquaculture system itself and in the interrelated geological, hydrological and ecological systems. The Budj Bim Cultural Landscape is the result of a creational process narrated by the Gunditjmara as a deep time story. For the Gunditjmara, deep time refers to the idea that they have always been there. From an archaeological perspective, deep time refers to a period of at least 32,000 years that Aboriginal people have lived in the Budj Bim Cultural Landscape. The ongoing dynamic relationship of Gunditjmara and their land is nowadays carried by knowledge systems retained through oral transmission and continuity of cultural practice.*[8]

The remarkable cultural values are cited by UNESCO in addressing one of the criteria for inclusion on the World Heritage List:

> *The Budj Bim Cultural Landscape bears an exceptional testimony to the cultural traditions, knowledge, practices and ingenuity of the Gunditjmara. The extensive networks and antiquity of the constructed and modified aquaculture system of the Budj Bim Cultural Landscape bears testimony to the Gunditjmara as engineers and kooyang fishers. Gunditjmara knowledge and practices have endured and continue to be passed down through their Elders and are recognisable across the wetlands of the Budj Bim Cultural Landscape in the form of ancient and elaborate systems of stone-walled kooyang husbandry (or aquaculture) facilities.*

> *Gunditjmara cultural traditions, including associated storytelling, dance, and basket weaving, continue to be maintained by their collective multigenerational knowledge.*

This landscape of basalt rises, watercourses and swampland was formed by volcanic lava flow when Budj Bim (formerly Mount Eccles) erupted 37,000 years ago.[9] As UNESCO notes, evidence shows that from at least 6600 years ago, the Gunditjmara manipulated this volcanic landscape, which extends from Budj Bim to the sea and encompasses a series of waterways that include Lake Condah and the Fitzroy River. They built the oldest and largest aquaculture system in the world. In managing and harvesting the short-finned eels whose migratory route bring them to this area annually, they created an economy and culture that thrived due to the great natural wealth that they harnessed. They built houses with stone walls at their base and permanent settlements arranged in family groups along the waterways and channels, expanding them in each generation, and passing on from generation to generation a rich waterworld of engineered channels, ponds and villages. As well as its cultural importance having been recognised by UNESCO, its natural values, sustained and managed by the Gunditjmara People, are also extraordinary. Their determination to preserve and maintain the biodiversity and environmental health of the area is expressed in the vision of the Master Plan in the following way:

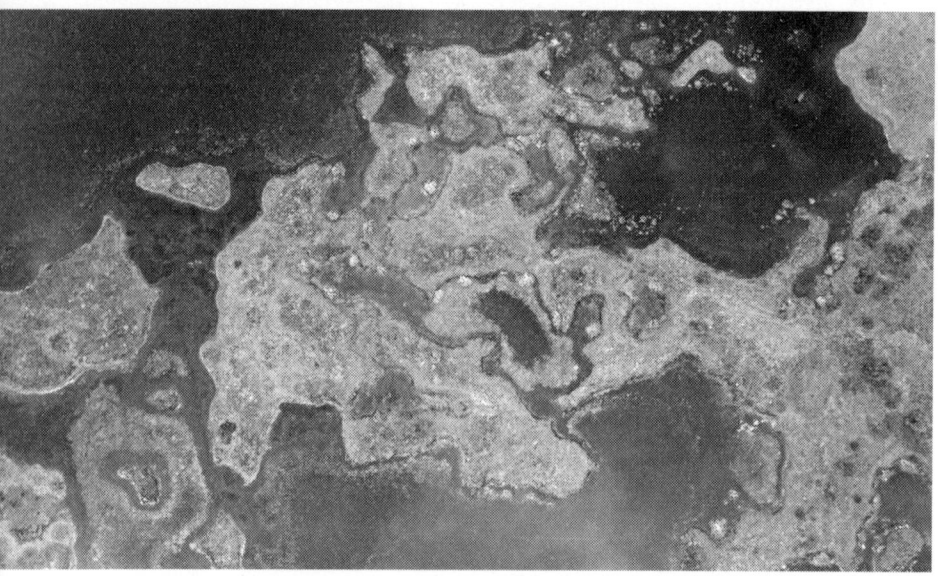

Eel traps in south-west Victoria – Aboriginal people are the original conservationists, caring for and protecting Country (photo Wayne Quilliam)

Budj Bim Connections aims to improve the condition of native vegetation, increase connectivity of aquatic habitats and foster sharing and integration of Aboriginal knowledge.

Already the project has delivered landholder management agreements to over 60 ha, including fencing and weed management. These works will enhance recreational opportunities along the waterway and benefit rare and threatened species such as Australasian bittern, growling grass frog, Yarra pygmy perch and Glenelg spiny crayfish.[10]

Archaeologist Professor Ian McNiven of Monash University, and many others, have worked with the Gunditjmara People to document their preservation and restitution of this remarkable cultural heritage. As McNiven tells the story, 'In the 1970s, Dr Peter Coutts of the Victoria Archaeological Survey carried out site surveys at Lake Condah (Tae Rak), the centrepiece of the Budj Bim cultural landscape':

Coutts and his team found what local Gunditjmara people had long known about – extensive Aboriginal fish-trapping systems comprising hundreds of metres of excavated channels and dozens of basalt block dam walls constructed over innumerable generations before European contact. Coutts estimated that the volume of basalt blocks moved measured in 'the many hundreds of tonnes'.

Determining how the Budj Bim traps operated was made difficult after European alteration of Lake Condah's water flows through installation of drainage channels in the 1880s and 1950s. Luckily, heavy winter rains in 1977 revealed how some Aboriginal-made channels fed water and eels into natural depressions that Coutts termed 'holding ponds'. In addition, numerous C-shaped basalt block structures, averaging 3–4 metres across and representing house foundations – possibly clustered into villages – were recorded in the same area as the fish traps.

Coutts hypothesised that the fishing facilities were up to 3,500 years old, based on radiocarbon dating of habitation sites in the region such as earthen mounds and shell middens. Reconstruction of ancient water levels in Lake Condah by pollen expert Leslie Head revealed that while some traps could have operated 8,000 years ago, most traps corresponded to water levels of the past 2,000 years.

Working at the same time as Coutts was Harry Lourandos, a PhD researcher from the University of Sydney. Lourandos examined Chief Protector George Augustus Robinson's 1840s journals in detail and investigated a huge Aboriginal fish trap at Toolondo, 110km north of Lake Condah.

> *Here again was further evidence of Aboriginal people digging an earthen channel (some 3km long) to move eels into a swamp to dramatically increase their range and availability. Lourandos' excavations revealed that it was up to 2.5m wide and over a metre deep. Aware of Coutts' Lake Condah holding ponds, Lourandos had the intellectual foresight to call the Toolondo and Mt William facilities for what they were – eel 'farms' associated with eel traps.*[11]

The work these researchers undertook with the Gunditjmara confirms the sophistication of the Gunditjmara's economic system and engineering:

> *These large-scale fishing facilities and associated aquaculture ponds rupture traditional representations of Aboriginal people as simply hunter gatherers.*
>
> *Rather than living passively off whatever nature provided, the Gunditjmara actively and deliberately manipulated local water flows and ecologies to engineer a landscape focused on increasing the availability and reliability of eels.*
>
> *Manipulation of the landscape involved stone structures (such as traps and channels) dating back at least 6,600 years. Eel aquaculture facilities (ponds and dam walls) pre-date contact with Europeans by many hundreds (and possibly thousands) of years ...*
>
> *The Budj Bim cultural landscape provides an outstanding example on a world stage of the scale, complexity and antiquity of a well-preserved Aboriginal fishery that continues into the present. And it is an exceptional example of Aboriginal environmental manipulation and management that blurs the distinction between foragers and farmers.*[12]

The staff and members of the Gunditj Mirring Corporation who manage the Budj Bim Cultural Landscape continue to collaborate with scientists, archaeologists, engineers and other researchers to document the aquaculture system, stone houses and settlements, cultural heritage, environment and history and to manage their inheritance and preserve it for future generations. To date, using LiDAR (Laser Imaging, Detection and Ranging) sensing, other imaging technology and drones, as well as on-ground research, five sophisticated fishtrap systems that were built around the lake's edge have been documented. They have also worked with authors to publish a series of books and other material to educate their own children and visitors about their heritage.

I highly recommend *The People of Budj Bim: Engineers of Aquaculture, Builders of Stone House Settlements and Warriors Defending Country* by the

Gunditjmara People with Gib Wettenhall (em PRESS Publishing). It was overall winner of the Victorian Community History Awards in 2011 and was reprinted due to popular demand in 2018. The stories of the Gunditjmara People and their deep understanding of their own history brings to life the science and heritage values of the place and its people. With a permanent freshwater supply and an abundance of eels, fish and water plants, the Gunditjmara lived in permanent settlements.

Their way of life was disastrously impacted by frontier violence. Their battle against squatters from the mid 1830s until the 1860s, with the most intense period being between 1834 and 1844, was made famous by Rolf Boldrewood as the Eumeralla Wars in his book *Robbery Under Arms*, set in Gunditjmara Country around the Eumeralla River. Thousands of lives were lost and regaining ownership and control of their homelands – and ancient rights to stewardship – after the devastation of colonisation has been another long battle over several decades.

There are Gunditjmara-owned-and-managed enterprises and not-for-profit organisations that offer immersive experiences in their fascinating Country, guided by local Gunditjmara rangers who are extremely knowledgeable about Country, its features and biodiversity.

Elsewhere in Aboriginal Australia, other groups of Traditional Owners are maintaining our natural and cultural heritage.

Kimberley rock art

The Kimberley region, in the north-west of Western Australia, has one of the largest concentrations of Aboriginal rock paintings in Australia. This rock art must be one of the oldest continuous art styles practised anywhere in the world. Archaeologist Peter Veth and others, working with Dambimangari and Balanggarra Traditional Owners and rangers, are undertaking studies to determine the age of these paintings. Some are at least 16,000 years old on present evidence, and some could have been produced 50,000 years ago. There are thousands of paintings in the region. The most famous are the Wanjina (also spelt Wandjina) figures. The distinctive figurative styles are said to span periods of cultural change and major climatic events over thousands of years.

These art sites are sacred places for the Traditional Owners, and many artists are continuing these artistic traditions.

Some people believe that the rock art is not just paintings but the Wanjina themselves in the rock. The religious belief of the people of this region is that the Wanjina are sacred creative beings, or sacred ancestor beings. They believe these beings created the people and the laws, and

Wuuyuru (Bigge Island) is a resting place for Gayarra Wanjina Aarwarrndju – the boss for all this place (photo Wunambal Gaambera Aboriginal Corporation)

shaped the geography and climate of their world. They are associated with rain and the seasonal regeneration of the land with each monsoon. It is believed that they and their power are eternal and ever-present.

There are many groups and languages in this region. Mowanjum artist Leah Umbagai has learnt that in her homeland there are three distinct peoples. With Rosita Holmes, the art development coordinator for Mowanjum Art and Cultural Centre, which represents these peoples, Leah explained her artistic depictions of Wanjina.

> There are three tribal groups. They are Worrorra, Ngarinyin and Wunambal Gaambera and the tradition of the three tribes is combined under Wandjina, which combines the three in shared customs and the law of country. We believe that Wandjina is the creator. He created the country, the people and the land since the beginning when people were first together.

Rosita added that the 'three groups share a kinship system different from other places in the Kimberley'.

> Wandjinas are associated with family groups, tribal groups, even people. It doesn't stop there; it is different in many different ways.
> It represents different areas. The Wandjinas gave the language,

the culture and the laws of the country. They told us how we have to work the country and how we have to live. So, all the laws, language and traditions we got from the Wandjinas. This is a very powerful person or spirit being that we believe in.

We are here because of the Wandjinas... The Wandjinas can only be painted by the Ngarinyin, Worrorra and Wunambal Gaambera people. We have had people in the past who didn't know the procedures and protocols for painting Wandjinas. It has really hurt us in the past that people have painted and done all sorts of stuff with Wandjinas. It only belongs to this one area. We were given Wandjina to look after this particular country and it belongs to only the three tribes.[13]

DINNER CAMPS OR SHELL MIDDENS

Middens are mounds of shells and sometimes also of bones and charcoal. They are found in the 'dinner camps' where many generations of ancestors of the local group gathered to feast on their harvest of shellfish and other foods. This makes them important Aboriginal heritage sites and sites of archaeological significance. They provide insights into the Aboriginal way of life in particular areas.

The Aboriginal Heritage Tasmania website notes that scientists can analyse the shell, bone, stone tools and charcoal to 'reconstruct past environments, and to understand Aboriginal occupation and land use patterns through time'. The information that can be gleaned from such research can include estimations:

about the size of the group that used the site, how long they occupied the region, and whether it was a regular campsite or the product of a single event. Charcoal samples may be tested to determine the age of each layer of occupation, and pollen samples may provide insight into past vegetation within the region.

Middens are a valuable archaeological resource not only for what they reveal about Aboriginal dietary habits, but also the technology that was utilized in gathering and processing food, seasonal trends of species exploitation, and also how humans adapted to environmental changes.[14]

The Aboriginal Heritage Tasmania website notes that in some middens, 'Charcoal and hearth stones from fires as well as other cultural items such as stone and bone artefacts can also be present', and that these 'distinct concentrations of shell' contain evidence of Aboriginal hunting, harvesting, gathering and activities to make food. They sometimes contain evidence of 'a more varied diet including fish, seal and kangaroo'.

Aboriginal shell middens are commonly found in estuaries and along the coastline, including in sand dunes and on beaches.

Kudjala/Kalkadoon Elder and educator Letitia Murgha explains that, for thousands of years, 'Aboriginal people caught and ate large numbers of shellfish species in and around the mangrove mud flats and coastal areas along the Queensland coast'. Depending on the type of shellfish, they were cooked or eaten raw. The discarded shells accumulated in these special cooking camps, creating large mounds of shells from one or several species that were harvested in the area. Some types of shells could be used for a number of purposes. For example, by grinding a shell to the right shape and adding a handle, it would become a sharp knife for cutting meat.

As Letitia Murgha says, middens 'tell the story of the Aboriginal peoples' diet, food sources for that particular area, what species were available, the impact of biodiversity, environmental changes and marine ecosystems'.[15]

Aboriginal shell middens are not easily detected unless you know what you are looking for. They may be 'small shallow discrete scatters to extensive deposits that run along a coastline for hundreds of metres'. They may appear 'on the ground surface as sparse scatters or concentrations of broken shell, and are often associated with dark, ashy soil including charcoal. Middens can also be visible in eroded or collapsed sections of dunes, where they may appear as a dark, ashy band with layers of shell throughout', according to the Aboriginal Heritage Tasmania website.

Shell-wash deposits might look like an Aboriginal midden, but they aren't made up of the same shells. They are caused by storms and high tides, and often appear at the high tide mark, but contain only shells from small species, such as Venus clams and dog cockles.

The oldest known Aboriginal shell midden place on the Victorian coast is nearly 12,000 years old. As explained in a Victorian Government fact sheet:

> At this time sea levels were lower because icecaps at the north and south poles were much larger than today. The shoreline was many kilometres away from its present position, at times creating a land bridge with Tasmania. Sea levels stabilised between [6000 and 7000] years ago, and most middens along the present coastline were formed since that time. The dates of middens, their location and their contents,

indicate that different areas of the coast were used at different times, generally when they were most productive. There were changes in shellfish species that were used, stone tool types and raw materials. The presence of exotic stone in places is evidence of contact between people from different areas.

In Victoria, all Aboriginal cultural places are protected by law. Aboriginal artefacts are also protected. It is illegal to disturb or destroy an Aboriginal place or remove an Aboriginal artefact from a site.

In New South Wales, Aboriginal rangers and New South Wales Parks and Heritage rangers protect Aboriginal sites, including shell middens.

As places with such rich evidence of ancestral life, shell middens are important to Aboriginal people everywhere. All Australians should feel a sense of responsibility to preserve them as part of our national heritage. They are important because they offer clues to the way people lived in this country for thousands of years.

This ancient shell midden is evidence of a 'dinner camp' where many generations of ancestors of the local group gathered to feast on shellfish and other foods, making it an important Aboriginal heritage site. (Photo by Melinda Sawers, Birany Birany, Northern Territory, June 2018.)

Listening to Country

Elders often say that if you sit quietly in the places where our ancestors left traces of their lives, on middens where they ate seafood in the sand dunes, or in rock caves where they left their paintings, you can hear them and feel their presence. This sense of being connected to a deep history is at the core of our being. Even if we have grown up with it, coming upon one of these special places always thrills us.

Listening to the stories that Elders tell gives me a feeling of being spoken to from the deep past. In those places where archaeologists look for signs of the past is our history. If all Australians could feel that attachment to our Country, they might respect this great legacy more.

When I was young in the 1960s, I saw so many more animals and birds, the seas and rivers teemed with fish, and the rocks were covered with oysters and mussels. Now it is much more difficult to catch a fish or find oysters. It is important for all Australians to understand what was there, what our ancestors left for us – a beautiful world – and to care for it as our ancestors did.

The modern Australian citizen should know about the history of the First Peoples because that is what makes this country distinctive. It should be a source of national identity and pride for everyone. Understanding the contributions Aboriginal and Torres Strait Islander peoples made over at least 65,000 years is also a way of respecting their descendants, continuing cultural traditions, practices and knowledge. It is a way to recognise their ability to contribute to this country by maintaining those practices that have helped to shape the environment and landscapes since ancient times.

Dancers gather at the 3 Rivers Festival on the Murray River (photo Wayne Quilliam)

2
Becoming Australia

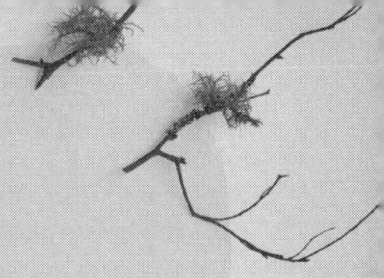

In 1770, Captain James Cook declared Britain's possession of the east coast of what was still a mysterious continent to the Europeans. He was standing on Bedanug, which came to be called Possession Island, off the coast of North Queensland.

When the British arrived in force in 1788 with eleven ships under the command of Captain Arthur Phillip and established the British settlement at Port Jackson on the shores of Eora Country in Warrane, what became known as Sydney, the future of Indigenous Peoples across the continent and islands was fated. At the time the penal colony was set up at Port Jackson, the British had lost the War of Independence in North America. After the American Revolution and the Declaration of Independence, the British could no longer send convicts to America and instead sent eleven ships, the first of 608 ships over 60 years, to Port Jackson to establish a penal colony on Gadigal land.

The Colony of New South Wales was the first, and Arthur Phillip its first governor, in charge from 1788 to 1792. Although the British had negotiated treaties with Native Americans, they did not do this in the Australian colonies. Governor Phillip and the governors who followed him all responded with violent force to the resistance from the Aboriginal people. The frontier was bloody. Eventually, six colonies were established, each with its own history of attempts to exterminate Aboriginal people. Huge numbers of Aboriginal people died, the population fell from an estimated one million at first settlement to less than 100,000 a century later.

White Australia

The men who wrote the Constitution believed that the 'Aboriginal race' would die out. This was one of the core tenets of their ideas about superior and inferior races, and the ideology of the 'survival of the fittest'. They believed that the 'problem' of the existence of the first peoples – 'aborigines' to use their term – would 'disappear'. On 29 and 30 March 1901, the first federal election was held in accordance with the voting legislation in each of the states (in some states already enrolled Aboriginal men could vote). On 9 May, at the Exhibition Building in Naarm/Melbourne, the Duke of Cornwall and York, later King George V, opened the Commonwealth Parliament in front of 12,000 invited guests and many more who lined the streets.[16] Four months later, on 12 September 1901, Attorney-General Alfred Deakin said that Australia needed a policy to secure a 'white Australia'. The parliament set about ensuring that no other non-white people would come to Australia without a strict policy, positioning them as other 'inferior races'. To limit non-British migration to Australia, they developed the White Australia policy and drafted legislation.[17] The *Immigration Restriction Act* was enacted on 23 December 1901.

It was Alfred Deakin who established a white nation and laid the principles for racial exclusion for the next 75 years. He stated his vision of 'white Australia' and how it would be achieved, in this way:

> That end, put in plain and unequivocal terms ... means the prohibition of all alien coloured immigration, and more, it means at the earliest time, by reasonable and just means, the deportation or reduction of the number of aliens now in our midst. The two things go hand in hand and are the necessary complement of a single policy – the policy of securing a 'white Australia'.[18]

This was the constitutional and legal state of affairs from 1 January 1901 until the successful referendum of 1967 that asked Australians to remove two racially discriminatory phrases from the national rule book. More than 90 per cent of Australians voted in that referendum in favour of removing race from the constitution.

The question was phrased, however, so that racism remained at the core of the nation's foundational document. The White Australia policy did not end until the Harold Holt government dispensed with it in 1966 when Australia needed immigrants, and when the disgrace of a racially determined immigration policy was provoking international criticism. The Whitlam government finally eliminated it in the 1970s, and later backed it up with the introduction of policies like the *Racial Discrimination Act 1975*, but still these ideas sit just below the surface of Australian public life.

As you learn more about what happened to the First Peoples of this land in the years from the arrival of the British to the present, you may find yourself rethinking the idea of 'Australia' and your idea of what is involved in being an 'Australian citizen'. There are some core ideas that you will need to understand to develop your own idea of what it means to be 'Australian'. The idea of 'race' is one of them and, by extension, the idea of being 'white' and 'not white'. Most Australians do not know or understand the history of the idea of 'race' and the White Australia policy nor how deeply they are etched into the national psyche. This has impacted on many new arrivals, but its most lasting impact is on the perception of the First Peoples and their descendants.

At the University of Newcastle, a group of researchers led by Professor Lyndall Ryan are researching the frontier violence that led to this terrible outcome. The First Australians were not passive victims:

> From the moment the British invaded Australia in 1788 they encountered active resistance from the Aboriginal and Torres Strait Islander owners and custodians of the lands. In the frontier wars which continued until the 1960s, massacres became a defining strategy to eradicate that resistance. As a result, thousands of Aboriginal men, women, and children were killed.[19]

Ryan and her team have documented the massacres of First Australians, mapping their locations, 'timelines, and information about massacres in Central and Eastern Australia from 1794 when the first massacre was recorded until 1930'. Their research includes the whole of Australia from the start of British settlement up to 1930 and is based on the most reliable information available on these events which were often concealed: 'Only events for which sufficient information remains from the past and can be verified'.

Their findings show that the way massacres were carried out changed over time and involved soldiers, settlers, mounted police and/or native police usually with firearms and sometimes with poison.[20]

The findings of the research project on frontier massacres are based on the records and cannot give an accurate picture as so many of the massacres were not recorded. At this stage, their conclusions are therefore conservative but worth repeating here.

> 421 sites of frontier massacre, in which 11,257 were killed, are included in Stage 4 [the final stage of the project]. The number is indicative rather than definitive and may vary as new information emerges.
>
> The map timeline indicates that frontier massacres of Aboriginal people spread steadily across southern Australia from 1794 to 1860 with notable peaks in the 1820s in Tasmania and the 1840s in NSW, Victoria, South Australia and Western Australia. From the 1860s when the frontier shifted to Northern Australia, massacre peaks took place

in Queensland in the 1860s to 1870s and 1880 to 1930 in the Northern Territory and the Kimberley region in Western Australia. The number of Aboriginal people killed in a frontier massacre increased from 1860, with the average number killed in each incident increasing from 23 to 32.

Group massacres: 18 clusters of frontier massacres, comprised of 58 separate incidents. The first cluster was recorded in Tasmania in 1827 and then Gippsland in Victoria in 1843. They intensified in Queensland in the 1870s and 1890s and continued in Western Australia and the Northern Territory until 1928.[21]

Preliminary Statistics

The following statistics relate to massacres of 6 or more people only and are subject to change as more information becomes available. Other factors affect the history of Aboriginal and Torres Strait Islander populations such as disease, loss of land, abduction of children, control of movement, and combined flow on effects to the community.

The statistics are indicative rather than definitive. They are minimum estimates only, not estimates of the full extent of massacres. It is likely that more massacres occurred than were reported and recorded.

Recorded massacres between 1788 and 1930 in Australia by current State and Territory borders

	Australia	Tas.	Vic.	NSW	Qld	SA	NT	WA
Est. Total Massacres	305	36	52	50	72	15	35	42
Est. Aboriginal and Torres Strait Islander victims of massacres	8178	487	1110	1929	2032	255	1350	1015
Est. Colonist victims of massacres	146	0	8	8	96	26	8	0
Est. Average Aboriginal and Torres Strait Islander victims of massacres	28.01	13.16	21.76	39.37	31.26	18.21	39.71	24.17
Est. Average colonist victims of massacres	13.27	0	8.00	8.00	13.71	26.00	8.00	0

The above information was retrieved from the Colonial Frontier Massacres website, 21 July 2021 (https://c21ch.newcastle.edu.au/colonialmassacres/)

These colonial beginnings of the nation are a hotly debated issue in Australia, especially on Australia Day on 26 January. Indigenous people hold their own events, such as the Yabun Festival in Warrane/Sydney, and since 2017 some local councils have voted to celebrate the founding of the nation on a different day.

The Federation Movement to bring the colonies together under one national government began in 1889. In that year Henry Parkes, the premier of the Colony of New South Wales, gave a speech in the country town of Tenterfield, calling for the six separate colonies to unite and create a national government for all Australia – a federation. At that time the Australian colonies reported to the Home Office in London on matters of state and were, in most important ways, governed from the Home Office.

Constitutional conventions were held, first in Warrane/Sydney and then in other cities around the country, to discuss the draft constitution. Aboriginal people were excluded from these conventions in all colonies except South Australia. Nor did they have any right to vote in the referendums on the proposed constitution.

Australia came into existence in 1901 following the enactment of the *Commonwealth of Australia Constitution Act 1900* by the House of Commons in the British Parliament. The Imperial Parliament exercised ultimate authority over the colonies and agreed to the Constitution Act on 5 July 1900; Queen Victoria approved it on 9 July 1900, and it came into force on 1 January 1901. The six English colonies of Queensland, New South Wales, Victoria, Tasmania, South Australia and Western Australia formed the Commonwealth of Australia under a new constitution, and Australia became a nation.

Aboriginal and Torres Strait Islander Peoples were not citizens after the constitution was enacted. At best, they were treated as wards of the state under Acts of Parliament in each state and territory that set out the laws for Aboriginal labour, confining Aboriginal people to reserves, and many other rules. In the constitutional referendum of 1967, Australians were asked to vote on whether the Commonwealth Parliament should be able to make laws for Aboriginal people, and whether Aboriginal people should be counted in the Australian census. After the referendum's success – a resounding 'yes' vote – all the states and the Northern Territory permitted Aboriginal people to vote. It took another couple of decades before it became compulsory as for the rest of Australia.

A change of the federal government in 1972 brought about sudden policy changes, including the recognition of Aboriginal land rights, the recognition of distinctive Aboriginal cultures, and the need for Aboriginal

LAND AND RATIONS

The military and, later, free settlers forced many Indigenous people from their land. British graziers and farmers altered most Australian landscapes by clearing trees to make way for their animals and crops. These changes brought to an end the ancient hunting, gathering and fishing economy of the First Australians across most of the continent. It meant that people had to rely on handouts of food rations to survive. The colonial administrators and settlers in New South Wales first started handing out rations to Indigenous people to secure their trust. Later, they gave out food to stop Aboriginal people from spearing their cattle. During droughts, they were forced to distribute the rations more widely. From the 1880s, government-funded rations were distributed to Aboriginal people in Queensland through missions, settler stations and government food-relief centres. The ration system had become widespread in the colonies by the late 1890s.

Above: Collecting the daily milk ration for babies and nursing mothers at the Snake Bay Government settlement on Melville Island, Northern Territory

Left: Men at work in a ration store in Delissaville, Northern Territory

organisations. A new prime minister, Gough Whitlam, initiated the legal recognition of Aboriginal land rights by handing over a land lease to the Gurindji People at Wattie Creek, now called by its proper Aboriginal name, Daguragu, in the Northern Territory.

Whitlam appointed Justice Woodward to the Aboriginal Land Rights Commission of Inquiry and, in 1976, the Commonwealth Parliament enacted his principles in the *Aboriginal Land Rights (Northern Territory) Act 1976*.

As the century proceeded, the impact of colonisation on Aboriginal people became a major human rights issue. The stealing and removal of thousands of Aboriginal children, incarcerating them in institutions throughout the twentieth century under the so-called 'assimilation' policy became the subject of a human rights inquiry, as discussed further in The Stolen Generations chapter of this book. The *Bringing Them Home* report was tabled in Parliament in 1997 and eventually, in 2008, led to the government apology to the Stolen Generations.

The practice of jailing Aboriginal people in such numbers that in parts of Australia the imprisonment rate was the highest recorded in the world became another human rights issue. The Royal Commission into Aboriginal Deaths in Custody was established in 1987, and the final report of the commission, published in 1991, remains the most comprehensive survey of Indigenous law and justice issues and of the underlying causes that bring Aboriginal people into excessive contact with the justice system. Despite the Royal Commission's 339 recommendations, Indigenous people are still fourteen times more likely to be imprisoned than non-Indigenous Australians. The Royal Commission recommended a reconciliation process, and the Council for Aboriginal Reconciliation was formed, consisting of both Indigenous and non-Indigenous members who initiated programs leading to many changes in attitude and practice. In 1997, a National Reconciliation Convention was held.

A number of national institutions, such as the National Museum of Australia, the Australian Museum, the Australian Broadcasting Commission, and the Australian Human Rights and Equal Opportunity Commission, have produced timelines of the many events in Australian history that are significant to Aboriginal and Torres Strait Islander Peoples in remembering their past, and increasingly to more Australians as historians reveal this past.

The timelines, which can be found on their websites, are a good guide to the history of Australia since 1788.[22]

Culture as a pillar

It is difficult to define what culture is. We might say, for example, that culture is the set of beliefs, customs and ways of life unique to a specific group of people. This definition is limited, though, because it doesn't tell us how we discover and define what 'beliefs', 'customs' and 'ways of life' are, and how they combine to evolve and create a unique culture. Also, these things are constantly changing. They change with the political situation, historical influences, the climate and the economy. In modern Australia's multicultural, global society, it is hard to define the cultural beliefs and practices of any group. And if you do, not everyone will agree with the one definition.

What are Australian values? Fairness is often said to be an Australian value, but for many First Australians there's not much fairness. About half the Aboriginal and Torres Strait Islander people are worse off than other Australians in terms of income, access to services, housing, employment and education. They are also much more likely to be in jail. It must also be said that although thousands of Aboriginal and Torres Strait Islander people are very poor, they are also the most culturally productive people in the country.

They are celebrated for their performances and artistic creations. Most Australians will have seen at least one example of Indigenous cultural expression, an artwork, a 'Welcome to Country' ceremony or a dance performance. However, according to the *The State of Reconciliation in Australia Report* published by Reconciliation Australia, most Australians have never met an Indigenous person.

Many people do not know that Indigenous Australia is enormously diverse and complex, both culturally and linguistically.

Many ideas that came to Australia from Britain and Europe led to stereotypes and ignorance about Aboriginal and Torres Strait Islander cultures. These misconceptions started in colonial times and persisted for much of the twentieth century. Even today, many Australians don't understand the full importance of the cultures of the First Peoples.

These cultures are thousands of years old and they are always changing. But as Noel Pearson said in his 2022 Boyer Lecture: 'Let me point out what is incontrovertible: Australia doesn't make sense without recognition. Until the First Peoples are afforded our rightful place, we are a nation missing its most vital heart.'

3
On Survival

As the settlers spread out across the lands of Aboriginal Peoples in the nineteenth century they seized control, assisted by the British troops. The history of twentieth century Australia was also brutal. So brutal that in many parts of the country, the historical facts have been suppressed and contested, and many still deny the terrible treatment that Indigenous people experienced.

With little choice but to congregate and wait for rations, Aboriginal people were drawn to the pastoral stations and the missions. Missionaries followed, and Aboriginal people were eventually rounded up and placed in missions and government administered settlements. By the end of the 1940s, only a few Aboriginal groups retained their pre-contact lifestyles. When people today refer to an Aboriginal community, they are often unaware of the history of these places. Government rations were small and irregular, so the handouts by the missions became a better option. In many missions the local Aboriginal people became a permanent working community and a 'no work no food' policy was followed. The missionaries' intention was to 'civilise' these people and train them in Christian ways of living.

The Gulag Archipelago: institutional control

After colonisation, Indigenous people continued to live in traditional societies in Cape York, Central Australia and the Western Desert, in some areas of the top end of the Northern Territory and in the Kimberley region of Western Australia. Even there, though, they were now controlled by the Europeans; this was the case across Australia. Charles Rowley was a public servant and Aboriginal rights advocate who referred to the thousands of scattered reserves and administered settlements to which thousands of Aboriginal and Torres Strait Islander people were confined under legislation as the 'gulag archipelago', comparing these 'institutions of total control' to the Soviet prison camps about which Aleksandr Solzhenitsyn had famously written in 1973.[23]

Elsewhere, the surviving Indigenous populations became involved in the new economy that had taken over from their own. They became cheap or even free workers and were often exploited by their employers. Despite this, from the hop growers of Coranderrk in Victoria to the pearl-shell divers of the Torres Strait, the ingenuity of the First Australians in these terrible circumstances was seen across the country.

In the first half of the twentieth century, the state and territory governments brought in assimilation policies that controlled the lives of Indigenous people. They became a low-paid labour force for governments, farmers and businesses and worked as domestic labour, usually unpaid, in households. Governments could also regulate whom Indigenous people were allowed to marry and removed 'half-caste' children from their families.

This way, they sought to control the Aboriginal 'race'.

People who were identified, at least formally, as 'full-bloods' were meant to stay on Crown Land – the reserves. The reality, though, was quite different. Reserve populations were mixed, with people from many different language groups and Country. The goal of segregating 'full-blood' and 'half-caste' people was never achieved.

In 1997, the Human Rights and Equal Opportunity Commission published *Bringing Them Home*, a report about how Australia's social

Children from settlements and missions play tunnel ball at Centralian School Sports Day in Alice Springs, Northern Territory

security regulations were used to control peoples' lives. It documents some of the examples of discrimination that Indigenous people had to live with for decades.

> *Seven years after federation, national aged and invalid pension schemes were enacted, and in 1912, maternity allowances. However, 'Aboriginal Natives' were disqualified from all payments. Throughout the Great Depression, Indigenous people continued to be excluded from eligibility for any benefit. After World War II, a comprehensive and universal system of social security existed in Australia, except for Aborigines. The first payment to which Indigenous people had access was a child endowment payment introduced in 1941. In 1942, 'Aboriginal Natives' became eligible for Commonwealth pensions, but as the Racial Discrimination Commissioner pointed out, the 1942 amendments excluded 'Aboriginal Natives' who were covered by the 'provisions of a state or territory law relating to the control of Aboriginal natives.' There were also exclusions for Indigenous people who were deemed 'nomadic' or 'primitive' and, despite the existence of entitlements: '... Social Security Act continued to discriminate against Aborigines by adding amendments that restricted access to pensions and allowance payments and placing Aboriginal Australians under the control of non-Aboriginal administrated Aboriginal departments, missions, settlements and pastoral properties.'*[24]

This policy of racist exclusion continued until the late 1960s. In 1966, the Department of Social Services removed all specific references to Aboriginal people from the *Social Security Act*. Indigenous people living in remote communities continued to be excluded from participation in Australia's social security system well into the 1970s.

Full, effective access to social security benefits did not occur until the late 1970s and in some remote communities not until the early 1980s.

In the 1960s, Aboriginal people who were in the workforce, or wanted to be, began to fight for equal pay. In 1968, the Conciliation and Arbitration Commission ruled that Indigenous workers in the pastoral industry should be paid the same as other workers. This victory didn't improve the lives of these workers, though, because many employers claimed they couldn't afford to pay the same wages to Indigenous and non-Indigenous people. In truth, some small operators probably could not afford to do so, but others could. In the upheaval that followed, thousands of Aboriginal people lost their jobs and families had to leave the properties where they had lived for generations.

The Aboriginal Land Commission, established in 1972, purchased pastoral leases for resident or nearby Aboriginal groups who had been marginalised by the white pastoralists who refused to pay equal wages to their Aboriginal workers.

When their stake in the industry dramatically increased, Aboriginal pastoralists found that small holdings could only support an owner-manager and their family. Agribusiness on a much wider scale, or involving more diverse and profitable uses of land, could support communities of several hundred Aboriginal people. Today, Indigenous people own and manage huge properties and mix their traditional culture with modern business, farming and grazing practices.

In the late 1960s and 1970s, it became clear that the Commonwealth Government would have to invest in desperately needed infrastructure for Indigenous communities. It also had to stop corrupt or poorly informed Aboriginal Affairs officials in the states and territories from managing these communities and controlling people's lives.

Missionaries were asked to leave, and reserve superintendents were replaced by community councils. People with jobs managing cattle, and in sawmills, bakeries, butcheries, on farms and in cottage industries on the missions, disappeared. These businesses were slowly run down, or simply closed overnight.

Many families fled from the reserves during the 1960s and 1970s to look for work in larger centres. However, Aboriginal people had been largely excluded from educational training, apprenticeships and employment. This led to a rapidly growing Indigenous underclass in the towns and cities, where people found it hard to get jobs and accommodation.

Aboriginal communities in urban areas, such as Redfern in inner Sydney and in Sydney's western suburbs, grew quickly as people moved from the rural areas. New communities also sprung up, such as in Inala in Brisbane. Aboriginal organisations were established at this time to service these highly disadvantaged people.

Young doctors and lawyers who supported Aboriginal rights worked as volunteers in the new cooperatives that opened in shopfronts to provide urgently needed services. The model of 'community-controlled' Aboriginal medical and legal services quickly spread across the country. It was a form of popular Aboriginal governance that empowered Aboriginal communities in their dealings with governments and with neighbouring non-Indigenous populations.

Indigenous communities are extremely diverse. Broadly speaking, Aboriginal and Torres Strait Islander people today live in three different types of communities. There are 'urban' Indigenous people who live in the larger cities and towns, although many have come from rural and remote areas to live there. This group makes up the largest percentage – about 82 per cent of the Indigenous population.

Then there are those who live in small towns and settlements that were established as Aboriginal reserves, missions or outposts during the 'protection and segregation' era. These communities are usually made up of the descendants of many different Indigenous clan groups who were forcibly removed from their traditional lands. Over time, Indigenous people living in these communities have been able to gain more control over their lives through campaigns for land rights and political empowerment.

Lastly, there are those Indigenous people who live on their own ancestral lands, usually in remote parts of Australia. Many Aboriginal and Torres Strait Islander people live and move across these different types of communities and have family and kinship connections in all three.

The notion of community arose out of the administration of Indigenous Peoples in remote and rural areas. In Australia today, Indigenous communities are villages where people live and work. Some remote communities are also administrative centres for Indigenous groups who live in homeland centres, and for highly mobile populations. Many originated as missions and government settlements and have been redesigned by Indigenous communities since the 1970s to maintain culture and possession of land. The aim is to survive as distinctive social and cultural entities.

Community gather in Warrane/Sydney in a sign of unity (photo Wayne Quilliam)

4
A Rightful Place

Australia's state governments controlled the lives of the Aboriginal and Torres Strait Islander Peoples well into the twentieth century. As well as the 'assimilation' policies under which these governments used their legal power to remove Aboriginal children from their families, destroying family life for thousands of Aboriginal people for several generations, Indigenous people were incarcerated on Crown reserves across the country. Superintendents or 'managers' of various kinds ran these reserves, settlements and missions. Indigenous people could not work, travel or even move from these places unless the superintendents gave them permission. Often this permission was not granted, and these people lived as if they were in prison.

Many were starving. They were given only small quantities of rations, sometimes once a week in the large settlements and less often in smaller

Indigenous and non-Indigenous people walk together in the spirit of reconciliation (photo Wayne Quilliam)

ones. As their movement across their land was restricted, they could not hunt or bring in the food their families had traditionally lived on.

Indigenous people across the country stood up against these racist policies. The movement for Aboriginal rights gained momentum in the 1920s and has continued to grow ever since. In Tarndanya/Adelaide in 1958, a national body was created: the Federal Council for the Advancement of Aborigines (FCAA). It aimed to gain 'equal citizenship rights' and a national approach to Indigenous affairs. It campaigned for equal pay and land rights, and to change the Australian Constitution.

In 1964, the organisation's name was changed to the Federal Council for the Advancement of Aborigines and Torres Strait Islanders (FCAATSI). Hundreds of FCAATSI's members, both Indigenous and non-Indigenous volunteers, campaigned for a referendum to remove discrimination against 'Aborigines' from the Constitution.

No other constitution in the world is as difficult to change as the Australian Constitution – any change needs a majority of people in the majority of states. As a result, only eight out of forty-four referendums in Australia's history have succeeded. The most overwhelming was the referendum which fundamentally changed the way Australia as a nation related to Indigenous people.

In 1967, a referendum was held and the campaign, 'Vote Yes for Aboriginal Rights', was an outstanding success. An overwhelming majority of Australians, and a majority of the states, voted Yes. The Constitution was amended. The change meant that Aboriginal and Torres Strait Islander Peoples were included in the national census and the discriminatory clause preventing the federal Parliament from legislating for 'Aborigines' (which was interpreted to include Torres Strait Islanders) was deleted.

Before the 1967 referendum, the Commonwealth Government could not legislate for Aboriginal and Torres Strait Islander Peoples. That meant there were only state policies – except for Aboriginal welfare officers and patrol officers in the Northern Territory.

The question put to the Australian people was:

> *Do you approve the proposed law for the alteration of the Constitution entitled 'An Act to alter the Constitution so as to omit certain words relating to the people of the Aboriginal race in any state so that Aboriginals are to be counted in reckoning the population'?*[25]

This question proposed to delete two parts of the Constitution. First, it proposed to remove the words 'other than the Aboriginal people in any state' from section 51(xxvi). Before the referendum, this section read:

Australians rallying for Aboriginal rights in the 1967 referendum (image courtesy of AIATSIS, item HORNER2.J01.BW-N04612_12)

> *The Parliament shall, subject to this Constitution, have power to make laws for the peace, order and good government of the Commonwealth with respect to ... The people of any race other than the Aboriginal people in any state for whom it is necessary to make special laws.*

This meant the federal Parliament didn't have any law-making power in relation to Indigenous people.

Second, the referendum question proposed to repeal section 127, which had prevented Aboriginal people from being included in 'reckoning the numbers of the people of the Commonwealth' – that is, the census. Section 127 prevented Aboriginal people from being counted for the purpose of determining the size and distribution of electorates for the federal Parliament. However, the impact of this section on Aboriginal and Torres Strait Islander people was much wider. As the 'Expert Panel on Constitutional Recognition of Indigenous Australians' reported in 2012:

> *At the first Australian census in 1911, only those 'aboriginal natives' living near white settlements were counted, and the main population tables included only those of half or less Aboriginal descent. Details of 'half-caste' (but not 'full-blood') Aboriginal people were included in the tables on race. Details of 'full blood' Aboriginal people were included in separate tables. The practice was followed in all censuses up until 1966.*

The effect of the section was that the government underestimated the number of Aboriginal and Torres Strait Islander people. This reflected the view, widely held at Federation in 1901, that Indigenous people were not entitled to take part in Australia's democratic processes.

In the 1967 referendum, 90.77 per cent of people voted in favour of amending the Constitution, the highest ever Yes vote recorded in a federal referendum. Section 127 was deleted from the Constitution and the words 'other than the Aboriginal people in any state' were removed from section 51(xxvi).

This extraordinary support for Aboriginal rights was a victory for the many hundreds of people who had held street marches, wrote to the newspapers and campaigned for decades. Professor Megan Davis wrote in *The Monthly* in July 2016, 'progress on Indigenous rights has never originated in the parliament'. If we have learnt anything from decades of Indigenous campaigns, she wrote:

> Indigenous rights, land rights, native title rights have come from Indigenous activism – tents on the lawn – and the courts. Parliament is always playing catch-up. The unwavering aspiration of Indigenous people for decades has been a settlement between Aboriginal polities and the state.[26]

The 1967 referendum was a step in the right direction. We still have a long way to go to make sure that the Aboriginal and Torres Strait Islander Peoples are given their rightful place within the nation and are empowered within its legal and political systems.

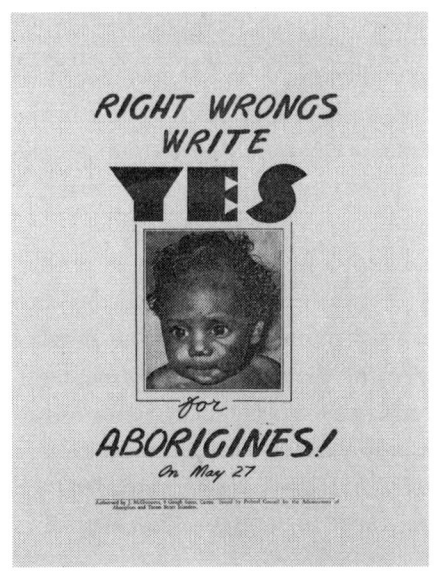

A pamphlet handed out in the campaign for Aboriginal rights in the 1967 referendum (image courtesy of AIATSIS, item DAA.003.BW-N04528_13A)

War service

Slowly, there is a recognition of the frontier wars, or the defence of their lands and peoples by the First Peoples when the British and others set out to take territory forcibly. Rachel Perkins investigated in journeys across the country the bloody battles fought on Australian soil and the wars that established the Australian nation – the Australian Wars. Perkins sought to change the narrative of the nation from the myth of a 'peaceful' settlement by the British and the nonsense about Aboriginal people as easily subjugated by the colonisers. The Australian Wars were waged well into the twentieth century and some of the wars lasted for more than a decade. New research about these battlefields is presented in *The Australian Wars* and movingly explained by Rachel and the descendants of those who fought the invaders. Rachel visited the Australian War Memorial during the making of her three-part documentary and called for the nation to acknowledge the First Peoples who died in these conflicts and for the Australian War Memorial to recognise them.[27]

Even though they had experienced the frontier wars, fighting against the colonists, hundreds of Aboriginal men enlisted in the Australian Army to fight in the First World War of 1914–1918. Some had even enlisted to fight in the Boer War in southern African in the nineteenth century.

Many of the men who campaigned for the 1967 referendum had served in the Australian Defence Forces (ADF) in World War II. They served overseas and in northern Australia as military and non-military personnel. They fought for the country that discriminated against them.

An Aboriginal Reconnaissance Unit in Arnhem Land was established by anthropologist Donald Thomson, who was a commissioned officer and Torres Strait Islanders provided a full battalion. When the Second World War ended and Indigenous Australian soldiers came back home, they faced the same discrimination as before, and were discriminated against in the Soldier Settlement Scheme. They were not citizens. Most did not get the right to vote until seventeen years later, after a long fight to achieve that and other citizenship rights.

Aboriginal and Torres Strait Islander people have served in every conflict and overseas commitment involving Australian defence contingents since Federation. The Australian War Memorial records 'even a small number of individual enlistments in the colonial defence forces before that'. Indigenous people served in both world wars, as well as in South Korea, Vietnam, Afghanistan, Iraq and other deployments. Their contribution was not recognised until the 2000s, when the ADF, the War Memorial and the Australian Government acknowledged them in several ceremonies. That only happened after the Indigenous servicemen and women themselves campaigned for recognition.

Then Chief of the Australian Defence Force General David Hurley stated in his 2016 memorial service speech, 'More than 3000 Indigenous Australians enlisted during World War II. Another 150 to 200 served as de facto servicemen, patrolling and performing other military duties along the north Australian coast, while 3000 Indigenous Australians supported the World War II defence effort as civilian labourers'. And yet, the Australian War Memorial board cannot recognise the Australian Wars and memorialise them appropriately.

NAIDOC Week and the burden of Australia's political history

NAIDOC Week, Australia's annual celebration of Aboriginal and Torres Strait Islander Peoples and cultures, is held in the first week of July every year. It is a way to make sure that we never return to the dark days of the Australian colonies, when the efforts to wipe out our peoples almost succeeded.

Originally, the acronym NADOC stood for 'National Aborigines Day Observance Committee', which organised the activities. From 1991, recognising the distinct cultural histories of Aboriginal and Torres Strait Islander Peoples, NADOC was expanded to include Torres Strait Islander people and culture. The committee then became known as the National Aborigines and Islanders Day Observance Committee (NAIDOC). This new name has become the title for the whole week, not just the day.

Now NAIDOC Week has grown to become a part of Australian life. Aboriginal and Torres Strait Islander people in communities and urban areas, as well as government agencies, local councils, schools, and workplaces, organise events in towns, cities, rural and remote areas around the country. The celebrations include dancing, singing, storytelling and other events.

Awards ceremonies are held in each state and territory to recognise the achievements of outstanding individuals, young and old, from a wide range of fields. The week culminates in the National NAIDOC Awards Ceremony, hosted by a local NAIDOC committee in a different city each year. During the week, the Aboriginal and Torres Strait Islander flags are flown across the nation, on buildings and schools and on flagpoles lining avenues and streets. Permission is not required to fly either the Aboriginal or Torres Strait Islander flag, which are recognised as official Australian flags under the *Flags Act 1953*. It is, however, essential to apply for permission if you want to reproduce the flags.

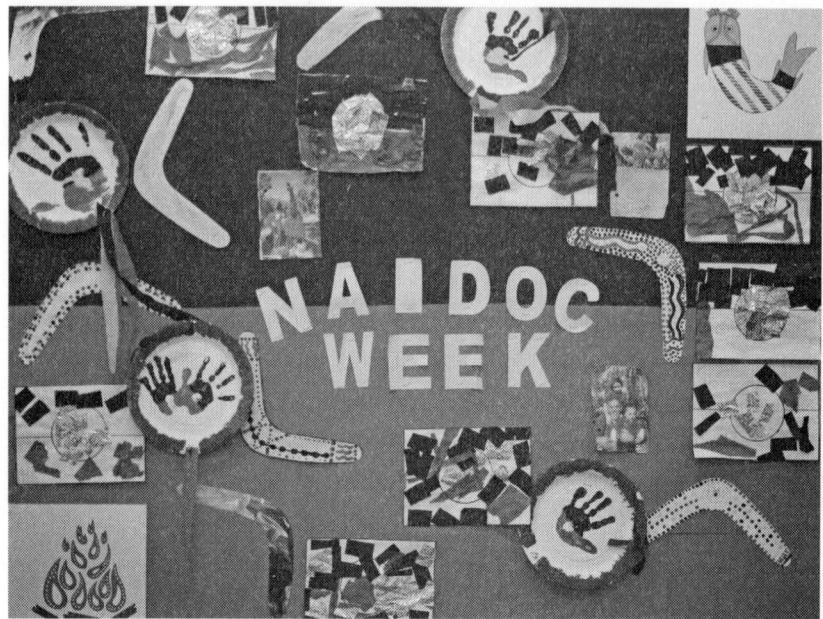

A display celebrating NAIDOC Week (photo Wayne Quilliam)

These celebrations are organised to reflect the issues that matter the most to us: cultural survival, wellbeing, our political rights, our languages, and our children. Indigenous people in the host cities form their own local communities and organise the celebrations, including cultural and civic events, and the local and national annual balls. The celebrations are open to all Australians.

Each year there is a different theme for NAIDOC Week. These themes express the concerns of Aboriginal and Torres Strait Islander Peoples. The first theme was announced by the then NADOC Committee in 1972. This came soon after police violently removed the Aboriginal Tent Embassy from outside Parliament House in Canberra in July that year. The theme 'Advance Australia Where?' was a response to the refusal by most politicians of the day to consider reforms in the ways our people were treated. They did not agree to negotiate land rights or stop the ongoing formal racism and racial segregation that most Indigenous people experienced.

The theme of NAIDOC Week 1980 was 'Treat Us to a Treaty on Land Rights'. It showed the desire to be formally recognised and treated as First Peoples, not as wards of the state, as we had been since colonial days. The demands for a treaty or treaties grew over the years. Many efforts were made to convince governments to consider treaties as a way of overcoming the long history of racism towards Indigenous Peoples in our country.

The National NAIDOC Committee, which until 2008 was chaired by former Senator Aden Ridgeway, has made key decisions on national celebrations each year, and it has representatives from most Australian states and territories.

In 2004, the theme was 'Self-determination – Our Community – Our Future – Our Responsibility'. This expressed a widespread dissatisfaction with governments that continued to marginalise and exclude us from policy development.

The only national body that gave Aboriginal and Torres Strait Islander people a say in their own affairs was the Aboriginal and Torres Strait Islander Commission (ATSIC). In 2004, the federal government began a campaign in the media designed to close it down. ATSIC was finally closed the following year when then Prime Minister John Howard's government repealed its legislation. From 2008 to 2018, Anne Martin and Ben Mitchell co-chaired the Committee.

One of the themes for NAIDOC Week 2012 was 'They dared to challenge', celebrating and Aboriginal and Torres Strait Islander people who have encouraged or brought about change. In 2017, the theme was 'Our Languages Matter'. As the National NAIDOC Committee explained, this was to 'emphasise and celebrate the unique and essential role that

Jannawi Dance Clan in Hyde Park, Warrane/Sydney, New South Wales

A Rightful Place

Indigenous languages play in cultural identity, linking people to their land and water and in the transmission of Aboriginal and Torres Strait Islander history, spirituality and rites, through story and song'.

In 2018, Anne Martin and Ben Mitchell announced the theme, 'Because of her, we can!' A glittering ball held in Sydney that year honoured many Aboriginal and Torres Strait Islander women who served their peoples and the nation. In 2019, under new co-chairs John Paul Janke and Patricia Johnson, the theme was 'Voice Treaty Truth', acknowledging that 'Aboriginal and Torres Strait Islander peoples have … wanted an enhanced role in decision-making in Australia's democracy'.

> We celebrate NAIDOC because of the important contributions that Aboriginal and Torres Strait Islander people make to the Australian nation. We celebrate because we have survived here for over 60,000 years and continue [to] practise our cultures and speak our languages – we want to share this with all Australians. We celebrate because this nation always was, and always will be our land.

In 2020, the theme of 'Always Was, Always Will Be', recognised that 'First Nations people have occupied and cared for this continent for over 65,000 years', and acknowledged that:

> It's about seeing, hearing and learning the First Nations' 65,000+ year history of this country – which is Australian history. We want all Australians to celebrate that we have the oldest continuing cultures on the planet and to recognise that our sovereignty was never ceded.

The 2021 theme, 'Heal Country, Heal Our Nation', was a call for stronger measures to maintain our cultures and heritage. In 2022 it was 'Get Up! Stand Up! Show Up!' and in 2023 it is 'For Our Elders'.

We are not young, we are ancient

For most of Australia's history since the arrival of the British, the First Peoples have experienced formal racial discrimination. Aboriginal and Torres Strait Islander Peoples didn't have any rights as citizens in their own land. Today, there is still no formal means for our peoples to have a say in their own futures. Although two of several racist clauses in the Constitution were changed in the referendum of 1967, there is still no formal recognition or treaty.

It is right that the federal Parliament can make laws for Aboriginal and Torres Strait Islander Peoples. But we need to find a way to make sure these laws are fair, and to prevent racist discrimination by the Parliament.

The proposal for an Indigenous Voice to Parliament and Government has been developed gradually over three decades since the inception of the first Council for Aboriginal Reconciliation in 1991. It was legislated to have 25 members of Indigenous and non-Indigenous Australians to bring about within a set timeframe 'A united Australia which respects this land of ours; values the Aboriginal and Torres Strait Islander heritage; and provides justice and equity for all.' At the conclusion of the final Council term in 2000, a report was delivered to the Australian Government, then led by Prime Minister John Howard. At the event called Corroboree 2000, the Council presented two documents to John Howard and others on 27 May 2000: the Australian Declaration Towards Reconciliation and the Roadmap for Reconciliation. Among the recommendations for the future was constitutional reform aimed at recognising Indigenous Australians in the Constitution. It also recommended an apology to the Stolen Generations.

In 2000, John Howard and his government rejected the recommendations of the report by the Council for Aboriginal Reconciliation in its road map for reconciliation. Howard continued to reject the call for an apology, recommended again in this report, and also rejected a treaty and a referendum to be held to change the constitution's preamble to recognise Indigenous Peoples.

When the Act's sunset clause was triggered on 1 January 2001, a group of committed people established a foundation called Reconciliation Australia so that the remaining challenge of reconciliation became a people's movement. The successes of these three decades of bringing about a greater understanding are often taken for granted, but also, too often, treated with contempt by politicians and others to score cheap points in their own campaigns.

Cabinet papers released at the beginning of 2023 are replete with the language of his speech in 1997. A national apology would be 'inappropriate' as it could imply 'that present generations are in some way responsible for the actions of earlier generations'. A treaty would be 'divisive' and would 'not solve the critical issues facing Indigenous Australians'. This is, of course, wrong.

In 2008, Kevin Rudd's apology to the Stolen Generations united the nation. Hundreds of thousands of people listened. It was a healing gesture. Its importance to the remaining victims of those vicious policies and their descendants cannot be overestimated.

The apology brought a new understanding of our nation, and so too would constitutional recognition of a Voice for Aboriginal and Torres Strait Islander peoples to make representations to the parliament giving advice on policies and laws that affect us. Such a unifying moment can be imagined in the light of the healing of the nation that the apology to the Stolen Generations afforded.

In 2014, Indigenous lawyer and activist Noel Pearson suggested a simple change to the Constitution to establish a body of Indigenous people with the power to review all legislation in Parliament which affects Aboriginal and Torres Strait Islander people.

After dialogues around the country, the first Indigenous Constitutional Convention was held at Uluru, in the heart of Australia, in May 2017. On the final day of the First Nations National Constitutional Convention, the 250 Aboriginal and Torres Strait Islander delegates agreed unanimously to support the 'Uluru Statement from the Heart'. This is a document that was written at the Convention and now forms the basis of the referendum that will be held to recognise First Nations people in the Constitution. This body would solve the problem of our status as a small minority, making up about 3 per cent of the population, with ancient roots in this land, and our desire for a rightful place in the nation.

The Uluru Statement called for:
- a First Nations' Voice to Parliament to be enshrined in the Australian Constitution
- a Makarrata Commission 'to supervise a process of agreement-making between governments and First Nations
- 'truth-telling about our history' to acknowledge Australia's treatment of First Peoples.

The word 'makarrata', from the Yolŋu languages of north-east Arnhem Land, expresses the idea of negotiating an end to historical conflicts and a settlement of grievances. The NAIDOC Committee's announcement that 'Voice Treaty Truth' was the theme and the focus of the week of NAIDOC activities in 2019 reflected these three pillars of the Uluru Statement.

The view among most Aboriginal and Torres Strait Islander people is well expressed by delegate Thomas Mayo, a Zenadth Kes Torres Strait Islands man, who lives in Darwin: 'The Uluru Statement from the Heart is a compelling and historic document, not just because of the joyous and hopeful national consensus that it came from, but also because it is a reasonable and achievable proposal.'

THE ULURU STATEMENT FROM THE HEART

We, gathered at the 2017 National Constitutional Convention, coming from all points of the southern sky, make this statement from the heart.

Our Aboriginal and Torres Strait Islander tribes were the first sovereign Nations of the Australian continent and its adjacent islands, and possessed it under our own laws and customs. This our ancestors did, according to the reckoning of our culture, from the Creation, according to the common law from 'time immemorial', and according to science more than 60,000 years ago.

This sovereignty is a spiritual notion: the ancestral tie between the land, or 'mother nature', and the Aboriginal and Torres Strait Islander peoples who were born therefrom, remain attached thereto, and must one day return thither to be united with our ancestors. This link is the basis of the ownership of the soil, or better, of sovereignty. It has never been ceded or extinguished, and co-exists with the sovereignty of the Crown.

How could it be otherwise? That peoples possessed a land for sixty millennia and this sacred link disappears from world history in merely the last two hundred years?

With substantive constitutional change and structural reform, we believe this ancient sovereignty can shine through as a fuller expression of Australia's nationhood.

Proportionally, we are the most incarcerated people on the planet. We are not an innately criminal people. Our children are aliened from their families at unprecedented rates. This cannot be because we have no love for them. And our youth languish in detention in obscene numbers. They should be our hope for the future.

These dimensions of our crisis tell plainly the structural nature of our problem. This is the torment of our powerlessness.

We seek constitutional reforms to empower our people and take a rightful place in our own country. When we have power over our destiny our children will flourish. They will walk in two worlds and their culture will be a gift to their country.

We call for the establishment of a First Nations Voice enshrined in the Constitution.

Makarrata is the culmination of our agenda: the coming together after a struggle. It captures our aspirations for a fair and truthful

> relationship with the people of Australia and a better future for our children based on justice and self-determination.
>
> We seek a Makarrata Commission to supervise a process of agreement-making between governments and First Nations and truth-telling about our history.
>
> In 1967 we were counted, in 2017 we seek to be heard. We leave base camp and start our trek across this vast country. We invite you to walk with us in a movement of the Australian people for a better future.[28]

In his book *Finding the Heart of the Nation* (2019), Thomas Mayo also explains why he believes constitutional recognition for Indigenous Australians is needed:

> Constitutional enshrinement of a Voice ... can only be achieved by way of a referendum. A successful referendum will make it a permanent and politically strong voice. It will speak with a mandate from the Australian people that must be heard ... No one is asking for a third chamber of Parliament. The Voice proposal is constitutionally conservative. The proposal for a Voice isn't new and it isn't too much to ask. First Nations have been struggling for fairly chosen representation and the right to self-determination since before Federation.[29]

The intention of the delegates at the May 2017 convention at Uluṟu was that there should be a referendum on the question of whether or not we should have a Voice in Parliament and this became the first election promise Anthony Albanese made when he was elected Prime Minister in May 2022.

The NAIDOC Committee in 2019 found it necessary to issue a statement elaborating on the meaning of 'Voice Treaty Truth', saying:

> It's time for our knowledge to be heard through our voice.
>
> For generations, we have sought recognition of our unique place in Australian history and society today. We need to be the architects of our lives and futures.
>
> For generations, Aboriginal and Torres Strait Islander peoples have looked for significant and lasting change.
>
> Voice. Treaty. Truth. were three key elements to the reforms set out in the Uluṟu Statement from the Heart. These reforms represent the unified position of First Nations Australians ...

> *Aboriginal and Torres Strait Islander people want their voice to be heard. First Nations were excluded from the Constitutional convention debates of the 1800s when the Australian Constitution came into force. Indigenous people were excluded from the bargaining table ...*
>
> *Australia is one of the few liberal democracies around the world which still does not have a treaty or treaties or some other kind of formal acknowledgement or arrangement with its Indigenous minorities ...*
>
> *A substantive treaty has always been the primary aspiration of the Aboriginal and Torres Strait Islander movement.*
>
> *The true story of colonisation must be told, must be heard, must be acknowledged.*[30]

The world has changed dramatically since 1967, but at the time of writing some sections of the media and some politicians seem likely to oppose to the Voice. Social media is alive with the old racist ideas that have tarnished Australia ever since Federation. As noted earlier, Australia has a racist political legacy which is well known to historians, but is conveniently suppressed in the mythology about Australia's founding. Alfred Deakin, who later became Australia's second Prime Minister, declared in 1901:

> *In another century the probability is that Australia will be a White Continent with not a black or even dark skin among its inhabitants. The Aboriginal race has died out in the South and is dying fast in the North and West even where most gently treated. Other races are to be excluded by legislation if they are tinted to any degree. The yellow, the brown, and the copper-coloured are to be forbidden to land anywhere.*[31]

There are people who still today would like to believe this. They oppose the survival and wellbeing of Indigenous Australians, and have flocked to the fanciful vision of One Nation, and say there should be no 'special' treatment.

It is likely that if a Voice is established and becomes a part of the machinery of government, most Australians will find the proposition uncontentious.

In 2019, Minister for Indigenous Australians Ken Wyatt pledged that a proposal to recognise Indigenous people in the Constitution will be put to a referendum within three years. He was later overruled by Prime Minister Scott Morrison. Ken Wyatt then appointed that a Senior Advisory Group to present him with a detailed report on a 'Voice to Government'. I was appointed Co-Chair, with Professor Tom Calma AO, and after almost eighty meetings conducted largely online during the COVID-19 pandemic, we presented our interim report to the minister in October 2020. The 52 members of the

Indigenous Voice co-design was made up of a majority of Indigenous people. The minister presented it to the Cabinet and then released it to the public on 9 January 2021. The report explains proposals for an Indigenous Voice that, if they became law, would provide a way for Indigenous Australians to provide input to the Parliament and Government on matters that are important to improve our lives. Our interim report is available at voice.niaa.gov.au/node/107 and the final report is available at voice.niaa.gov.au/final-report.

When Linda Burney became the Minister for Indigenous Affairs in 2022, she also appointed a Referendum Advisory group, a Referendum Engagement Group and a Referendum Legal Expert Group. I was also appointed to the first and second group. All were tasked with advising the Minister for Indigenous Australians, the Attorney General Mark Dreyfus, Senator Patrick Dodson, the Special Envoy for Reconciliation and the Implementation of the Uluru Statement from the Heart, and Senator Malarndirri McCarthy, the Assistant Minister for Indigenous Australians. With a tight schedule for planning and campaigning for the referendum to be held in late 2023, the Advisory group members have advised on matters such the proposed Constitutional amendment and referendum question, as well as the parliamentary consideration of the *Referendum (Machinery Provisions) Amendment Bill 2022*. The Prime Minister Anthony Albanese has announced that the Australian Government is funding the pamphlet setting out the Yes case and the No case, and a civics education campaign because most younger Australians and new citizens will not have ever voted in a referendum, as the last one was held in 1999.

The question to be put to the voters at a referendum in late 2023 was announced by Prime Minister Anthony Albanese on Thursday 23 March, 2023, in Parliament House in Canberra, following months of deliberation by the Referendum Working Group, made up of Aboriginal and Torres Strait Islander people with a long history in the cause for constitutional change to recognise the First Peoples. The Group was chaired by Minister for Indigenous Affairs Linda Burney and included Special Envoy for Reconciliation and Recognition Senator Patrick Dodson, Attorney-General Mark Dreyfus and Assistant Minister for Social Services Senator Malandirri McCarthy. The Group was advised by a Constitutional Advisory Group consisting of constitutional experts, the majority of whom agreed with the final form of the question. The alteration to the Constitution, if approved by a majority of voters in a majority of states, will give constitutional recognition to Aboriginal and Torres Strait Islander Peoples by enshrining a Voice. This is the question to be answered Yes or No by the voters at the referendum:

Proposed referendum question

A Proposed Law: to alter the Constitution to recognise the First Peoples of Australia by establishing an Aboriginal and Torres Strait Islander Voice.

Do you approve this proposed alteration?

A majority Yes vote will result in a change to the Constitution as a new Section 129:

Proposed addition to Constitution

Chapter IX Recognition of Aboriginal and Torres Strait Islander Peoples

129 Aboriginal and Torres Strait Islander Voice

In recognition of Aboriginal and Torres Strait Islander peoples as the First Peoples of Australia:
- *There shall be a body, to be called the Aboriginal and Torres Strait Islander Voice;*
- *The Aboriginal and Torres Strait Islander Voice may make representations to the Parliament and the Executive Government of the Commonwealth on matters relating to Aboriginal and Torres Strait Islander peoples;*
- *The Parliament shall, subject to this Constitution, have power to make laws with respect to matters relating to the Aboriginal and Torres Strait Islander Voice, including its composition, functions, powers and procedures.*

The question is accompanied by these three provisions, and the Prime Minister also agreed to the publication of the Design Principles for the development of the Voice agreed by the Referendum Working Group. These are detailed and the summary that follows gives a good idea of the way that the Voice would be legislated by the Parliament should the referendum be successful:

Design principles for a Voice to Parliament

- *The Voice will give independent advice to the parliament and government*
- *Will be chosen by Aboriginal and Torres Strait Islander people based on the wishes of local communities*
- *Will be representative of Aboriginal and Torres Strait Islander communities, gender balanced and include youth*

- Will be empowering, community-led, inclusive, respectful and culturally informed
- Will be accountable and transparent
- Will work alongside existing organisations and traditional structures
- Will not have a program delivery function
- Will not have a veto power

If the referendum fails, the readers of this book will inherit this 'unfinished business'. Should this happen it will have dire consequences not just for my people, but the nation. As mentioned previously, no other constitution in the world is so difficult to change; only eight of forty-four questions voted on in referendums in Australia's history have succeeded. One of these was the referendum in 1967, when there was only a Yes case funded by government, and the proposition was sufficiently popular that no parliamentarians sought a No case. Before the details of the 2023 referendum question had been agreed by the Parliament, the National Party decided in December 2022 to oppose it.

The outcome in the case of a no vote to these questions will doom Aboriginal and Torres Strait Islander people to a permanent status as marginalised peoples, denied the rights that other Indigenous peoples enjoy in democratic settler states such as the United States of America, Canada, New Zealand and several nations in the Pacific and South America. Australia is an outlier in the world with respect to a postcolonial settlement with its First Peoples. This is recognised throughout the international bodies in which Australian representatives seek to exert influence on a range of matters such as defence, trade, cultural affairs, aid programs, human rights, the climate crisis, food security, health responses to pandemics, and many other issues.

Our predicament is known the world over, and in other countries where there has been a reckoning with the colonial past, such as coming to terms with slavery in Britain and the United States of America, or the impoverishment of former colonies with the centuries of extraction of human labour and local resources, all taken in what is now recognised as mass larceny. Repatriation of stolen cultural heritage, development and aid programs, compensation, and other measures are part of the global human rights response to the legacy of imperialism and colonialism. Pretending that Australia has no such obligations is a head-in-the-sand approach, politically immature and distinctly unhelpful in overcoming the problems that we have inherited.

What will happen if Australians vote yes in the referendum in 2023?

The blame game and political theatre of white guilt will end when the First Peoples of Australia have a genuine right to take responsibility for our own futures by advising Parliament and Government on the best way forward. The Uluru Statement from the Heart, like all the reconciliation statements and reports before it, makes clear that we are not blaming and not demanding a response of guilt.

An honourable status would be accorded to Indigenous Australians as the First Peoples, creating a foundation for a new idea of the nation that once looked to Britain as the 'mother country' and has since changed with waves of migration from countries other than the United Kingdom and the few European nations that were acceptable under the White Australia Policy. Most Australians of the future will be citizens of a rapidly changing world at risk from the climate crisis, ongoing violent conflicts and wars, and political upheaval. There is a security for citizens of a nation that has reconciled with its past treatment of Indigenous peoples and is able to genuinely claim pride in its nationhood. Our vision of the Voice as a constitutional plank for a new idea of the nation incorporates 65,000 years of human history with the British tradition of parliamentary democracy, the modernity of multiculturalism and all the benefits that migrant groups have offered to our way of life.

Whatever the outcome of this referendum, whether Australians are able to overcome their colonial burden will ultimately depend on their understanding of Aboriginal and Torres Strait Islander Peoples and their nation's past, including its pre-colonial past stretching back at least 50,000 years and more likely 65,000 years on present evidence. It is my hope that this book gives all Australians a better understanding and knowledge, and the tools to strengthen their own role in making our country a better place for all, with a place of dignity for the First Peoples.

5
Cultural Diversity and Resilience

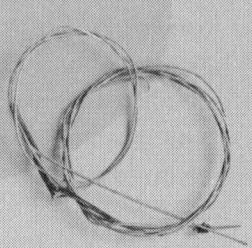

The cultural practices of Indigenous Australians in cities, towns, communities and remote regions vary greatly. They are grounded in different cultures, histories, socio-political conditions and the experience of colonisation and segregation. In many remote areas and a few urban and rural areas, pre-colonial traditions have survived. Many are being revitalised.

Family life is a fundamental aspect of any society, particularly for First Australians. Colonisation destroyed the old clan systems in many parts of the country. The practice of forcibly removing children from their families to 'assimilate' them as domestic and field labourers also damaged Aboriginal family life and the legacy of trauma continues today. While strong ties to family often – thankfully – remain, in many areas the kinship systems

Indigenous people from across Cape York in Far North Queensland gather at the Laura Dance Festival for three days of ceremony (photo Wayne Quilliam)

and the ways that people connect with extended family and 'tribes' have changed dramatically. The following chapter on kinship explains some of these traditions and the changes that followed the decimation of Aboriginal societies, as they were forced from their land with heavy losses of life.

Aboriginal and Torres Strait Islander languages, music and performance traditions are also becoming more endangered each year. Events such as the Barunga and Garma festivals have proved very effective in encouraging people to maintain these traditions, which are explained more in the following chapters.

Religious life and rituals continue

Religious life has been profoundly affected by colonisation. But rituals continue and many have been revived. The idea of the sacred is a strong organising principle, and this is pronounced when people have access to their traditional lands and the important sites where their ancestors are said to remain in the land.

Today, Aboriginal and Torres Strait Islander people around Australia follow various traditions and carry out important rites and rituals that mark the sacred in everyday life. Welcome to Country rituals for visitors, and some of the rituals of funerals, are good examples. By performing rituals, people bring their sacred spiritual beliefs and traditions into their daily lives, and the lives of those who witness them. This is the way that Aboriginal and Torres Strait Islander religious life is practised.

A powerful feature of Aboriginal life is the regard that is held for ancestors and supernatural beings that played a part in the creation of the world during a time that anthropologists call 'the Dreaming' or 'the Dreamtime'. There are terms in Indigenous languages for the sacred world. One such word in some Central Desert languages is Tjukurrpa, which is also spelt Tjukurpa or Jukurrpa in some Central Desert languages.

These great spiritual beings are recorded in rock art and are still celebrated in songs and ceremonies today. Some of them travelled, and their sacred travels and the stories that record them are expressed in song series, often called 'songlines', a term popularised by the British writer Bruce Chatwin in his 1987 book of the same name. For the first time non-Indigenous people learnt something about the ancient cultural traditions and beliefs, and the way spiritual ancestors, revered as the 'Old People', are sources of great power.

Sometimes this power is dangerous and must be mediated by the Elders, who guide visitors through the landscape where the Old People live in spirit. Because the sacred past resonates in places, Indigenous Owners follow traditions that will give safe passage to visitors. That is why the custodians will carry out smoking or water blessing rituals. These rites of mediation are often called 'Welcome to Country' ceremonies. In many places, Elders introduce visitors to the ancestors, because driving or walking to a place where they live eternally without the permission of Traditional Owners can invite their anger.

Traditional Owners perform welcome ceremonies in many different ways. Some groups light smoky fires with wet eucalyptus or paperbark leaves, so that the smoke wraps around the visitors and makes them one with the place. Another type of welcome ceremony involves throwing water on visitors; another involves wiping the sweat of an Elder on the visitor's face so that the visitor smells like the Traditional Owner.

One rite observed in many parts of the country is the taboo on saying the names of someone who has recently died. Instead, you refer to the deceased with a substitute name, and use the substitute name for everyone else with the same name as the deceased. In the deserts, the terms used are Kumanjayi and Kunmanara; Birrinjymal is the word in Arnhem Land in the Gupapuyŋu language; in western Cape York, Tayipity is used; and there are similar terms elsewhere. The deceased are remembered in various ways: with special words, in designs and visual art, funerary objects, songs and dances.

Respect for the spiritual Old People and ancestral beings is strong throughout the cultures of the First Australians. The idea of Old People corresponds to the perception of stars as being representations of the past. The Old People are encountered in the landscape, just as we see stars when we gaze at the night sky. We know that stars are what can be seen now of some cataclysmic event in the universe many thousands of light years ago. That is, the light of the explosion emanates through time and space and is visible to our eyes in the present.

Likewise, Aboriginal people perceive the spiritual presence of Elders in the landscape as something that has come through time since the ancestor died.

The influence of the ancestors is felt in the Indigenous knowledge systems that tell us about how the world works and how humans should live together and in the world. The ancestors created kinship systems, laws for the ownership of land, sacred sites, and systems of relationship between people and the natural world.

All of these are reflected in a variety of ways across Aboriginal and Torres Strait Islander cultures. Some of the different ways are explained in the chapter on kinship. Kinship and descent are the main structuring forces that bring people together into clans, 'tribal' groups and customary identities.

Most Aboriginal and Torres Strait Islander people will be required to assert their identity and sometimes to prove that identity. Because of legal and social complexities, many choose to announce themselves by customary or language identities, such as Iman (which I do, as my grandfather was born into the Iman-speaking people in eastern central Queensland). They may also speak of their 'mob' or clan name.

The current legal definition for an Aboriginal or Torres Strait Islander is based on the 1981 parliamentary *Report on a Review of the Administration of the Working Definition of Aboriginal and Torres Strait Islanders*. It is a three-part definition based on (1) descent, (2) self-identification and (3) community recognition. This definition has since been adopted by various federal and state departments.

Debates over the legal wording for an Indigenous Australian rage on. Yet Aboriginal and Torres Strait Islander people themselves find certainty in following their own family lines or genealogical connections. Stan Grant is a Wiradjuri man from Griffith in New South Wales. His book *On Identity* explains how the idea of 'kinship' is in fact universal for all humans:

> Put two or more of us together and it is the first question asked: 'Where are you from, who are your people?' It is genealogy, but it is more than that. It is survival. We all do this in our own way – people everywhere. It is the family crest, the clan's tartan, a sepia-tinged photograph, a convict ship's manifest, a long-dead soldier's pocketbook, the tattooed wrists of the death camps – tangible proof, because we so need it.

Gender identities

Gender identities are also important in the Indigenous world. For example, in the deserts and parts of the Kimberley region, there are women's societies where widows live together. In some cases, the women stop speaking to each other, instead communicating in hand sign language to be used only by widows. Men's ritual groups are similarly rule-bound. Men in these places often have martial arts traditions involving heavy clubs.

Gender roles across Indigenous Australia can also be significantly different from Anglo-Australian practices. In her book *Aboriginal Woman: Sacred and Profane* (1939), Phyllis M. Kaberry writes about her time living in the Forrest River Mission, later known as Oombulgurri (but no longer exists), in the Kimberley between 1935 and 1936. She depicted strong independent women with their own rituals, beliefs and traditions that were the privilege of women. More recent books include Diane Bell's *Daughters of the Dreaming* (1983), which describes a women's society in the area around Tennant Creek, and

(left) Campaign poster (2012) for Sistergirl leader, Crystal Johnson; (right) poster promoting the rights of brotherboys and sistergirls (2014)

Making Aboriginal Men and Music in Central Australia (2015) by Åse Ottoson, a fascinating account of Aboriginal men in Alice Springs whose manhood is shaped by their love of country, rock and reggae music.

INDIGENOUS LGBTQIA+ CULTURAL LIFE

Now that same-sex marriage is legal, young Indigenous people have felt encouraged to claim their gender and sexual identities, whether gay, bisexual, trans or other. Their important cultural contributions are being recognised and they are flourishing. I have asked some young people who participate in LGBTQIA+ Indigenous cultural events and happenings – irrespective of their identities – to contribute to this chapter.

But first, it is important to include some history of the fight by LGBTQIA+ people for their rights, because their human rights have only very recently been recognised at law.

The first Pride march or parade to be held in Australia was on 28 June 1970, a year after the Stonewall Riots in New York, which took place in 1969 when, fed up with constant police violence, gay people at the Stonewall Inn in Greenwich Village fought back, and five days of riots ensued, inciting a global movement.[32]

Homosexuality was still illegal in Australia in 1978 when a brave group of gay men and lesbian women organised a street festival to celebrate gay rights. They are remembered as the '78ers and are honoured for their role in fighting for the rights of gay and lesbian people in Australia. The organisers called themselves the Gay Solidarity Group, and after a week of events, on Saturday 24 June 1978, held the first Mardi Gras street festival. Their aim was to decriminalise homosexuality and they were also planning the 4th National Homosexual Conference.

Two Indigenous people were among the '78ers – Annie Pratten and Darug man Chris Bourke (deceased). Indigenous people have become more visible in the subsequent Pride marches now held annually (except during COVID-19 restrictions) across the country. The first featured Indigenous contingent in the Sydney Mardi Gras was in 1998.

The first Sydney Mardi Gras was a sedate affair, compared to the recent parades that last for hours with float after float of spectacular displays, dancing and music processing down Oxford Street to the noisy adoration of, as 2019 figures attest, half a million people from around Australia and the world. But the night of Saturday 24 June 1978 ended in violence. Although the NSW Police have since issued an apology for their behaviour and violence, the horror of the police attack on the festival attendees has not been forgotten. On that night, several hundred gay and lesbian people and their supporters, 'some in fancy dress and some simply rugged up against the cold – gathered at Taylor Square and followed a truck with a small music and sound system down Oxford Street to Hyde Park.' The Sydney Gay and Lesbian Mardi Gras 1978–2020 Timeline is an excellent resource and its account of what happened that night in Sydney and, although brief, resonates still, because it inspired thousands to join the '78ers and protest at the discrimination against gay and lesbian people. At the 2019 AGM of the Sydney Gay and Lesbian Mardi Gras (SGLMG), a resolution was passed giving the '78ers Lifetime Membership.

The Mardi Gras in Sydney has evolved to become a world-renowned celebration of queerness and it has grown from the one-night grand parade to events held across several weeks. The official title is the Sydney Gay and Lesbian Mardi Gras and for those unable to join in person, the parade is broadcast live on SBS (the Special Broadcasting Service).[33]

In 1982, Narrandera man Roger McKay marched alone in the parade, wearing the Aboriginal flag. This significant moment is widely acknowledged as the first time the Aboriginal flag appeared in the parade.

'He was determined to make the point that, no matter how much Oxford Street was seen as the gay "Golden Mile", it was still on Aboriginal land.' (Colin Clewes, Gay in the 80s)

'The first person to carry the Aboriginal flag up the guts of Oxford Street was Roger McKay from the Sandhills of Narrandera.' (Esther Montgomery, Gay in the 80s)

The parade has also been a means of contesting history-making for the LGBTQIA+ community. Before the 1988 Mardi Gras, a debate over how to acknowledge the bicentenary was resolved by featuring Malcolm Cole, an Indigenous gay man, dressed as Captain Cook. His version of Captain Cook was later commemorated in an exhibition along with Indigenous drag queens dressed as superheroes, and portraits of the well-known Noel Tovey and Raymond Blanco.

In 2019, First Nations Rainbow helped the SGLMG win WorldPride, an international event promoting LGBTQIA+ rights, cultures and issues through sporting events, festivals, conferences, a parade and other cultural events. They were Graham Simms, Gadigal; Ben Graetz, Iwaidja, Malak Malak and Badu Islander; and Joseph Cardona, Iwaidja, Malak Malak and Badu Islander.

Members of the worldwide InterPride network of Pride organisations voted between Sydney, Montreal and Houston as the host city for WorldPride 2023. Sydney won with 60 per cent of the vote. The biennial WorldPride festival was held over February and March to coincide with the 2023 Sydney Gay and Lesbian Mardi Gras. First Nations Rainbow helped to make the announcement, with a Gadigal man who attended the Athens Pride conference, congratulating Australia on its unprecedented win in a video on Twitter.[34]

The '78ers inspired a nationwide movement, and Pride marches are now held throughout Australia every year. Today the Australian Pride Network is the umbrella organisation for LGBTQIA+ festivals and events for the entire community to celebrate, reflect and promote their cultures and human rights. Across Australia, a diverse selection of festivals and events takes place throughout the year. Events are listed on the Australian Pride Network by state and territory.

The Sydney Gay and Lesbian Mardi Gras website also lists all events. The diversity and contributions of First Peoples members of the LGBTQIA+ communities are widely acknowledged and respected.

SYDNEY'S MARDI GRAS by Luke Pearson

The first Mardi Gras, held in Sydney on 24 June 1978, was an add-on to a demonstration marking the anniversary of the Stonewall riots in New York in 1969. The parade held that night led to an excessive police response in the form of violent arrests, and eventually a riot between police and those participating in the march at Kings Cross.

It is believed that a number of Indigenous people were involved in this violent clash, both as participants in the parade and as bystanders who joined in to support the protesters.

Miss First Nation Australia 2018 contestants in the Miss Photogenic shoot at Mrs Macquarie's Chair, Warrane/Sydney. From left: Shaniqua, Timberlina, Zodiac, MadB, Bailey Legal, Felicia Foxx, Lasey Dunaman.

While there has been a long history of Indigenous LGBTQIA+ participation in Mardi Gras, it was not until 2017 that an Indigenous float led the parade. Sydney's Mardi Gras has since become a month-long series of events with significant Indigenous inclusion, including Koori Gras, an Indigenous-led event involving performances and exhibitions. There is also an online timeline showcasing the history of Indigenous involvement in the Sydney Mardi Gras parade at tiki-toki.com (which can be found by searching history of First Peoples in Mardi Gras).

INDIGENOUS LGBTQIA+ CULTURE AND LIFESTYLE
by Jessie Lloyd

Lesbian, gay, bisexual, transgender, queer, intersex, asexual and pansexual people have always been a part of the Aboriginal and Torres Strait Islander community. But due to various religious or cultural practices in some communities, many people are often marginalised or remain 'in the closet'. As a result, people migrated to capital cities to connect with other LGBTQIA+ groups or began working in queer-friendly spaces.

Indigenous queer folk participate in cultural events such as drag shows, dance and performance works, and pride marches across the country, incorporating their unique cultural identity and themes into the queer space.

There are Indigenous communities that are more open and supportive of LGBTQIA+ members such as the Tiwi Islands, which has a high percentage of transgender people known as 'Sistergirls'. *Top End Wedding* (2019), starring Miranda Tapsell, features some of the Sistergirls in the film. In other regional places like Broome in Western Australia, community diversity is easily accepted from generations of intermarriage between Aboriginal, Japanese, Malay and Chinese people. Mikka Polina of Broome in Western Australia says, 'Being gay in the Kimberley and Broome is amazing ... You are first accepted as a family member and a community member and ... being gay is not an issue.'

Indigenous LGBTQIA+ people have always had a strong online presence, with Black Rainbow on Twitter and Beautiful, Talented & Deadly on Facebook. There is also the radio program *Rainbow KINection* on Noongar Radio. Issues such as sexual health, suicide or homelessness are the driving factors behind queer programs and support networks.

MELBOURNE'S LGBTQIA+ MIDSUMMA by Mark Nannup and Todd Fernando

Melbourne's LGBTQIA+ MIDSUMMA Festival was established in 1988 after local LGBTQIA+ people became tired of heading to Sydney for the Mardi Gras.

Since 1988, Aboriginal and Torres Strait Islander people have taken part in the festival but 2017 was the first year that the festival was led by Aboriginal and Torres Strait Islander people down Fitzroy Street in St Kilda, with a smoking ceremony from local Traditional Owners, the Boon Wurrung People. It was a huge success and over sixty people turned up to celebrate this special occasion.

MIDSUMMA's organisers now make sure Indigenous people continue to be a part of this festival by working very closely with the Aboriginal and Torres Strait Islander community to make their voices present within it.

In 2017, the Victorian NAIDOC Committee decided to incorporate an LGBTQIA+ night in the calendar, to showcase inclusivity within our community. This night came to be because of all the hard work and determination of a group called OutBlack, which has been running the Aboriginal and Torres Strait LGBTQIA+ Pride Night for the last thirty years in Victoria.

ACCEPT AND EMPOWER OUR LGBTQIA+ BROTHERS AND SISTERS by Ruby Langton-Batty

A young Aboriginal LGBTQIA+ friend of mine told me that he doesn't think homophobia is a big issue within the Aboriginal community. Unfortunately, there is still some homophobia within the Aboriginal community. I have seen this kind of discrimination first hand, and I have seen the harm it does. According to LGBTIQ+ Health Australia (formerly the National LGBTI Health Alliance), the Indigenous LGBTQIA+ community 'are an invisible minority ... and there are currently no protocols for identifying them in the suicide and self-harm statistics', but it is understood they are more vulnerable to risk of suicide than other minority populations. I can barely imagine how painful and exhausting it must be to battle daily against both racism and homophobia. We must all stand up against homophobia and racism and ensure that our LGBTQIA+ brothers and sisters are treated with respect and receive the same rights as any other Australian.

Tiwi Islander Crystal Love-Johnson is the first Indigenous trans person in the Northern Territory to come out as 'Sistergirl' and to live a trans life in a modern way. She has faced incredible hardship and adversity but has fought for her rights and demanded to be treated with respect. She is the first trans person to be elected to a local government in Australia, becoming a member of the Tiwi Shire Council in 2012.

Actor, writer and musician Steven Oliver, of *Black Comedy* fame, makes light of being a gay Aboriginal man in Australia in his brilliant song 'Minority within a Minority'.

His lyrics always reduce his audience to tears of laughter. You can watch the song on YouTube. Oliver's work epitomises how the Aboriginal and Torres Strait Islander LGBTQIA+ community copes with, and fights against, homophobia and racism: with humour.

TJay (Lasey Dunaman) and Dallas (Nova Gina) are the Indigenous drag duo the Dreamtime Divas. These prolific performers travel far and wide around Australia, sharing positivity and acceptance of diversity. One of their stated aims, as they explain on their Facebook page, is to 'raise awareness for youth depression and teen suicide [as a result of] homophobia, violence and bullying'. I have a deep admiration for all drag queens, and especially Black queens, because they are like warriors for love and peace. Their beautiful, glamorous, bedazzling and hilarious resistance is a barrier against all forms of oppression. Even the most complacent and backward audience members can't help but crack a smile.

I went to the Miss First Nation pageant (aka the 'Olympics for Aboriginal drag queens') for the first time in 2017 at the Imperial Hotel in Sydney. The contestants were Bailey Legal, Felicia Foxx, Lasey Dunaman, MadB, Timberlina, Zodiac and Shaniqua. The performances were epic and the competition was fierce. More than anything, it was a powerful explosion of joy. It is incredibly liberating to be in a space where everyone feels safe to truly be themselves, no matter who they are.

It was in this small corner of the world where I glimpsed our possible future. In that future, no one experiences hatred or violence because of who they are. All people and expressions are celebrated. Instead of 'freedom of speech', there is 'freedom of being'. That night, Lasey Dunaman was crowned Miss First Nation Australia.

Our traditions and cultures deserve respect

There are hundreds of Indigenous cultures with many customs specific to them and others that are continent-wide, such as managing fire with fire. Many customs, such as ceremonial practices and rituals, vary greatly across the continent. We speak many languages; we are cultural beings. This is the universal case for humanity. We are no less 'cultural' for embracing different customs and practices.

Aboriginal and Torres Strait Islander cultures offer unique ways to see and be in the world. They have been mostly invisible throughout Australian history – misunderstood, denied, vilified and lied about. The price our people have paid for being Aboriginal is not only a tragic and unwarranted loss of life. The frontier deaths, discrimination, marginalisation and stigmatisation are part of the burden that we carry. What is encouraging, though, is the extraordinary resilience of First Australians to maintain and preserve our cultures and tell the world about them.

The increasing interest of students, scholars and historians and others who have investigated our traditions tells us that there are people who prefer the facts over the mythologies. The mythology about First Australians is that we are trapped in the imaginary 'Stone Age' and incapable of change. The facts show otherwise. First Australians have always been innovators, finding ways to create and develop the longest living cultures on the planet throughout tumultuous periods of climate change, radically altered environments, colonisation and more than a century of extreme violence and dispossession. Despite this, traditions that began when our ancestors started to arrive here at least 65,000 years ago continue and are relevant today. There is a great deal to learn. This brief chapter has explored a few aspects to show the very different, but no less valuable, ways of knowing and being in the world of the First Australians.

6
Language and Country

More than 600 distinct language dialects and at least 250 languages were spoken across the continent before colonisation. Many of these languages were completely different from one another, and most people spoke more than one language.

There is a strong cultural association between language and land. Many organisations are now using the name of the language group to describe their location. For example, Australia Post recognises traditional names for mail delivery, and the capital cities are increasingly known by the traditional name for the area: Naarm/Melbourne, Meanjin/Brisbane, Warrane/Sydney, nipaluna/Hobart, Tarndanya/Adelaide, Garramilla/Darwin, Boorloo/Perth and Ngambri/Ngunnawal/Canberra. This recognition helps redress a major loss.

When the Indigenous Peoples lost their land, in many cases they also lost their language. Australia is one of the world's hotspots for language loss. Many Indigenous languages are no longer spoken; for some languages, only a few words are remembered. Since colonisation, governments and organisations banned or discouraged Indigenous people from speaking their languages. It is remarkable that 120 of those languages are still spoken.

Aboriginal languages strengthen the connections people have with their land, culture and identity. This is one of the reasons why it is important to preserve, record and learn them. The level of information that is available about Indigenous languages varies greatly across the country. Some are well supported with stories, dictionaries and multimedia resources in the language. In the case of many others, very little is known. Many Indigenous languages are at risk of disappearing as the remaining speakers pass away.

The First Peoples are working with linguists and other interested groups to record and revive their languages. They are also teaching them to young people in schools and communities. Some projects that record and share Indigenous knowledge also preserve the language. For example, projects to collect information about Indigenous weather knowledge also preserve the

William (Bill) Wentworth tape recording Aboriginal words and songs with four Elders from Maree region, Western Australia (image courtesy of AIATSIS, item WENTWORTH.B03. CS-000168946)

language of weather knowledge, including the words for seasons, weather phenomena and seasonal indicators such as flowering plants.

While it is possible to learn about Aboriginal and Torres Strait Islander languages, it is much more difficult to learn to speak them. They are different from English in every way – in their pronunciation, tone, vocabulary and sentence structures.

Thanks to an innovative policy in New South Wales, Aboriginal languages have a greater chance of surviving there than elsewhere in Australia. In 2017, the New South Wales Government introduced a law to protect the Aboriginal languages within the state's boundaries. The *Aboriginal Languages Act 2017* is the first legislation in Australia to acknowledge the significance of First languages.

This Act seeks to promote, reawaken, nurture and grow Aboriginal languages across New South Wales. It has three parts:

- a preamble that acknowledges the importance of Aboriginal languages. It also recognises the importance of reawakening, nurturing and growing Aboriginal languages and Aboriginal custodianship of languages.

- establishment of an Aboriginal Languages Trust to resource local language activities, among other functions
- a five-year Strategic Plan to guide investment and activities in language revival in New South Wales.

The New South Wales *Aboriginal Languages Act* is the strongest legal expression of our right to speak our languages. This right is expressed in the United Nations Declaration on the Rights of Indigenous Peoples.

One remarkable example of Indigenous language revitalisation has been initiated for the Wiradjuri language, which is spoken in the heartland of Wiradjuri Country around Orange, Parkes and Forbes in the central west of New South Wales. Dedicated Wiradjuri language workers and teachers are introducing their language to students in the state school system, especially in Warrane/Sydney. St Andrew's Cathedral School in Sydney also has a program for Aboriginal and Torres Strait Islander primary students. The children taking part in this program, which is called Gawura, start Wiradjuri lessons in kindergarten. The other primary school students at St Andrew's start learning Wiradjuri from Year 3.

This revitalisation strongly contrasts with the belief held in the nineteenth and twentieth century by many linguists and anthropologists who claimed that our languages and cultures would become extinct.

Aboriginal English

Many people assume that speakers of Aboriginal English have not learnt Standard English very well and so they are poor speakers of English. This is not the case: Aboriginal English is a dialect of Standard English in its own right. Dr Diane Eades from the University of New England points out, 'Aboriginal people in areas where there was no pidgin language made English into an Aboriginal English by bringing into it accents, grammar and ways of speaking from their traditional languages'.

Speakers of Aboriginal English can also learn Standard English and switch between the two, depending on the situation. Among other Aboriginal people, instead of saying, 'You are very well dressed', I would say, 'You too flash' or 'You lookin' deadly'.

In some communities, Aboriginal English and several creoles have replaced the original Indigenous languages, or are spoken in addition to those languages. Creoles are languages that have developed from a pidgin version of English to become the main language. According to an estimate from the 2011 census, Kriol is spoken across much of northern Australia by around 4000 people. However, the number of speakers is probably higher than that.

Narrm (also spelled Naarm) is the traditional name for the location where the city of Melbourne is built (photo Wayne Quilliam)

Linguist Dr Greg Dickson wrote in *The Conversation* in April 2016, 'Linguists put the number of Kriol speakers closer to 20,000, knowing that census data struggles to accurately capture high levels of multilingualism in remote Aboriginal communities.' He also tells us: 'Creole, as a linguistic term, is a type of language typically born out of abrupt and often brutal colonisation processes. Creoles are generally based on the dominant language of the colonisers.'

In Australia, there are two creole languages that have large numbers of speakers. One is Kriol, spoken in the savannah regions of northern Australia. The other is Torres Strait Creole, which is spoken alongside multiple Indigenous languages in the Torres Strait.

The languages of the Torres Strait Islands

The eastern languages of the Torres Strait Islands are not related to the Aboriginal or, properly speaking, the Australian languages of the mainland, while the western and central languages are. A handy summary of the languages of the Torres Strait Islands is provided by the State Library of Queensland. It shows the great complexity of language in just one region of northern Australia.

> There are two traditional languages of the Torres Strait Islands, Meriam Mir and Kala Lagaw Ya. Meriam Mir (also written as Miriam Mer) is the

language of the Eastern Islands of the Torres Strait. Linguistically, it is connected to the Papuan languages of the Austronesian family of languages. There are two regional dialects:

- **Mer dialect** – Mer (Murray), Waier, Dauar.
- **Erub dialect** – Erub (Darnley) and Ugar (Stephen).

Kala Lagaw Ya (also written as Kalaw Lagaw Ya) is the traditional language owned by the Western and Central islands of the Torres Strait. It is linguistically connected to the Aboriginal languages of the Australian mainland and has four distinct regional dialects derived from this language:

- **Mabuyag** – The dialect of Mabuiag, Badu and St Paul's Village.
- **Kalaw Kawaw Ya** – The dialect of the top western islands of Saibai, Dauan and Malu Ki'ai.
- **Kawrareg** – The dialect of the south-western islands of Kubin, Kaiwalagal, Muralag (Prince of Wales), Nurupai (Horn), Giralag (Friday), Waiben (Thursday), Keriri (Hammond), Maurura (Wednesday), Moa (Banks). It is also known as Kawalgau Ya.
- **Kulkalgau Ya** – The dialect of the central islands of Aurid (Aureed), Damut (Dalrymple), Iama (Yam or Turtle-backed), Masig (Yorke), Mauar (Rennel), Naghir (Mt Earnest), Poruma (Coconut) and Warraber (Sue).

The dialects are determined geographically and developed over time with influences by traditional trade, visits, intermarriage and kinship ties.

The contact with missionaries and others since the 1800s has led to the development of Torres Strait Creole; it has developed from a Pidgin and now has its own distinctive sound system, grammar, vocabulary, usage and meaning. Torres Strait Creole (also known as Ailan Tok or Yumplatok) is spoken by most Torres Strait Islanders and is a mixture of Standard Australian English and traditional languages. It is an English-based creole; however, each island has [its] own version of creole.[35]

By learning another language, we begin to understand the role of language in our lives. The vocabulary of another language, or the words that make it up, gives us an insight into how other people see the world. Some languages have many terms for rain, for example, because the people live where rain is common. It comes as deluges or drizzles, storms or raindrops. Others have many terms for snow because the people who speak to them live in environments that are subject to snowfall for much of the year.

How we speak about something using the words in our language determines a great deal about how we think about it. In many ways, our perception of the world is defined by language. When we lose a language, or our mother tongue is lost to us and replaced by a dominant language such as English, we lose not just the language but all the special meanings that language held for us. This applies to how we understand our environments and our family, our kinfolk and our inner selves.

In many parts of the Aboriginal world, languages are sacred, as they were given to us by the ancestors. Indeed, languages are owned by those people who can claim a sacred genealogical link to an ancestral speaker of that language. Place, identity and the laws that apply among the people who live on the same area of land are bound together by their language.

The different languages spoken around the country, especially in coastal areas, distinguished the many groups of people who lived there. The social relations of language bring people together under one language-speaking identity. They show them as being different from others who speak other, closely related languages in a web of close and distant kin.

The loss of a mother tongue is a destructive burden for Indigenous Peoples who are marginalised minorities. Indigenous people face discrimination on the basis of ethnicity, race, lifestyle, religion and especially language. This is why UNESCO has developed tools to help preserve the world's linguistic diversity. To answer the question of why we should preserve languages, the UNESCO project known as the 'Atlas of the World's Languages in Danger' states: 'Languages are vehicles of our cultures, collective memory and values. They are an essential component of our identities, and a building block of our diversity and living heritage.'

To be free to speak our mother tongues is a human right. This right is expressed in the United Nations Declaration on the Rights of Indigenous Peoples, at Article 13:

1. Indigenous peoples have the right to revitalize, use, develop and transmit to future generations their histories, languages, oral traditions, philosophies, writing systems and literatures, and to designate and retain their own names for communities, places and persons.
2. States shall take effective measures to ensure that this right is protected and also to ensure that indigenous peoples can understand and be understood in political, legal and administrative proceedings, where necessary through the provision of interpretation or by other appropriate means.

Australia declined to become a signatory to this Declaration when the member states of the UN General Assembly voted on 13 September 2007.

By eventually becoming a signatory, Australia has indicated a commitment to uphold the rights contained in it.

The Aboriginal and Torres Strait Islander Social Justice Commissioner Tom Calma released a Social Justice Report in 2009 highlighting the problem. 'The perilous state of Indigenous languages in Australia', he pointed out that it was only in August that year, for the first time in Australia's history, that the Commonwealth Government launched a strategy for preserving Indigenous languages. *Indigenous Languages – A National Approach 2009* set out the government's plan to preserve Indigenous languages through targeted actions. Those actions are:

- increasing information about Indigenous languages in all spheres of Australian life
- improving coordination of language centre activity
- supporting language programs in schools
- undertaking a feasibility study to develop a National Indigenous Languages Centre.

While there is still much work to do to implement Article 13 of the United Nations Declaration on the Rights of Indigenous Peoples in Australia, there has been some progress. First Languages Australia has developed essential resources for speakers of our languages and is rescuing endangered languages and those thought to be extinct. First Languages Australia explains that the

An example of how language is used to convey important values and principles (photo Wayne Quilliam)

human rights of speakers of Australia's First languages are a foundational motivation for their work. In 'Why maintain our languages?', which you can find on the First Languages Australia website, the authors cite chapter 3 of the Social Justice Report 2009: 'As Aboriginal and Torres Strait Islander people we know we have a unique place in this country and we value our languages. They are precious to us, and there is a sense of loss amongst those of us who no longer speak our languages.'

Tom Calma noted other benefits of maintaining our languages in some detail in his report: promoting resilience, improving health, improving cognitive functioning and increasing employment options. He also presents an economic argument about the costs of losing our languages.

THE LANGUAGE WORK OF THE NGANGKARI TO HEAL

The ngankari, the traditional healers of the Pitjantjatjara, Yankunytjatjara and Ngaanyatjarra Peoples, have a profound understanding of the meaning and role of their languages. Pitjantjatjara is one of the widely spoken languages in northern South Australia and in the south of the Northern Territory. Some of the neighbouring languages are Yankunytjatjara, Ngaanyatjarra and Luritja.

The women of this region who speak the three dominant languages formed an organisation more than forty years ago to ensure their wellbeing and survival of their cultures. The NPY Women's Council has among its programs the Ngangkari – Traditional Healers service. Its most innovative project, the Uti Kulintjaku initiative, uses language to strengthen emotional wellbeing. As explained on the council's website, npywc.org.au, uti kulintjaku is a Pitjantjatjara phrase that means 'to think and understand clearly'.

The ngangkari give young people ways to speak about their feelings in their own language and give their families the language for listening. They do this by providing the words in the languages that describe and name emotional states and states of being, and by doing so in engaging ways. Their tools also give parents the words for understanding the stages in their children's development.

Uti Kulintjaku 'works at the interface of knowledge systems and languages to better understand mental health and wellbeing and develops resources to promote this shared bi-cultural understanding more broadly'.

The project is no longer funded but, during its short period of funding support, it brought together:

ngangkari, senior A*n*angu, interpreters, and mental health practitioners in workshops to strengthen communication between A*n*angu and non-Aboriginal health professionals ... to improve the emotional vocabulary of A*n*angu children and explain how trauma can affect their behaviour.

The Uti Kulintjaku Project helped 'A*n*angu address mental health and related issues using their own language and culture, and their knowledge of western mental health'. As explained on the website:

*It also strengthens the capacity of local mental health professionals to engage with and communicate more effectively with A*n*angu people, to 'see through their eyes'.*[36]

The Words for Feelings Map is an illustrated poster that is designed to help people to 'find the right words to express different feelings' using words from Pitjantjatjara and Ngaanyatjarra. 'We believe that if people can find the words to express their feelings, then they are better equipped to ask for the help they need.' The map is one item in a set of word tools created by the ngangka*r*i. Other tools in their kit are posters, magnets and flashcards, children's books such as *Tjulpu and Walpa: Two Children, Two Roads*, and colouring books for meditative practice 'to help improve mental health literacy'. The project also produced the award-winning Kulila! app (*kulila* means 'listen up'). My personal favourite is the set of Uti Kulintjaku magnets. I have them on my refrigerator.

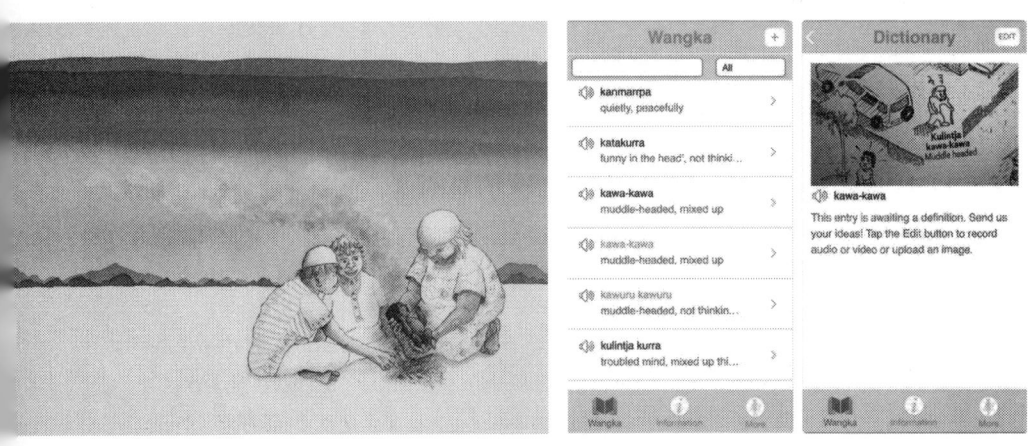

Left: *Tjulpu and Walpa*, NPY Women's Council 2017, illustration by Katelyn Griffin.
Right: A screenshot of the Uti Kulintjaku Project's dictionary app, designed to help people translate and communicate their feelings.

Language and Country

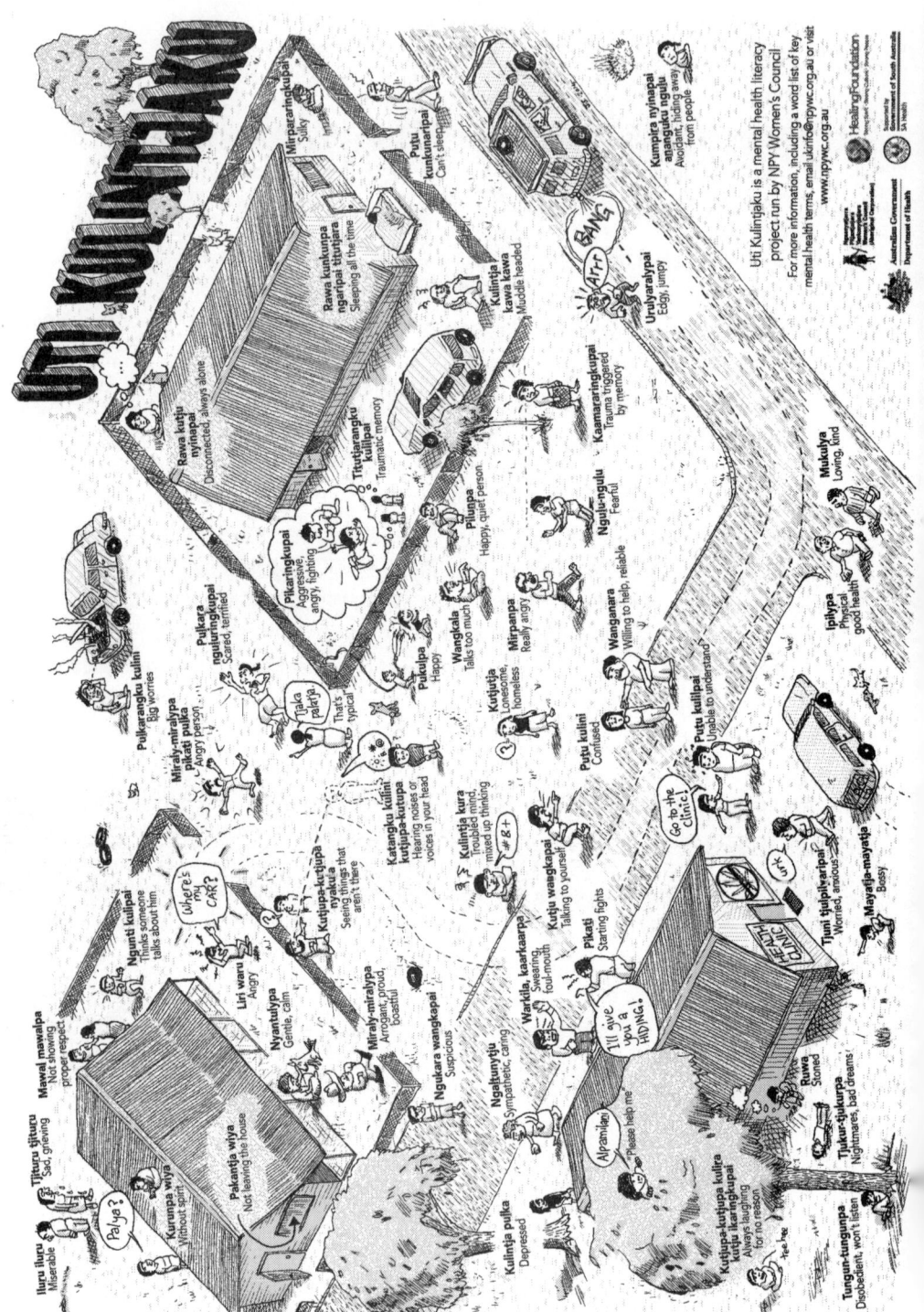

Uti Kulintjaku means 'to think and understand clearly' in Pitjantjatjara. This poster assists the discussion of mental health with 'words for feelings'.

You can watch films made in Aboriginal and Torres Strait Islander languages. In one of my favourites, *Ten Canoes*, directed by Rolf de Heer and Peter Djigirr and released in 2006, the actors speak entirely in their language, Ganalbiŋu. It is easy to follow as it has some subtitles and is narrated by the awarding-winning actor David Gulpilil. *Ten Canoes* is a story of events that took place in the distant past among the Yolŋu Peoples of the Arafura wetlands region, in Arnhem Land in the Northern Territory. It involves stolen wives, revenge and war, and while it is a dark comedy, the storyline is carried by the superb acting of local people. They re-create a Dreaming story within a Dreaming story. It also shows the traditional customs and traditions from one area of Australia.

Many Indigenous musicians sing in both English and their own languages. My favourite band, Yothu Yindi, cut several beautiful tracks in the Gumatj tongue of the Yolŋu matha languages. Their song 'Tribal Voice' is the best example. Several of their most popular hits, such as 'Djäpana: Sunset Dreaming', had fans around the world singing in an Aboriginal language. It is a public ceremonial song in the Manikay style of the Yolŋu musical tradition. Among other things, it is about the sacred sunset. Sunset is the divide between night and day, and is regarded, like dawn, as a sacred event.

The term 'djäpana' refers equally to the yellow colour of clouds at sunset, the particular clans that are linked by the waŋarr (ancestral beings) and

To watch is to hear, to listen is to understand (Baker Boy performance, photo Wayne Quilliam)

Language and Country

their journeys, and other matters. The colour yellow is one emblem of the Gumatj clan, of which Dr Mandawuy Yunupiŋu, the late lead singer of Yothu Yindi, is a famous son. Sunset is when the wind blows through the forest, the leaves rustle, white cockatoos swoop down to their roosts in the branches, and the inflamed sky darkens. It is customary for ceremonies to begin sometime just before sunset; even if the ritual itself is delayed, people gather at this time, waiting for it to begin. Baker Boy (see page 143) is continuing this new tradition of singing popular music in Yolŋu matha, and so too are many other singers. The annual National Aboriginal and Torres Strait Islander Music Awards in Garramilla/Darwin showcase these multilingual singers.

Every time you say the word 'kangaroo' you are speaking an Aboriginal language, Guugu Yimithirr. Captain James Cook wrote down this word at the place called Wabalumbaal, which he named Endeavour River, where the town of Cooktown now stands. It was where he moored to undertake repairs on his ship. Cook and his men encountered Guugu Yimithirr speakers, who told him their name for this marsupial that is now on Australia's coat of arms. Each language has its own vocabulary and there are hundreds of words for the animal now called kangaroo. Hundreds of Aboriginal words from other First Australian languages have entered modern Australian English, although some have changed from the original: koala, coo-ee, kookaburra, wallaby, billabong, dingo and wombat are just a few examples.

7
Kinship and Country

The hottest topic in Aboriginal get-togethers is often kinship – how people are related to each other. Determining this by exploring personal histories is regarded as a matter of utmost importance. If a biological kinship link cannot be identified, there are ways to create kinship relationships that are often just as meaningful as close family ties. Many Aboriginal and Torres Strait Islander people follow ancient kinship rules in their everyday relations with others. They believe that these kinship rules are laws left by the sacred ancestors who created the living environment and its people.

Kinship nomenclatures, or the names for kinship status, such as mother, father, etc., and the system of relatedness of each Aboriginal or Torres Strait Islander group are fundamental to a group's identity. A group may be named from a language that was spoken by their immediate or even distant ancestors. Many are named after an English surname that was given to their ancestors who were forced onto reserves. Many Indigenous people in Australia today state their group identity or traditional origins when they introduce themselves.

Kinship systems of the Torres Strait Islander Peoples are very different. Only Aboriginal kinship systems are discussed here.

Each person is born into a kinship network. It stretches back through the generations, beyond grandparents and great-grandparents into the distant past, and also outwards socially. You may have heard the expression 'He's like a brother to me' or 'She's like a mother to me'. Familial relationships can be created as acts of friendship. These quasi-kin friendship networks have operated throughout human history as people have helped each other and worked together to ensure food and water for all. Aboriginal kinship logic continues to operate in this way, even if the local or regional languages are no longer spoken.

Exclusion from the Australian economy and exploitation for indentured and slave labour created intergenerational poverty for thousands of Indigenous people. It made sense, then, to keep the old traditions of

Aboriginal kinship networks stretch back through generations, and also outwards socially (photo Wayne Quilliam)

sharing so that no one starved. These traditions have changed, especially in the areas where colonisation impacted first, yet they are still recognisable as Aboriginal kinship and social structures. Helping family and friends in one's social network was, and remains, normal and is often governed by rules in those societies that operated in a more collective fashion, such as tribal and clan-based groups.

All human societies have kinship systems and nomenclature – systems of names – as well as other social structures that bind people together. They vary greatly around the globe. There are several different types of Aboriginal kinship systems operating across Australia. They are far more complex than English or European systems of kinship. Most Aboriginal systems recognise twenty-eight types of kin roles, many more than in the English system of kinship that many Australians use. In the Aboriginal world, everyone is kin, either close or distant. But all relationships, whether or not people are biologically related, are determined by kinship and classification laws. In addition to kinship systems that name kinship roles, there are classifications, such as moieties and 'skin systems'. These classification systems operate together with the kinship system, binding everyone into a world of relatedness and giving them principles of behaviour to live by.

Aboriginal kinship systems are difficult to learn and understand, and it is not expected that outsiders do so. What is important to know is that in all Aboriginal societies, all people and ancestral beings, as well as named and recognised plants and animals, natural features and tracts of land and sea, are part of a structured web of connections that is called kinship.

These systems are governed by rules or laws that prescribe marriage between certain types of kin and preclude marriage between other types of kin. There are variations to these rules that are found to be acceptable, or at least are not considered offensive.

There are also ways of referring to people who have married the 'wrong way' or not quite the 'right way'. In many Aboriginal kinship systems, there are also avoidance relationships, especially between mothers-in-law and sons-in-law, who cannot speak to each other. Also, there are rules for showing respect between brothers and sisters and brothers-in-law.

Where the original Aboriginal kinship systems are no longer used because languages are no longer spoken or are spoken only by a few Elders, new Aboriginal ways of addressing people as kinfolk have been developed. You may hear Aboriginal and Torres Strait Islander people refer to Elders as 'Aunty' or 'Uncle' even though they are not related. They are used as terms of address that show respect for Elders and a sense of belonging and identity.

Children hold photos of their family at the Apology in Ngambri/Ngunnawal/Canberra (photo Wayne Quilliam)

Skin names

In addition to the named kinship roles, such as mother, father, daughter and son, some Aboriginal societies have what anthropologists call a 'section' or 'subsection' system. Aboriginal people call these 'skin names'. Skin names tie people together as a kind of kinship group, even though there might be no relationship through descent or marriage, or only a very distant one. Skin names allow people to identify a kinship relationship between them even if they have never met. 'What is your skin name?' people ask. This is a typical way to engage a stranger or newcomer in those societies where these systems operate.

There are only a few such systems operating, although they are widespread across very large regions. The most famous are:

- the Arrernte section system with its four categories
- the subsection systems (with eight categories divided into sixteen by gendered subsection names) of the Warlpiri People and Western Desert Peoples, whose Country extends northwards from the Central Desert
- the Arnhem Land systems. The subsection system is thought to have been introduced into some areas, such as Arnhem Land, perhaps not more than 150 years ago.

When a person from outside these systems is bestowed a 'skin name' by an Aboriginal person, the outsider is incorporated into the wider kinship network in a kind of adoption. A kinship relationship is then established and sanctioned. A local woman will declare to another woman who is visiting, 'You are my sister', and the rules of behaviour among sisters will be explained. The husband of this woman becomes the brother-in-law of this newly acquired sister, and her sisters and brothers, and children will call her 'mother' in the local language.

Where these traditional kinship systems are followed, people often do not refer to each other by their personal names but by kinship terms, as this is considered polite and proper. A great example of the everyday kinship and skin name structure that underpins Aboriginal societies and connects us to the fauna, flora and all the named phenomena in the natural and spiritual worlds is the story of the white corella of Galiwin'ku. Pets or other domesticated animals, and even semi-domesticated wild animals, often have skin names. The white corella is known by the skin name of Ŋarritj. Ŋarritj achieved fame when he featured in a documentary about his life in the township at Galiwin'ku, a Yolŋu community on Elcho Island in the Northern Territory.

Ŋarritj enjoys a complex network of social relations in the township, speaks Yolŋu matha well enough to make his demands, intentions and thoughts clear to others, and interacts in a variety of ways with his adoptive family, the school children, the police, the shop staff, and other residents of the town. Ŋarritj's adoptive family members and the residents of Galiwin'ku refer to him in the appropriate way, using kinship terms or his skin name. Ŋarritj's encounters with people at home, in the shops and on the streets shows kinship and skin names in action.

The use of these names shows respect for the animals themselves and it recognises the close relationship between the human and non-human worlds. The documentary, *Ŋarritj*, has been broadcast on NITV and other broadcast services and is available online.

Gurruṯu, kinship

Through my associations with Yolŋu People from north-east Arnhem Land, I refer to my sisters as yapa and my brothers as wäwa, and their mothers and their mother's sisters as my mother, or ŋändi.

In the Yolŋu matha – the languages of the Yolŋu – the term for kinship is gurruṯu, but it has a much broader set of meanings. It takes in relationships with traditional land estates, ancestral beings and all things associated with them. The named world is also in a set of kinship relationships with the Traditional Owner groups, members of which refer to neighbouring estates of clan groups in kinship terms.

All named entities in the world are in either the Dhuwa or the Yirritja moiety. This applies to almost everything, including the planets, wind, plants, animals, places and people. The saltwater crocodile is Yirritja, while the crow is Dhuwa, for instance. There are also the spiritual meanings associated with these relationships. As an example, from a female perspective, yothu–yindi means 'child–mother', and gutharra–märi means 'daughter's child–mother's mother'. These terms also express people's relationships to places and are loaded with spiritual meanings.

Clan groupings are the major form of social organisation in Yolŋu society. They are determined by descent from the most distant remembered male ancestor. They operate as the corporation that owns the clan's land estate and other property, both spiritual and physical.

My friends and colleagues, ethnomusicologist Aaron Corn and the late Yolŋu Elder and scholar Joe Gumbula worked closely together to describe gurruṯu through various lenses. They wrote in *Boundary Writing*, published in 2006, that Yolŋu society is an expansive network of more than sixty clans, or mala, that own numerous homelands in north-east Arnhem Land. Children are born into the clans of their fathers and share hereditary ownership of their fathers' homelands. All Yolŋu People, clans, homelands, ancestors and bodies of law are classified as being either Dhuwa or Yirritja.

The Yolŋu understand themselves to be 'direct descendants of the waŋarr (ancestral progenitors) who originally shaped, named and populated northeast Arnhem Land, and remain sentient and ever-present in its lands and waters'. These sacred ancestral entities are further said to inform the souls of all living Yolŋu People upon conception. They travel through ancestral waters back to their spiritual homes following death.

Through this sacred birthright, all Yolŋu are born as owners or wäŋa-wataŋu (Country-holders) of their clan's homelands, and rom-wataŋu (law-holders) in associated canons of names, songs, dances and designs that prove their clan's ownership of its homelands under ancestral law.

Marriage rules are laws in all Aboriginal kinship and classification systems. In the Yolŋu system, as shown in the top diagram in Appendix A in the colour insert based on an original painting by Joe Gumbula, a person born into a Dhuwa clan must marry a spouse from a Yirritja clan, and vice versa.

As shown in the bottom diagram in Appendix A in the colour insert, in addition to being born into one's father's clan, Yolŋu People, whether Dhuwa or Yirritja, also use the gurrutu system to trace their relationships to other clans through the mother's lineage.[37]

In this way, a Yolŋu person will also identify strongly with the clans of people from whom they descend and who are descended from them in the relationships of mother (1), mother's mother (2), mother's mother's mother or woman's child (3), and mother's mother's mother's mother or sister (4). Father's mother (5) and marriage (6) relationships are also important. A Yolŋu person will also recognise the importance of their fathers' full female lineage and the complete female lineages of the children of each clan's men.

The diagram in Appendix B in the colour insert, by Aaron Corn, shows how the Yolŋu recognise such chains of yothu–yindi (child–mother) in relationships between different clans (in smaller grey Roman text, such as 'Wangurri') and homelands (in larger black Roman text, such as 'Matamata'). These homelands include tracts of sea (in black italic text), which is a distinctive feature of the Yolŋu land-tenure system in this rich coastal landscape. Hereditary knowledge of how the ancestral entities associated with each of these clans passed through each other's homelands is commonly said to bind these clans together in yothu–yindi relationships today.[38]

The Yolŋu place great emphasis on their binary Dhuwa and Yirritja classifications, and less emphasis on their skin system. By contrast, desert peoples, such as the Yothu-yindi relationships between selected Yolŋu clans and homelands and the Warlpiri, place much greater emphasis on skin systems.

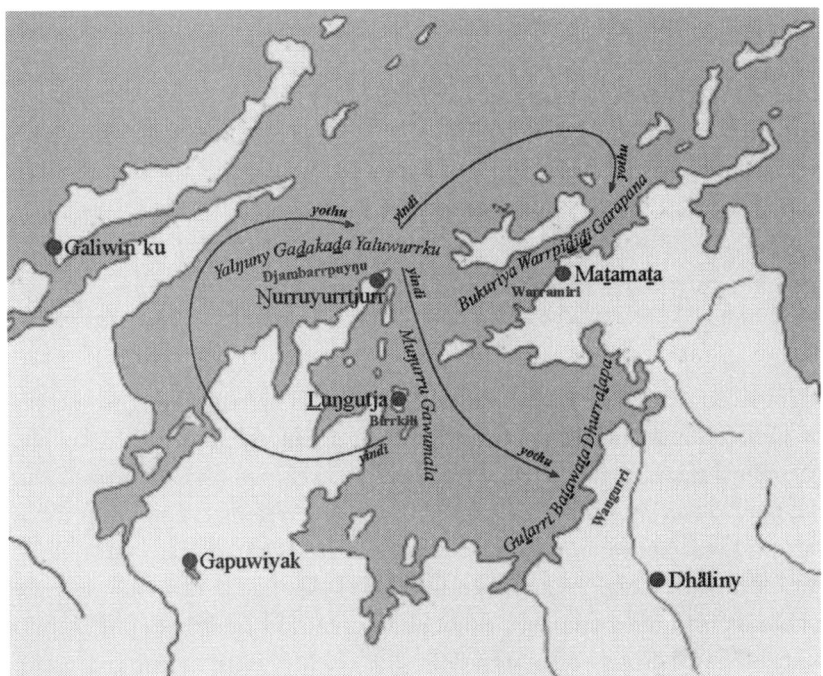

Yothu–yindi relationships between selected Yolŋu clans and homelands © Aaron Corn, University of Melbourne

According to a skin system, each person in society is born with a standard skin name that marks their various kinds of relationships with everyone else. Skin systems are another means of linking people in family relationships. The diagrams in Appendix B in the colour insert, drawn from Aaron Corn's writing, show the ideal Yolŋu mälk (skin name) system for relationships through marriage and descent and equivalent expressions in Kriol and Burarra.[39]

8
Knowledge

Many Australians have heard of the remarkable abilities of Aboriginal people to track animals and people over very long distances. The character of the Aboriginal tracker has been made famous in novels and films. The tracker in the film *Rabbit-Proof Fence*, discussed in the Storytelling chapter, is perhaps the most well-known but there are many others. The tracker has entered the Australian mythology as an especially skilled Aboriginal man (trackers are always male in the mythology, although women read landscapes just as well) with uncanny powers of observation. The trackers were indentured police assistants who had the job of capturing escaped 'natives' and white outlaws or finding people who were lost. Gradually, non-Indigenous Australians are coming to realise that Aboriginal people also had an encyclopaedic knowledge of their environments and were keen observers of human behaviour.

There are Indigenous knowledge systems that explain how animals and plants survive, how environmental systems work, the movement of the stars and planets, weather systems and climatic change, as well as human relationships with other species.

As the sustainability of human systems and natural environments becomes a key challenge globally, environmental thinkers are looking at the ways Indigenous people managed the land for 65,000 years. They needed to be skilled at adapting and innovating: they witnessed an Ice Age, the disappearance of the megafauna, the rising of the seas and the drying up of the continent.

Today, Aboriginal and Torres Strait Islander Peoples maintain their philosophies and knowledge traditions that originated tens of thousands of years ago. They have been passed from generation to generation by knowledgeable people and taught during each person's lifetime. This takes place through experience living on Country and by learning about the world, the sacred origins of People and traditional estates, their responsibilities for management of the environment, and how to provide for the material needs of their families.

Tracker and constable on patrol, Western Australia

The First Peoples understood human nature and the natural world, environmental practices and traditions, medicine and healing, and much more. They conveyed this understanding through their teaching systems and practices, the sacred narratives such as song series (or songlines), art and designs, rituals and ceremonies, and storytelling. They also displayed it through knowledge used in daily life. This knowledge was both specific to local areas and spread regionally according to customs.

The ever-growing colonising population, with their herds of sheep and cattle and their lust for land and water, changed environments around the country forever. The impact on the continent-wide Aboriginal land management systems and the knowledge systems that supported them was profound. It is astonishing how much has survived.

As scientists and researchers come into contact with Indigenous people who practise their ancient traditions, they recognise the importance of these traditions and the elaborate knowledge systems. They acknowledge the relevance of Indigenous knowledge systems for dealing with Australia's many challenges, especially in relation to understanding and living with our environments. There is also greater respect today for the Aboriginal and Torres Strait Islander people who manage land and water. These people are often involved in research projects to help protect the environment and to learn about it.

By the end of the twentieth century, the evidence had mounted to show the First Peoples played a critical role in shaping the environment. It also proved that these societies had a co-evolutionary relationship with the continent's landscapes over at least 65,000 years.

As discussed earlier, two of the outstanding investigators of Indigenous knowledge about the environment are historian Bill Gammage and writer Bruce Pascoe. Gammage's book *The Biggest Estate on Earth: How Aborigines Made Australia* (2011) and Bruce Pascoe's book *Dark Emu: Black Seeds: Agriculture or Accident?* (2014) have fundamentally changed the simplistic characterisation of Aboriginal societies of pre-invasion times as 'hunters and gatherers' who harvested their food and basic needs from the 'wilderness'.

Bill Gammage explains that the Australian continent the British encountered in 1788 was no wilderness; rather, it was a managed series of landscapes, much of which looked like 'a gentleman's park'.[40] In his study of the historical records, scientific literature, paintings and images pertaining to Aboriginal use of the land and vegetation, Gammage writes that the Aboriginal Peoples created a continent-wide system of land management.

Three years after Gammage's grand study, Bruce Pascoe published his account of south-eastern Australia, and although not a trained historian, he brought an original interpretation to sources with the eye of a layman fascinated by the story in the archives that had been largely ignored. His book quickly became an extraordinary best seller and ignited a debate about the nature of the economic practices of the First Peoples. It set out another body of evidence that changed the way we think about Aboriginal economic practices and their food production, demonstrating that Aboriginal people practised agriculture and developed technological innovations in some areas of Australia. Even if a few of his contentions are not supported by the evidence in the records, Pascoe showed that much of the evidence was always there in plain sight, but it had been cloaked in old ideas about Aboriginal people as unsophisticated hunters and gatherers.

By examining historical documents written by the first European people to encounter Aboriginal societies, *Dark Emu* brings to life the Indigenous farming innovations implemented by various societies before colonisation. This is also well before the introduction of colonial farming practices that erased not only the First Peoples who starved as cattle and sheep polluted their waterholes and destroyed their grasslands, along with their agriculture, their dwellings and their material culture. Pascoe extends the work of Gammage by including evidence of food production methods, housing construction and even clothing. In his research, he 'came across repeated references to people building dams and wells, planting, irrigating and harvesting seed ...

and manipulating the landscape' (Extract from *Dark Emu* by Bruce Pascoe, published by Magabala Books, Broome WA, 2014).

Many examples of this community resourcefulness are presented in rich detail in the book. One such example that shatters the idea that Aboriginal people were merely passive consumers of the land's resources is that of grain production. Pascoe presents evidence that grain was grown and harvested, stored, and then ground into flour for making into bread. Pascoe also highlights evidence of other agricultural practices, including yam and onion production, aquacultural infrastructure, dwelling construction and native grass management that promoted soft and fertile soil. All of this led him to the realisation that 'the hunter-gatherer tag was a convenient lie'.[41]

The second theme of the book is Pascoe's exploration of the reasons why evidence of Aboriginal civilisation has been so comprehensively erased from Australia's national conscience. He describes how the detailed accounts of the very first explorers and pastoralists failed to make it to even the second generation of white settlers.

This is partly because the hard-hoofed animals, such as cows and sheep, compacted and destroyed all beneath their feet, while Aboriginal villages were burnt to the ground, obliterating the basis for these accounts. It is also partly because what he terms 'cultural amnesia' was necessary to legitimise the wholesale theft of the Australian continent. Pascoe explores this in some detail, explaining how and why the belief in the 'nomadic, hunter-gatherer lie' was so successfully adopted.[42] His book aspires to introduce an important shift in perspective when examining Australia's pre-colonial past and its people, and a new respect for its Aboriginal civilisation.

The debates about *Dark Emu* have been ferocious, with many of the contributions reciting old racist myths about Aboriginal people and attacking Pascoe's identity as a person of Aboriginal descent. The formal state records did not always record the details of the birth of Aboriginal children, their paternity, or their maternity, as we learnt during the inquiry into the stolen children. Even today, it is estimated that the birth records of about 25 per cent of Aboriginal children born in Victorian hospitals have had their Aboriginality denied on hospital records and birth certificates.

Those who have salaciously peeped into publicly available records and denied Pascoe's family history have delivered barbs that are clearly intended to insult and humiliate him. Their concerns have been less with the content of his work and more with policing the boundaries of 'race' as they imagine it. Leaving aside the largely racist attacks on him, the book has also been criticised by several old-school scholars who insist on their own superseded classification of a wide range of economic activities as 'hunting

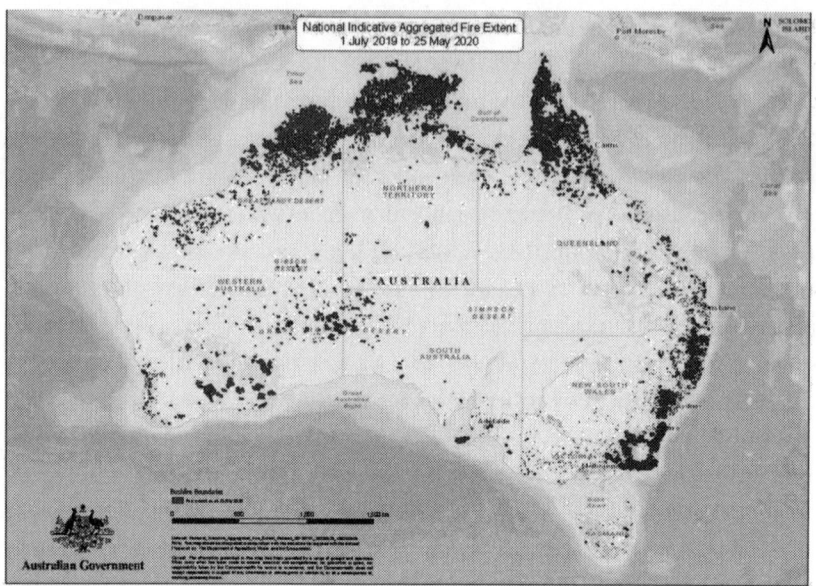

National Indicative Aggregated Fire Extent 1 July 2019 to 25 May 2020. Developed by the Department of Agriculture, Water and the Environment (DAWE). Retrieved from naturaldisaster.royalcommission.gov.au/submissions/summary-submissions, July 2021

and gathering'. These include anthropologist Ian Keen in a journal article,[43] and linguist Peter Sutton and archaeologist Kerryn Walshe in *Farmers or Hunter-Gatherers? The Dark Emu Debate* (MUP, 2021). They would deny a commitment to the trope of the 'noble savage' but they have clung to a sharp dividing line between humans who hunt and humans who farm. This ignores decades of literature on earlier societies where there is no evidence for such a division. Instead, contemporaneous hunting and farming and other gradual transitions over many centuries evolved from one dominant form of economic activity to another. Such evidence comes from societies across the globe but perhaps most aptly from historian James Boyce in his history of the Fens in eastern Britain, *Imperial Mud: The Fight for the Fens*. Boyce dismissed this 'fateful line' summarily:

> The Fens were full of fish, eels, and waterbirds, with the wild birds multiplying at the same time as farming was being successfully refined. Both forms of food collection became integral to Fennish life, further evidence as James C. Scott has explored, 'there is no fateful line that separates hunting and foraging from agriculture,' nor any empirical basis to the assumed superiority of farming for economic and cultural development. A predictable and easily countable grain harvest was more efficient for collecting taxes and asserting centralised authority, but this should not be equated with human progress.[44]

Keen suspects that there's a racist agenda in the media attacks on Pascoe, while Sutton and Walshe ignore the scientific evidence for Aboriginal engineering feats such as the world's oldest and largest aquaculture system at the UNESCO-recognised Budj Bim Cultural Landscape, which I described earlier. Sutton and Walshe not only ignored this evidence but that of anthropologists and others who documented what is called 'incipient agriculture' – the propagation of plants and grains for consumption. Sutton and Walshe have no expertise in southern Australia where most of the historical sources that Pascoe cites are relevant, and neither are historians. In north Australia, where their work is largely located, Yolŋu make bread from collected and leached cycad seed pods, baked into small loaves for special occasions; it is called ŋathu. I have seen it myself. I also know that I will be attacked for saying this by those who remain uncomfortable with Aboriginal ideas from the south because this fact blurs the neat racial boundaries of the colonial triumphalist myth of a 'superior' race over an 'inferior' race. Those Aboriginal people whose traditional economy includes hunting, fishing with traps, nets and harpoons, gathering shellfish, and harvesting bush fruit, nuts and vegetables have wondered what all the fuss is about. They love their economic practices and their lifestyles.

In these new culture wars between post-colonial and Indigenous versions of our past, one must read diligently and closely to keep up with the battle and the swings and blows against the mounting evidence that Aboriginal economies were varied, mixed and complex. I continue to recommend Pascoe's *Dark Emu* because it will inspire you to *think critically about the historical sources* and count as part of our Aboriginal traditions: eel farming, propagation of plants and grains for consumption (farming), hunting, fishing, foraging (including shellfish gathering) and food storage of many different types.

The Black Summer

In the Australian summer of 2019–2020, wildfires exploded in the forests and scrublands with fatal consequences for people, wildlife and environments in the path of the fires. This season of fire left Australians in a state of shock at the devastation. They recognised that climate change will trigger more intense and frequent fires. On 20 February 2020, the Australian government established the Royal Commission into National Natural Disaster Arrangements to learn from this devastation. The Royal Commission was established to ensure Australian governments better coordinate their responses to limit the deadly and destructive impacts of bushfires.

It published a map of the extent of the fires across Australia from 1 July

2019 to 25 May 2020, which presents a disturbing picture of the loss of biodiversity and natural resources.[45] The words of the Royal Commission are a stark reminder of that terrible summer:

> Over 24 million hectares were burnt. Many Australians were impacted, directly or indirectly, by the fires. Tragically, 33 people died and extensive smoke coverage across much of eastern Australia may have caused many more deaths. Over 3,000 homes were destroyed. Estimates of the national financial impacts are over $10 billion. Nearly three billion animals were killed or displaced and many threatened species and other ecological communities were extensively harmed. Every state and territory suffered fire to some extent. The fires did not respect state borders or local government boundaries. On some days, extreme conditions drove a fire behaviour that was impossible to control ... We heard stories of bravery and camaraderie – and luck. It was a true 'campaign season'. The season commenced in July 2019 and was not declared over until 31 March 2020.

For some species, this was the tipping point, and more have become endangered. Australian extinction rates were already among the highest in the world before the Black Summer. In the Proceedings of the National Academy of Sciences of the United States of America of April 2015, Woinarski, Burbidge and Harrison write:

> The 29 Australian endemic mammal extinctions comprise 35% of the world's modern mammal extinctions. Some 1.5% of the world's 5,500 mammal species are extinct, a proportion substantially less than for Australia. Our assessment of 30 Australian mammal extinctions is also appreciably greater than that recognized under Australian environmental legislation, which lists 20 Australian mammal species as extinct ...[46]

They describe 'an extent of recent and ongoing loss of its mammal fauna that is exceptionally high and appreciably greater than previously recognized', and they conclude that causes of loss are unlike biodiversity decline elsewhere in the world. While much of the evidence is unclear, there can be no doubt that the colonisation of Australia by the British is correlated with species extinction in 'a broad sequential wave ... beginning from the first settled areas in south-eastern Australia ... to the present day in much of northern Australia', and the 'loss of indigenous land management, particularly of fire'.[47] The losses are continuing: a further 56 Australian land mammal species are threatened and 52 species are near threatened. In summary, of the 273 Australian endemic

Burning Country – Ngurrurpa Indigenous Protected Area, Great Sandy Desert (image courtesy of AIATSIS, item POIRIER.S09.CS-000115846)

land mammal species, 11 per cent are extinct, 21 per cent are extant but threatened, and a further 15 per cent are near threatened.[48]

Cultural burning, or traditional Aboriginal fire management practices, provides a large part of the solution to this ongoing disaster, as the Royal Commission found. The Royal Commission report is an impressive document, containing 80 recommendations. The Commission Chair, Air Chief Marshal Mark Binskin AC (Retd), presented the report to the Governor-General on 28 October 2020. It was tabled in Parliament on 30 October 2020.

In two recommendations, the Royal Commission urged that 'Australian, state, territory and local governments should engage further with Traditional Owners to explore the relationship between Indigenous land and fire management and natural disaster resilience' and to 'further opportunities to leverage Indigenous land and fire management insights, in the development, planning and execution of public land management activities'.

These recommendations were based on evidence from across the country about cultural burning. A comprehensive chapter of the report, Chapter

18 on Indigenous land and fire management, presents a compilation of evidence – and the evidence of Aboriginal land managers who fight fire with fire should be required reading for all Australians who live on land at risk of wildfire.

I draw the reader's attention to parts of one submission in particular because of its concise summary of Indigenous knowledge and science in an urgent call for greatly expanded Aboriginal fire management, or cultural burning.

Aboriginal fire management practices

A group of Indigenous and non-Indigenous experts on Australian wildfires and Indigenous fire management made a submission to the Royal Commission. Their primary concern was the urgent need for traditional Aboriginal fire management practices to be implemented to manage wildfires and limit their impacts in the long term:

> it is fundamental that an implementation of Cultural Burning be planned, led by, undertaken and administered by Indigenous groups that are local to the site of practice. Effort, then, needs to be made to resource and support the formation of Indigenous bodies, such as the highly successful Ranger programs across Australia ... Communities and Elders still hold much information which is not widely known or shared, and in many areas there have never been Indigenous-led initiatives which allow a safe place for knowledges to be activated. Transformational change is required in the way Country is being managed and we assert that resourcing and partnering with Aboriginal knowledge holders to reinvigorate Cultural Fire practice, ensuring empowerment and not appropriation, represents a necessary and powerful piece of the suite of measures required for transformational change ...[49]

They explained how cultural burning will build Australia's resilience to natural disasters:

> Indigenous Australians have managed Australian landscapes for more than 65,000 year[s] using a highly effective holistic land management practices and a suite of Country-specific management regimes that have persisted through, and have been shaped by, massive environmental changes ... All Aboriginal land management practices have been the result of intimate knowledge of Country developed over many, many millennia of careful observation, continual interaction and active custodianship (Olsen & Russell 2019). Arguably the most profound

Victor Steffensen, author of *Fire Country*, demonstrating fire management

influence of Indigenous Australians on the Australian environment was achieved through Cultural Burning. Empirical and ethnographic data clearly demonstrates that the Australian environment of 1788 was radically different to the landscape we see today, and that this difference can be seen as largely as a result of the negation of cultural burning regimes ... This landscape change aligns with significant impacts of colonisation, which have prevented Indigenous Land Management and cultural burning across the region ...

FIRE COUNTRY

Aboriginal Peoples used fire to promote and distribute plant communities, such as grasses or open forest. They also used it to distribute trees and plants, which in turn promoted and protected animals, birds, reptiles and insects. By using fire as an intrinsic part of land management, Aboriginal people managed the wildfire-prone Australian landscapes.

Fire and symbols of fire are important features in Indigenous religious rituals and ceremonies, including many that are still practised today. Fire also features in myths and stories about the sacred past, when life and the world were being created. The video *Yagun Gulinj Wiinj (How Man Found Fire)*, made in 2016, shows a sacred ancestral story about the origin of fire.

Through careful observation of weather and winds, and the seasonal changes in many plant and animal species, Aboriginal people used fire in Country to keep it healthy. Its use was carefully and skilfully regulated so that different parts of Country were burnt in the appropriate season, at appropriate intervals, and with a suitable intensity. Cool burns (that is, low-intensity fires) were used to maintain low fuel loads in the forest understorey without harming the forest canopy, to protect the trees and resident biodiversity.

Burning was also used in relatively small patches of vegetation. This produced a 'mosaic' pattern across the landscape, which meant that when a wildfire started (for example, through lightning) it would be less likely to develop into a large blaze. An occurrence such as a firestorm would have been devastating to Aboriginal society. Fire was also used to maintain grasslands, to ensure the reproduction of fire-adapted vegetation and to protect fire-sensitive plants. In modern terms, traditional Aboriginal fire practices had the overall effect of promoting greater biodiversity.

The term 'firestick farming' was devised by prehistorian Rhys Jones in 1969 to indicate that these practices were deliberate and governed by rules.

Bill Gammage showed that Aboriginal people made fire an ally, not an enemy. Among its advantages, Aboriginal landscape fire:

- gave every species a favourable habitat, letting them flourish and preventing species extinctions
- promoted drought-shielding native grasses and shrubs
- minimised the impact of bushfire ('wildfire') by reducing fuel, and by creating firebreaks to break up or isolate areas with dangerous fuel loads.

In a review in *The Monthly* in 2011, historian James Boyce observed:

> Gammage is determined to open our eyes to the fact that in 1788 there was no wilderness, but a landscape that reflected a sophisticated, successful and sensitive farming regime integrated across the Australian landmass. Fire was not an indiscriminate tool of fuel reduction or grass promotion, but carefully employed to ensure certain plants and animals flourished, to facilitate access and rotation, and to ensure resources were abundant, convenient, and predictable.[50]

In many parts of Australia, the traditions of using fire ceased when Aboriginal societies were disrupted – during the colonial period, when many populations were removed from their traditional land, and later, under the protection and assimilation period. Urbanisation, particularly in parts of New South Wales, Victoria and Tasmania, means it is no longer possible in many areas of Australia.

However, Traditional Owners and Indigenous rangers continue to practise these traditions on Aboriginal land, especially in northern Australia. Scientists debate whether the practices can be used to control wildfires in those areas where Aboriginal populations are no longer living on the land. Trials of fire management regimes are run to experiment with burning practices, to understand ecological complexity and variation in species response in different communities. Firefighters now routinely attend field days to learn Aboriginal burning techniques.

In northern Australia, where traditional land management continues to be widely practised, a few communities are harvesting carbon credits by using traditional fire management. This is because, as both Aboriginal and non-Aboriginal experts agree, frequent small fires release less carbon than infrequent, larger, wildfires.

Towards the end of the Black Summer, as the rains came and the fires were finally extinguished, a remarkable book was published that explains cultural burning through the eyes of a man who learnt about this ancient body of Aboriginal traditional knowledge from two Elders in Cape York, George Musgrave and Tommy George.

Victor Steffensen wrote *Fire Country: How Indigenous Fire Management Could Help Save Australia* to help 'heal the wounds inflicted on the people and the environment' by 'putting the right fire back onto the land. The fire is just the beginning of an important journey for us all.'[51] Victor first met George and Tommy in the little town of Laura in the middle of Cape York, where their strong presence was immediately obvious:

> *I could see two old men from a distance, sitting with their families ... I was told that they were brothers and had a reputation as among the most respected and knowledgeable men in the area. I was instantly intrigued by their status and wanted to learn more about them. As I peered over at them I could see that they were watching me. Even when they weren't looking at me, it felt like they were watching me. They had a really strong presence that I was drawn to, but it made me nervous to think of approaching them.*

By the end of the day, Tommy George had invited Victor to live in his house, and the story of how ancient knowledge is passed along to the next generation begins in Victor's inimitable bush way with words that are often called 'yarning'. This is a precious written account because it is the only one. Both Tommy and George have passed away – they were the last Awu-Laya Elders who could give the traditional knowledge and stories of their Country to their young people. Others will do so through the oral traditions and being on Country. This legacy is a fragile one, as Victor explains:

It was an honour to learn from them, but it didn't come without many challenges along the way. You have to develop trust, not just with the old people, but the whole community. It took some time before the old people really started to teach me things. They also found me useful to help them out too around other life matters. The main thing they wanted was to practise culture and get back onto their country. They wanted to apply their knowledge back onto the land, the fire, the water, looking after the story places. But most of all they wanted their younger ones to learn the language and get back onto country. It was vital because the two men were the last of the Awu-Laya Elders who knew the traditional knowledge and stories of that country. They wanted the young ones to inherit the knowledge and take over their role as leading Elders ... The healing knowledge using fire for the land comes from the same knowledge of maintaining country with fire. Healing the environmental problems becomes far more possible if you understand the land through ancient knowledge views. Knowing the values and indicators of each ecosystem allows you to work out ways to adjust the fire management to improve the condition of sick landscapes. Burning outside of the normal times you would burn the country, depending on its identity and condition.

The health status of a particular country determines the best possible application of fire. It's sort of like being a doctor for the land, giving a diagnosis and then the treatment.

Cultural burning can only be learnt on Country, and in this excerpt, we are treated to Victor's first lesson:

I will never forget that day Poppy lit the first fire on country in front of me. We were standing in the middle of a small community of boxwood trees about 20 kilometres out of old Laura town. The ecosystem was only as big as a couple of basketball courts and was surrounded by a small creek and stringybark country. The grass was quite thick, dead, and dry, and we were standing in it up to our knees.

'I'm gonna light the grass now, like the old people used to do,' Poppy said loudly and proudly. He walked over to the stringybark country and ripped off a long piece of bark from the closest tree.

'You look now.' He teased one end of the long piece of bark, lit it up and then walked through the boxwood patch in a repetitive, figure eight type movement. He was almost skipping as he dragged the bark along, making the fire follow him around. I watched him dancing through the flames like some kind of fire spirit sprinkling magic dust onto the land. I watched the fire go higher and the smoke fill the space *around him until I couldn't see him anymore. There was nothing but fire in front of me, but it was only seconds before it started to calm down. Then he reappeared in the middle of the fire, walking over the flames with his bare feet, giving me the biggest smile.*[52]

Scientists, ecologists, historians and many others have given us other versions of the knowledge that Victor shares, but their sources are the written record, not the Elders themselves. When Victor uses the word 'magic' he does so to convey the great subtlety of the practice of cultural burning and the finest understanding of fire and the environment that cannot be learnt from books. Yet, these books are important in their own way, because no Australians will ever again experience the teachings of Tommy and George.

Aboriginal fire management is both an ancient and a contemporary practice, which has altered the Australian landscape. European settlers thought the continent was a wild and harsh environment, but in fact what they encountered was a landscape that had been consciously and deliberately shaped by fire for thousands of years.

Extensive Aboriginal, scientific and ecological literature demonstrates that Aboriginal people have used fire as a technology of powerful proportions and effect to imprint the economic signature of the human species throughout much of the Australian continent. Wherever Aboriginal economic traditions have survived, researchers have discovered ordered, patterned and rule-governed Aboriginal burning practices.

Indigenous rangers: working on Country

Aboriginal and Torres Strait Islander Peoples have continued their tradition of caring for Country in many ways. One of the most important ways in which they do this today is through the workforce of environmental carers who manage Indigenous land and waters. The Australian government supports these Indigenous ranger projects, which were first funded in 2007 by the Working on Country Program but were established decades earlier by Indigenous volunteers. With government support, these projects acknowledge and reward a traditional practice of Aboriginal and Torres Strait Islander Peoples and benefit the environment as well.

The Department of Prime Minister and Cabinet has a webpage dedicated to the program, now called *Indigenous Rangers – Working on Country*. In April 2021, it reported that the government supported 129 Indigenous ranger groups across Australia, and 'has created more than 2,100 full-time, part-time and casual jobs in land and sea management around the country, including almost 900 Indigenous rangers and coordinators.'[53]

The Australian government's recognition of these ancient knowledge systems and environmental conservation and management practices has led to greater awareness of the need to involve Indigenous people in protecting our natural resources. This is acknowledged on the webpage:

> Indigenous ranger projects support Indigenous people to combine traditional knowledge with conservation training to protect and manage their land, sea and culture. Indigenous ranger groups also develop partnerships with research, education, philanthropic and commercial organisations to share skills and knowledge, engage with schools, and generate additional income and jobs in the environmental, biosecurity, heritage and other sectors.

Aboriginal and Torres Strait Islander seasons and weather knowledge

Unlike the four European seasons, most Indigenous Australian seasonal calendars have three seasons, each with three sub-seasons. These vary across the continent in accordance with the region's climate. In northern Australia, the monsoonal season is markedly wet and the dry season is markedly dry, while in the temperate zones, rainfall varies across the seasons.

While Europeans generally assign whole months to a particular season, Indigenous people say that a season commences and ends with the

Miriwoong seasonal calendar, copyright of Mirima Dawang Woorlab-gerring Language and Culture Centre (MDWg), also found at www.mirima.org.au/calendar

appearance of ecological indicators. This could be the flowering of particular trees or shrubs and the appearance of particular insects. Each season is also associated with particular weather patterns, such as wind directions and speed, temperatures, rainfall, dew or storms, clouds and the time of the day when these occur. There are names for all of these weather patterns as well. Wind patterns are an important part of Aboriginal seasonality and for some groups are the primary indicators of seasonal change.

The Miriwoong seasonal calendar from northern Australia is a good example of an Indigenous seasonal calendar. Miriwoong (Miriwung) is an Australian Indigenous language which is a part of the Jarrakan subgroup of languages, which today has fewer than twenty fluent speakers, most of whom live in or near Kununurra in Western Australia. Miriwoong People have an in-depth knowledge of climatic seasons and weather patterns. This Aboriginal traditional knowledge was documented to produce the Miriwoong seasonal calendar on page 98, showing the links between observed changes in weather patterns and the response of flora and fauna in the landscape. The calendar is being used as a management tool to monitor and evaluate the on-ground impacts of weather events and climate change.

There are many more examples of Indigenous seasonal calendars on the Bureau of Meteorology and CSIRO websites. For example, Bathurst and Melville islands of the Tiwi Islands have three major seasons and thirteen minor overlapping seasons, while Noongar Country in Western Australia has six seasons.

Aboriginal and Torres Strait Islander astronomy

> *In Aboriginal and Torres Strait Islander cultures, everything on the land is reflected in the sky. The sky serves as a scientific textbook – a map – that is home to a wealth of knowledge for those who are able to interpret and read the information it holds.*

This quote comes from Duane Hamacher's contribution to the National Aboriginal and Torres Strait Islander Curricula Project. His Aboriginal and Torres Strait Islander astronomy curricula can be found at: indigenousknowledge.unimelb.edu.au/curriculum

> *Did you know that Aboriginal and Torres Strait Islander people paid careful attention to phenomena such as eclipses and the complex motion of planets, and could determine the cardinal points with high accuracy? Did you know that they discovered that Betelgeuse, the ninth brightest star in the sky, pulsates in brightness over time, along with observations of other red-giant variable stars?*

Astronomers Ray Norris and Duane Hamacher have led research to document how the traditional cultures of Indigenous Australians include a significant understanding of astronomy. It is explored through storytelling, ceremony and art.

> This includes a detailed understanding about the motions of objects in the sky, which are used for constructing calendars and planning ceremonies. There is also evidence that traditional Aboriginal Australians made careful observations and measurements of cyclical phenomena.

Professor Norris and Associate Professor Hamacher have unearthed this knowledge from historical records, studying archaeological sites and working directly with Elders to build an extraordinary project. Their team includes Indigenous astronomers Dr Stacy Mader, Kirsten Banks, Krystal De Napoli, Peter Swanton, Peter Reeve, John South and William Stevens. They are documenting traditional star knowledge, including the movements of celestial bodies, and examining how this is handed down over many generations. Their work casts new light on the depths of traditional Indigenous knowledge and has led to new understandings of how Aboriginal and Torres Strait Islander Peoples organised their economic and social life by the cycles of the sky.

With their knowledge of astronomy, Indigenous people are able to read the weather and climate as it relates to food propagation. They can predict changes in the environment in relation to seasons, weather patterns and the behaviour of plants and animals. Their knowledge is used to manage harvesting, hunting and gathering, navigating across land and sea, and organising social and ritual life by the sun, moon and stars.

If you want to explore Aboriginal and Torres Strait Islander knowledge of astronomy, the website aboriginalastronomy.com.au hosts a treasure trove of published and audiovisual records and images of traditional knowledge and cultural astronomy. Duane Hamacher's book, *The First Astronomers: How Indigenous Elders Read the Stars* (Allen & Unwin, 2022), provides a comprehensive account of this research with Elders (thefirstastronomers.com).

SOLAR POINTS IN TORRES STRAIT ISLANDER ASTRONOMICAL AND TRADITIONAL KNOWLEDGE

Duane Hamacher learnt about traditional Torres Strait Islander knowledge of the Sun from Mua artist David Bosun. Bosun's father was a traditional astronomer, or Zugubau Mabaig, and taught him how to observe and interpret the Sun's setting position from the village of Kubin. Bosun explained:

people in the village of Kubin observe the position of the setting Sun with respect to the archipelago of islands to the west and southwest throughout the year. This informs them about seasonal change and food economics.[54]

They found further information in the historical records. The notebooks of Peter Eseli (1886–1958) were a treasure trove. Eseli was a Mabuyag man and the son of Peter Papi, one of the three chief assistants to the A.C. Haddon expedition sponsored by Cambridge University in the late nineteenth century. Eseli's notebooks, translated into English from Kala Lagow Ya, provide a wealth of knowledge about traditional seasonal knowledge in the western Torres Strait.

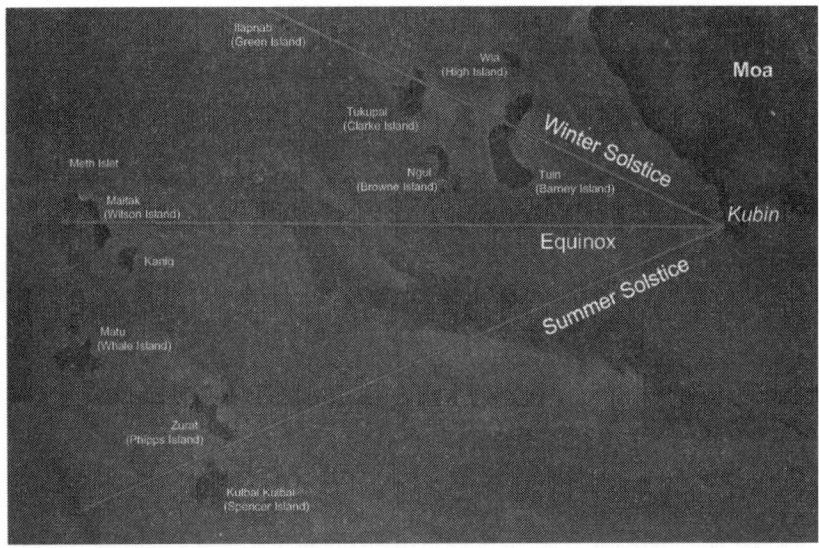

Figure 1: Islands to the west and southwest of Mua Island, western Torres Strait featuring their western and traditional names (where available), with the solstice and equinox lines in red. Image modified from Google Earth.

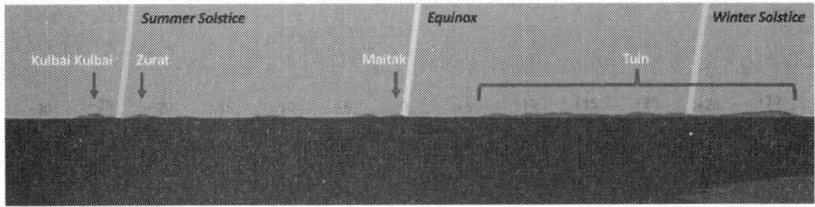

Figure 2: A simulation of the setting Sun as seen from Kubin village, taken from the Horizon software package, developed by Andrew Smith at the University of Adelaide (www.agksmith.net/horizon/)

> As the setting Sun moves southward each day, the weather gradually warms, the days lengthen, and the animals' behaviour changes. It reaches its southerly most point at the summer solstice when the rains of the monsoon season kick off. The Sun then moves northward each day until it passes the equinox, and the Dry season comes by late April. It reaches its northerly most point at the winter solstice during the Dry season in late June.[55]

They explain in considerable detail the movement of the Sun, the extreme setting position of the Sun at the solstices, and the meanings of these positions, such as the distinctive seasonal implications, the weather, the wind, the turtle mating season, when mating turtles float on the surface of the water, the wet season monsoon, the south-east trade wind in the drier season, the abundance of food at this time and the good conditions for easy travel on the water, and the yam harvesting season.

The diagrams on page 101 show a simulation of the setting sun as observed from Bosun's home, Kubin village on Mua Island, and the solstice and equinox lines as observed from Kubin village when looking towards the islands to the west and south-west.[56]

STAR MAPS

Aboriginal and Torres Strait Islander star maps have been transmitted by Elders over hundreds of generations through stories, teaching, maps and song series, or 'songlines'. They became the subject of research when Euahlayi Elder Uncle Ghillar pointed out a pattern of stars to Robert Fuller, an MPhil student at Macquarie University, as they sat under the clear, starry sky in Goodooga, in north-west New South Wales. Fuller was researching the astronomical knowledge of the Euahlayi and Kamilaroi Peoples in 2013 when he became aware of 'star maps' to teach navigation when going beyond one's local Country.

Ghillar pointed out that the pattern of stars to the south-east was used to teach Euahlayi travellers how to navigate outside their own Country during the summer travel season.

They were used not so much as a map but as a memory aid. As you can read on the website aboriginalastronomy.com.au:

> Robert did some research, and looked at a route from Goodooga to the Bunya Mountains northwest of Brisbane, where an Aboriginal Bunya nut festival was held every three years until disrupted by European invasion. It turned out the pattern of stars showed the 'waypoints' on the route. These waypoints were usually waterholes or turning places on the landscape. These waypoints were used in a very similar way to

navigating with a GPS, where waypoints are also used as stopping or turning points.

After Fuller's lesson from Ghillar, a series of star maps were developed. It became clear that these star maps would guide people to the easiest routes to take and were probably routes already established in song series and other oral and visual records. Some of the roads and highways used today follow these routes. Again from aboriginalastronomy.com.au:

> *Drovers and settlers coming into the region would have used the same routes, and eventually these became tracks and finally highways. In a sense, the Aboriginal people of Australia had a big part in the layout of the modern Australian road network. And in some cases, such as the Kamilaroi Highway running from the Hunter Valley to Bourke in NSW, this has been recognised in the name.*

Traditional Aboriginal medicine and healing

In many areas of Australia, Aboriginal men and women turn with great confidence to traditional healers to maintain their wellbeing. While scientists have generally dismissed them as being ineffective, Aboriginal

Gathering of bush medicine in central Australia (photo Wayne Quilliam)

people recognise the need to maintain these traditions. In the Indigenous world, the causes of disease are understood in the terms of ancient cultural knowledge that has served thousands of generations well.

We have so much yet to learn from the traditional healers and their techniques, such as the way they use their artistic works, including painting and weaving – healers use images, for example, to focus the patient's attention on ancestral power and the correct balance between the spiritual and ordinary, to achieve social order.

These extraordinary healers are called by many names: clevermen, marrŋgitj and ngangkari are just three. Healers, medical professionals, and scientists are beginning to collaborate. Health professionals sometimes invite healers into clinics and hospitals when Aboriginal patients are afraid and resistant to health care, as healers bring ancient Aboriginal values to the task. They understand that Aboriginal patients should use western medical treatments too, and often explain to them that they should go to the clinic or stay in hospital and not fear the doctors and nurses. Healers can be blunt about this and have said to me, 'I can't help you. Go to the hospital.'

Where there is no hospital, healers use traditional treatments for fever, some infections and wounds, diarrhoea, and other common ailments such as mental distress. They are reported to help patients who are overcome with the belief that they will die and bring them back to a state where they are engaged with life.

Aboriginal medical traditions and treatments are supported by encyclopaedic bodies of knowledge developed in an intimate relationship with the local environment, vegetation, climate and geography. Observations of the cause and effect of substances, the transformation of plant material by applying fire, water, smoke or other treatments all helped to build the traditional medicinal knowledge.

More mysterious and difficult to comprehend are the Aboriginal ways of understanding human physiology and psychology. These complex cultural principles and theories involve the idea of the interconnection of people and land, the spirit world, and the perceived world.

They also involve the many ancestral spirits and their influences on the world. These ideas and principles are such an important part of Aboriginal cultures across the continent, and I have come to understand some of them simply by listening and observing.

That so many Aboriginal people can maintain their ancient medical traditions against the odds presents us with an important opportunity. We should study the profound change in Aboriginal health since colonial times through the lens of the repercussions of the widespread destruction of traditional knowledge and practices. With these insights, we should find ways to preserve and reinstate these trusted practices in health care today.

BOOKS ABOUT TRADITIONAL ABORIGINAL HEALING

There are many books about traditional Aboriginal healing knowledge and its practice since earliest colonial times. One book filled with information is the beautiful, award-winning *Traditional Healers of Central Australia: Ngangkari*, from the Ngaanyatjarra Pitjantjatjara Yankunytjatjara (NPY) Women's Council Aboriginal Corporation.

Ngangkari are the traditional healers of the Ngaanyatjarra, Pitjantjatjara and Yankunytjatjara lands – 350,000 square kilometres of the remote Western Desert. As the publisher, Magabala Books, notes, 'To increase understanding and encourage collaboration with mainstream health services and the wider community, the ngangkari have forged a rare partnership with health professionals and practitioners of Western medicine.'

Dark Emu, by Bruce Pascoe, powerfully shows how the derogatory views of our ancient traditions are wrong. Research on these traditions is growing, as are efforts to revive and maintain them; for example, by the production of healing remedies for the market, and programs supporting the healers and their collaborations with the health workforce.

A very useful book is *Body, Land and Spirit: Health and Healing in Aboriginal Society*, a collection edited by Janice Reid. The article 'Bush Medicine: The Pharmacopeia of the Yolŋu of Arnhem Land', explores how the Yolŋu in Arnhem Land understand human suffering is based on Reid's experience living in and visiting Yirrkala.

Reid also wrote the book *Sorcerers and Healing Spirits: Continuity and Change in an Aboriginal Medical System*. Even though so much has changed in the last half-century, many of her descriptions of Yolŋu medicine are easily recognisable today. She reported very little on the herbal and other remedies that are still offered at women's healing events in north-east Arnhem Land. I suspect that the influence of missionaries drove many of these practices 'underground' or out of sight. But, as my own experience proved, these traditions continue and are a source of great pride for the families who hold the knowledge.

Research on these traditions is growing, as are efforts to revive and maintain them, from the production of healing remedies for the market, to programs supporting the healers and their collaborations with the health workforce.

Indigenous sorcerers

I have met sorcerers in Cape York, Central Australia and Arnhem Land – encounters that were fascinating and more than a little frightening. Sorcerers make no claim to the greater good. Sorcerers exist, but so too does fear of imagined sorcerers, who almost always live beyond the social boundaries of one's own group and can never be accurately identified. When I have been told to beware because sorcerers were afoot, the instructions were vague.

When sorcery-removing rituals are conducted, the consequences can be severe: affected families may be required to evacuate their homes, or hand over their worldly goods to their in-laws, while community assets such as stores and vehicles may be put out of action by the taboos that are invoked in ritual efforts to remove sorcery curses. The results of these encounters can be explained by understanding the context of each one.

When I worked for the Royal Commission into Aboriginal Deaths in Custody in the late 1980s, attribution of deaths to sorcery was common. The role of sorcery as an Aboriginal explanation for the rising mortality rates caused by chronic disease, contact with the criminal justice system, alcohol, vehicle accidents and violence was not well understood.

Janice Reid, in her book *Body, Land and Spirit*, writes the accepted view that has been put to me by healers, and one that supports my own observations:

> *The power utilised by both sorcerers and healers is ultimately from the same source. This power is morally neutral, it is not the nature of the power a marrŋgitj possesses which distinguishes him from a sorcerer but the choice which he makes about how he will use it ... this power is held in trust. People believe they use it to heal and to protect others. While the potential for its use to harm people exists, marrŋgitj and their families vigorously deny that they work sorcery, even on enemies, and they become offended and angry if anyone suggests such a possibility.*[57]

On racist stereotypes of Indigenous people and their origins

Colonial impressions of Aboriginal and Torres Strait Islander societies that cast them as 'simple' or 'primitive' remain the obstacle to understanding the depth of their knowledge. Ideas about the Indigenous people have shifted from insults based on impressions from fleeting observations to a much more profound knowledge of robust, adaptive societies.

From the first recorded encounters of Europeans with Aboriginal people, the idea of a 'backward people' developed. This idea has been remarkably resilient in Australian literature, school textbooks and public commentary. That is despite more than 200 years of experience, scholarship and research that has found to the contrary: Aboriginal and Torres Strait Islander Peoples developed complex systems of social and religious organisation, economic patterns and practices, and artistic, cultural and technological traditions that adapted to life in Australian environments.

English seaman and author William Dampier is credited with being the first European to observe Aboriginal people. His few notes on his glimpses of Aboriginal people have reverberated throughout Australian history.

In 1688, he sailed along the coast of what is now Western Australia, in the vicinity of King Sound. In 1699, he sailed his ship the HMS *Roebuck* near Shark Bay, also on that coastline. The *Australian Dictionary of Biography* noted:

> Dampier's direct contribution to Australian history was slight; indeed, his own impression of the west coast was unfavourable, since it seemed to him to be a long series of reefs and shoals behind which lay sandhills and barren country, apparently without water and inhabited by 'the miserablest People in the World'. There is nothing in this description of the topography to endanger his reputation for accurate observation. Nevertheless, the great interest in the southern continent roused by his books was sustained throughout the century and the final exploration of the Pacific was carried out by his fellow-countrymen.[58]

More than 400 years after Dampier's mistaken impressions were published, it has finally become obvious to non-Indigenous scientists and other researchers that the Aboriginal and Torres Strait Islander Peoples' intellectual traditions have been transmitted over hundreds of generations. It's now realised that they can explain with great clarity and detail their own traditions of knowledge, and fully engage in debates about their philosophies and ways of knowing and learning.

When the British arrived in 1788, their first encounters with Aboriginal people were remarkable. For a few years, Governor Phillip sought their friendship to gather intelligence about the lands beyond. The records from that time show genuine curiosity on the part of the British. Except for a few individuals, such as Bennelong, the Aboriginal people kept their distance.

Bennelong sought to befriend Phillip to obtain an ally. Some of Phillip's men were not motivated by the strategy of maintaining good relationships to help make the colony permanent. His gamekeeper, it can be ascertained

Crude sketch of Bennelong published in 1904 by T Egerton, Whitehall (image courtesy of AIATSIS, item MASSOLA.A01. BW-N02450_11)

from the records, was suspected of assaulting local women, and one of the local leaders sought revenge.

Attacks on the gamekeeper's lodge by Indigenous resistance fighter Pemelwuy drove Phillip, who had become dispirited by the difficulties he faced, to order Pemelwuy's head to be brought to him. After that, the relationships turned to war, and massacres of local people became more and more common as free men (as opposed to convicts) set out to stake their claim to what was then entirely Aboriginal land, owned by named clans and governed by a subtle system of laws implemented by a hierarchy of Elders.

The currency in the colony was rum for the convicts and wine for the senior officers. Once alcohol caught Aboriginal people in its grip, the decline of the Gadigal People in the area we now call Sydney (Warrane) followed.

A smallpox epidemic in 1789 killed more than half the local population and then spread inland. Some Europeans sought to understand the First Peoples. Much of what is known about the First Australians during early colonial times comes from their detailed records. Paintings, drawings and other illustrations also provide a window on Aboriginal life.

After these earliest encounters, the records present a hateful catalogue of unjustified opinions. What is often not properly understood is that these people were documenting the First Australians and their societies after they had been devastated by the horrors of the violent and brutal colonial invasion. Their observations were made after epidemics of disease that also greatly reduced Aboriginal populations, and when the First Australians were being rounded up and confined to reserves and missions. Apart from the few accounts of first contact, they were observing people whose social and environmental worlds had already been substantially destroyed or permanently altered. This was especially the case in south-eastern Australia where the colonisers arrived first. The pattern of observing people undergoing radical and often violent change continued as the colonists spread across the continent.

Many Europeans in the colonies were committed to the ideas of a racial hierarchy and regarded Aboriginal and Torres Strait Islander people as members of 'inferior races'. These ideas distorted their perceptions and their accounts. The nineteenth century fashion for 'scientific racism' has been discredited by reputable scientists. The perception of Aboriginal people as 'simple' and 'backward' has been shown to be a vile and destructive myth.

Aboriginal Elders and custodians of our knowledge traditions want all Australians to know about them. They especially want Indigenous children to learn about our knowledge traditions in school, and young people to learn about them at universities. They want teachers to understand that a sound education about Australian life, history, society, and environments must include our knowledge systems.

To understand the logic of Indigenous systems of knowledge requires Indigenous-born cultural experts. A few dedicated people in each society attain this status through a lifetime of cultural practice. However, it is important for everyone to be able to learn about the ancient knowledge traditions that enabled hundreds of generations of the First Australians to live here.

There are teachers scattered across our schools who have enriched their own lives and the lives of their students by teaching Aboriginal and Torres Strait histories and culture. By doing so, they have shown respect for our peoples and given joy and hope to Indigenous students in their classrooms who want to see themselves reflected in the school curriculum and given non-Indigenous students an insight into the oldest continuous human cultures. They have conveyed a deeper understanding of Australia's history to students who want to know about our peoples and their traditions.

9
Art

Australian Indigenous artists are acclaimed around the world and their works are held in major public and private galleries locally and internationally. The diversity of artistic styles of Indigenous Australia grows each year as communities, clans and families venture into the art market with renditions of their visual traditions. As well as this increasing diversity in style, the media and materials used by the artists also continue to expand, from bark painting and canvas and acrylic formats, to include fabric and fibre weaving, screen-printing, linocut prints, sculptures in materials such as metal, multimedia presentations using communications technology and computer imagery, virtual reality, photomedia and sound.

There are many more styles of Indigenous art than is generally understood. They range from adaptations of traditional ritual and rock art to the full spectrum of Modernist and Postmodernist art. Some of the regional styles are particularly distinctive, such as the works of the Pintupi art movement and other Central Australian and Western Desert styles, the Arnhem Land bark paintings, and the paintings and sculptures of the Cape York regions; and the artistic community in the Torres Strait Islands creates its own distinctive sculptures and linocuts also.

'Aboriginal art' is an umbrella term for many traditional, adapted and modern styles, forms, and genres from diverse and distant regions of the Australian continent and its islands. Many of these places are as remote and isolated as it is possible to be in this world. Yet a painting from a tiny Aboriginal settlement in an Australian desert or on a tropical savannah floodplain can be found in a gallery in a major international city – in New York, Paris, or Berlin – and be celebrated as a profoundly important expression of human creativity.

There are hundreds of Aboriginal and Torres Strait Islander artists. Their work can be seen at galleries, art competitions and art festivals throughout Australia. Each capital city has a public art gallery with significant Indigenous collections. There are also collections on exhibition in many leading international institutions, such as the British Museum, the Musée du quai Branly in Paris and the Kluge-Ruhe Collection at the University of Virginia in the United States of America, to mention just a few. Indigenous works also appear in many important private collections, such as that of Swiss art collector Bérengère Primat. Her gallery and Fondation Opale, in the rural Alpine town of Lens, is dedicated in large part to the artwork of Indigenous Australians.

Many collections in major galleries include artworks that are heavily influenced by classical Aboriginal traditions, as well as the works of Indigenous Modernist, Postmodernist and experimental artists. Museums have traditionally collected precious objects that their curators classify as 'artefacts', but which Indigenous people regard as the property of their ancestors. In this chapter, I will briefly introduce you to some Aboriginal and Torres Strait Islander artists – the Pintupi, Warlpiri and Yolŋu artists – and explain their social and historical contexts.

Aboriginal artist Wayne Quilliam shares his creations of connection to the land at a major installation in central Sydney (photo Wayne Quilliam)

APY Women's Collaborative, Amata, South Australia, 2017

Aboriginal art circulates in the global market as a kind of commodity, and yet it is difficult to say how its value is determined. This may be because an Aboriginal art object, or commodity, holds many values simultaneously. It is unlikely that any one person would identify both the market and the non-market values embedded in an object. These are discerned by a collection of people in the marketplace, some estimating the object's economic worth and others its cultural and historical significance.

While a painting from a tiny Aboriginal settlement can be found in a major international gallery in a big city, the artist might live in extreme poverty, and die at a young age from a treatable disease or condition. They might never see the world where their art will hang. We cannot ignore this contrast between wealth and poverty that is embedded in the material history of an Aboriginal art object in the global marketplace.

The impact of colonisation on Indigenous people is expressed in much Aboriginal artwork. This impact may not be obvious in the subject matter of the work, but by the way people in Australia and around the world view Aboriginal art images. In each work of art there is a specific personal story grounded in the historical and social past. This is why the contribution anthropologists and historians make to the work of the art historian is valuable. The transition of art traditions and history from ancient societies into the fast-changing world of post-colonial Australian life is complicated. So, the input of people in various fields helps the public understand and appreciate the artwork. Among other things, it is the meanings within Aboriginal art that make it so profound. And it is in the world of making meaning that the structure and fascination of Aboriginal art are to be found.

Worldwide audiences are attracted to Indigenous art because of the ancient traditions of the First Australians and, I believe, because of its extreme 'otherness': its difference from western art. The difference is partly to do with the Indigenous treatment of space. An almost universal meaning found in Aboriginal art is the connection between being and place. The idea of place is not of something 'out there' but of something that is part of the nature of ourselves, especially in relation to special places. This is the key idea that many Aboriginal artists offer to their audiences. Modern global living means people might live in a place without having a personal history that is connected to it. Indigenous people have spiritual and religious connections to places over countless generations, and they bring these connections into their art.

Spiritual and religious beliefs are an essential part of Indigenous social structures and the Indigenous interpretation of the world.

When we look at Aboriginal art and images, often it is possible to see the religious beliefs represented in them. The religious symbols sometimes show how Christianity became a part of many Indigenous people's lives after colonisation. The engagement and the conflict between two religious systems since the eighteenth century are sources of inspiration for a great deal of art today.

Art is central to Aboriginal life, identity and culture. One of the results of the unimaginably long period of human presence in Australia is the vast array of rock art that can be found in most parts of the country. Captured in this ancient art are many of the totemic icons and visual designs – or the 'Dreaming' elements – that appear in modern Aboriginal art and material culture, dance and storytelling. More than art alone, these are the signs of a great human migration across the oceans and the archipelago to our north, and across this vast continent. The remains of ancient Aboriginal life are to be found scattered across landscapes everywhere. Examples include the stone walls of houses in southwestern Victoria, the engraved trees on the inland plains of New South Wales and Victoria, the engraved concentric rings in rock faces that signal water sources in the arid areas, and stone tool-making sites.

Painting and engraving rock faces enabled people to write, read and, through time, negotiate the land's cultural meaning. The experience of standing in a rock-art gallery gazing at ancient paintings of people and times long gone is spine-chilling. I have stood on sand in a sandstone escarpment shelter where people had camped tens of thousands of years ago. Gazing up at their paintings, some of them gigantic and elaborate, is a kind of time travel. The paintings seem to resonate with the spirit of the people who made them. The hand stencils made by groups of Aboriginal people record their visits to these rock galleries. Each man, woman and child in the group held their hand up as an Elder blew liquid ochre over them to record their presence.

These beautiful images, often found at the base of large rock-art galleries, are a form of census. We can look at them and imagine the people who marked their presence at these places. Who among them were the artists, we wonder? Who painted the giant kangaroos, the barramundi and saratoga fish, the hunting scenes, and the magical ancestral figures across the walls of the escarpment shelters? Rock art plays a role in the definition of territory and identity. The artists painted themes in styles that portray the reality of a world view and a society.

We can imagine families at these rock-art galleries, sitting at night around their campfires, telling the stories of a good season hunting, fishing and harvesting; enjoying their meal cooked on the fire; celebrating a rich season on the grassy plains through their painting and storytelling; and taking shelter from the rain, the thunder, the lightning and storms. The Wanjina paintings

Artist Michael J Connolly (Munda-gutta Kulliwari) at Dreamtime Kullila-Art Gallery, Queensland

Artworks by (left to right) Noŋgirrŋa Marawili, Baluka Maymuru, Noŋgirrŋa Marawili at Buku-Larrŋgay Mulka Centre, courtesy of the artists, Buku-Larrŋgay Mulka Centre

in the Kimberley region of Western Australia show the faces of ancestors who came with these storms, and the lightning strikes are painted around their heads to depict their association with the wild storms of the monsoonal season.

When art collectors first approached Aboriginal painters to buy their work, there was no Indigenous art market as we know it today. Very little had been written about Aboriginal design traditions and material culture. The standard view was that only European works could be considered as art. The work of other 'races' was generally seen as merely primitive mark making. Paintings on bark and various funerary sculptures were collected as exotic objects for anthropological study and exhibition. Christian missionaries also collected them as part of their attempts to establish cottage art industries to financially support artists and their families.

Explorers in the eighteenth and nineteenth century collected objects and material culture as exotic trophies and evidence of their travels. Also, some came across rock paintings and revealed them to the world. Sir George Grey, later appointed Governor of South Australia, happened on the Wanjina paintings on sandstone escarpments in the Kimberley region during his exploration of the area in 1838. The Wanjina is the Rain Maker spirit and is often painted with headdresses that represent thunder and lightning.

In 1891, pastoralist Joseph Bradshaw saw ancient rock paintings in the north-west Kimberley region. That is the homeland of the Wunambal and Gaambera Peoples. These paintings are now known as the 'Bradshaws', but more correctly should be called by their Aboriginal names, which include *Gwion Gwion* and *Giro Giro*. These are finely detailed paintings of figures, and they are still the subject of research today.

Art historian Andrew Sayers surveyed nineteenth-century Aboriginal artists and their relationships with the European artists they met. He found that in the colonies of New South Wales and Victoria, European artists gave Aboriginal artists paint and other materials, and the Aboriginal men observed the painting styles of the newcomers. The result is a body of drawings and paintings that departs from the men's symbolic traditions.

Adopting to some degree the styles of the European artists they met, they painted and sketched detailed representations of the rapidly changing world around them. Sayers documented drawings by several artists, including works by a man called Black Johnny, which resulted from his meeting with Austrian artist Eugene von Guérard in Victoria's Western District in 1855. Sayers wrote that the work of these Aboriginal artists had two major themes: ceremonies, and traditional hunting and food gathering. Other subjects included encounters with Europeans, such as William Buckley, the 'wild white man', squatters – both sober and inebriated – Chinese men being chased by Aboriginal men and sailing ships.

In the first half of the twentieth century, Ronald M. Berndt and Catherine H. Berndt documented Aboriginal societies in Western Australia and the Northern Territory, and they also worked briefly in South Australia. During 1947, when they lived in Yirrkala in Arnhem Land in the Northern Territory, they gave some Yolŋu People brown paper and crayons and asked them to draw their world. The works these people produced represent a turning point in the understanding of Aboriginal art. They depict a range of subjects, such as ancestral figures, brightly coloured renditions of traditional ceremonial and body painting, with some variation from the classical forms. Ronald Berndt documented their subjects in detail, and this extraordinary collection is now registered with the Australian Memory of the World Register, a project of the UNESCO Memory of the World Register.

In June 1956, the Czech artist Karel Kupka arrived at Miliŋimbi in Arnhem Land with the intention of finding Aboriginal bark paintings as examples of the work of 'early man'. Basel Museum had commissioned him to bring back works to add to their small collection. Miliŋimbi, the oldest Yolŋu town, had become the location of a mission settlement established by the Methodist Overseas Mission. Visiting there, Kupka developed a friendship with artists Tom Djawa and Dawidi Birritjama to understand their art. He travelled to other communities as well. The result of his collecting and studying was a short book that told readers very little about these great traditions. It was translated into English as *Dawn of Art*, but its original title, *Un Art a l'État Brut (Art of a Brutish State)*, says a great deal about ignorant attitudes to Aboriginal people in the 1950s.

I have mentioned only a few of the early encounters Aboriginal artists had with Europeans. In the 1960s and 1970s, radical changes took place in the world of Aboriginal art and a better-informed audience and market for art developed with the emergence of the Papunya art movement.

In the early 1970s, an art teacher, Geoffrey Bardon, was sent by the Education Department to Papunya, a remote Aboriginal settlement in Central Australia. He soon found himself witnessing and supporting what was to become a major Australian art form of international standing. Bardon assisted the Luritja and Pintupi Elders to create their religious art with materials readily available on the settlement: acrylic paint on fibro at first,

Artists cutting bark in Miliŋimbi, Northern Territory, to make bark paintings, 1963

and later canvas. In 1971, he invited some of the men in the community to paint a blank school wall. The men took a great interest in the startling transfer of their ceremonial sand-sculpture designs to modern materials. Soon their works were being exhibited to great acclaim.

Bardon recognised the importance of the old men's wall paintings and encouraged them to paint more. They went on to paint murals on the Papunya school walls. Not satisfied with the results, senior men Long Jack Phillipus Tjakamarra and Billy Stockman Tjapaltjarri painted a Honey Ant Dreaming mural on the wall. This provoked such intense interest among the people living at Papunya that, in the same year, about fifty senior men produced around 620 small paintings on boards, using acrylic paint. In 1972, the artists successfully established their own company, which continues today as Papunya Tula Artists Pty Ltd in Alice Springs. This famous art cooperative brought the art traditions of a small group in the centre of Australia to the world. Their style came to be synonymous with Aboriginal art, despite the long history of many other regional styles.

The images in their paintings, before seen only as sand paintings in ceremonies, sent a clear message that here was a religion with meanings and explanations as deep and as relevant as any that Christian missionaries might follow. The paintings were commercially successful but, as anthropologist Fred Myers reported, dispute arose when Pitjantjatjara men from the Warburton Range area of the Great Western Desert saw an exhibition of these paintings in Boorloo/Perth. They did not agree with the sacred designs being put on public display. To overcome this, the sacred symbols were disguised by incorporating them into other designs or omitting them from the final works.

This movement spread throughout most parts of the Central and Western deserts. By the late 1970s, the style was attracting considerable interest in Warrane/Sydney and Naarm/Melbourne. It is now classified into 'genres' of the Western Desert acrylic art movement.

From the early 1970s, the Central Desert Peoples started to move off government-run Aboriginal settlements, such as Papunya. They returned to the homelands to renew their connections with their sacred places and their histories and meanings. This was an essential step in ensuring the survival of their cultures. They painted their sacred designs for an enthusiastic audience that was prepared to pay for the privilege of seeing the marks of the ancestors. This enabled the leaders of this cultural movement to pursue their philosophical traditions, and to offer the paintings to a marketplace as signs of their ownership of these stories and histories.

A firsthand account of this pivotal period in Australian art history is told in a book by Geoffrey Bardon and his older brother, James Bardon:

Papunya: A Place Made After the Story. It features images of more than 500 paintings, drawings and photographs from Bardon's personal archive, many of which are 'now regarded as some of Australia's most treasured cultural, historical and artistic items'.

Exhibitions in Paris and the United Kingdom, principally of the Papunya style of art with the distinctive lines and dots that appear to depict a bird's eye view of landscapes, excited the art world. Soon, paintings began to sell for high prices as collectors competed for the rare pieces that reached the northern hemisphere.

The paintings of the Papunya Tula movement tell us that these were people who lived in and knew an immense territory as their home. They journeyed on foot to their far-flung camps within these landscapes. Each camp, or ngurra, was reached after days of walking, sometimes carrying water in wooden vessels. On the way, side journeys were taken to hunt animals, gather vegetable foods or collect firewood. Reaching a ngurra, they cooked in their ground ovens, and before sleep, around their fires in the night, they could gaze at the other great sacred geography in the night sky where ancestors reside among their stellar marvels.

People who live in the open air read the light and shadow of the day, the movements of the stars, the colour, direction, and shape of clouds as they traverse the sky, the signs of smoke and dust in the landscape, the level of water in waterholes, the direction of birds flying across the sky in the evening and the tracks and scats of animals. They predict the weather from the rings around the moon, the seasons, and the movement of ants and birds. To eat and live well depends on attention to these details.

Understanding the landscape intimately, living under a vast sky and knowing what lies beyond the horizons is a geographical legacy that is represented in paintings.

These graphic designs were formerly marked out in sacred sand sculptures with feathers and sacramental matter, prepared by gatherings of men or women in groupings affiliated with particular ancestors and sites. They decorated these sculptures as if painting the body of a kinsman.

In 1985, keen to present their own works to the public and distinguish themselves from the Pintupi artists, the Warlpiri People formed Warlukurlangu Artists, now an Aboriginal Corporation. In the Warlpiri language, Warlukurlangu means 'belonging to fire'. In contrast to the subtle colour palette seen in the Pintupi paintings, the Warlpiri artists preferred bold, saturated colours.

The public first saw their distinctive style when the artists painted thirty doors at the Yuendumu school in the Northern Territory. Judith

Warlpiri artists Clarise Nampijinpa Poulson and Michael Japangardi Poulson with son Joel Japanangka Poulson in Yuendumu, 1989

Crispin, who worked with Warlpiri Elders, explains that in 1984, the school principal, Terry Davies, welcomed the approach by the artists, Paddy Japaljarri Stewart, Paddy Japaljarri Sims, Larry Jungarrayi Spencer, Paddy Jupurrula Nelson and Roy Jupurrula Curtis. These men went on to paint the doors with their most important Jukurrpa (the sacred narratives and laws referred to in English as 'the Dreaming') to teach the children about their traditional Country. Twelve years later, the South Australian Museum acquired the doors.

Paddy Japaljarri Stewart's account of painting the doors reveals that the designs, like so much of the art that emerged from the desert communities at that time, were inspired by the sacred ground paintings made for ceremonies. Here are his words, as quoted in an article by Crispin at kurdijiapp.wordpress.com:

> We can't leave our Jukurrpa behind, we have to keep it alive. When my father was alive this is what he taught me. He taught me the traditional ways like the traditional designs in body or head of Kangaroo Dreaming (that's what we call Marlu Dreaming) and Eagle Dreaming. He taught me to sing song for the big ceremonies.

The Warlukurlangu artists' cooperative commenced soon after the artists painted the doors. As recounted on the website, the motivation driving the Elders was their desire to maintain their cultural practices.

In 2014–15, the National Museum of Australia exhibited drawings by Warlpiri People. They had been sketched in the 1950s at the government settlement of Hooker Creek, now the township of Lajamanu, in the Northern Territory, when, in 1953, anthropologist Mervyn Meggitt invited Warlpiri men to draw with crayons on paper. The drawings were deposited with the Australian Institute of Aboriginal Torres Strait Islander Studies. Some sixty years later, the descendants of the artists were shown these works.

At the end of the assimilation period in the 1970s, Aboriginal artists were encouraged by the Australian government's establishment of the Aboriginal Arts Board of the Australia Council. This was also the time when the government responded to the first native title case, brought by the Yolŋu People of north-east Arnhem Land.

When Justice Blackburn handed down his decision in this case, the Yolŋu People and their supporters were shocked. Blackburn found that there could be no recognition of Aboriginal laws, despite the large amount of evidence of their existence submitted to the court. His argument rested on the ceded colony doctrine, better known as the 'terra nullius' doctrine.

The new federal government appointed Justice Edward Woodward to head a commission of inquiry to determine how Aboriginal rights in land could be recognised. He had been the Queen's Counsel representing the Yolŋu clans in the court. At the end of Woodward's hearings of further evidence from the clan leaders, in 1973, the Yolŋu People gave him gifts, including sacred bark paintings and objects.

He had become Sir Edward Woodward after a distinguished career and was chancellor of the University of Melbourne from 1990 until 2001. In early 2003, he entrusted the works to the University of Melbourne's Ian Potter Museum. They are works of art and sacred objects that record the life and history, the sacred narratives and land and sea estates, of the respective Yolŋu clans whose Elders at that time created them.

Art and country

Famous artist and leader of the Madarrpa clan Djambawa Marawili stated the link between art and Country when he spoke at the Garma Forum in 2003: 'Why do I look at arts? What does it mean? It is very important to me. Because it is the image of the art here in the country. The country is talking to me. We have knowledge.'

His work has featured in many exhibitions, such as the ground-breaking 'Saltwater' exhibition. The exhibition, initiated by Marawili, was part of important evidence of sacred sites that led to the successful 2008 Blue Mud

Bay High Court sea rights claim. The authors of the 'Saltwater' exhibition catalogue note that the 'Yolŋu artists had dual motives for selling their artwork: to purchase goods in exchange and to teach Europeans about the value of their culture'.

These beautiful images, as well as the manikay (songs) and buŋgul (dance and performances) associated with them, may be understood in western thinking as works of artistic and performative expression. For the Yolŋu People they have profound meanings and are associated with matters of law.

The Yolŋu universe has two parts – Dhuwa and Yirritja – and each person, animal and plant, all land or sea estate, sky, water, and other beings belong to one or the other. These moieties, or halves, are fundamental in the kinship and marriage system and the general order of things. The maternal connection is especially important in this regard. The yothu–yindi (child–mother link) and the gutharra–märi (daughter's child–mother's mother link) form foundational ties between clans and their estates. The bäpurru is a group of clans linked by songs, dances and designs associated with a particular waŋarr being, who travelled the land when it was first created. Bäpurru also refers to the members of a single clan who come together for ceremonial purposes to celebrate the sacred story that gave birth to them. It is from this story that their shared inheritance of sacred objects and rituals, resources and governing responsibilities comes.

In 1962–63, the clan leaders of north-east Arnhem Land presided over the creation of two large Church Panels painted with clan emblems, representing the Yirritja and Dhuwa moieties and the most sacred designs of the clan waŋarr. They were then displayed in the mission church at Yirrkala. These events marked a turning point in the relationship between Aboriginal people and the Yirrkala missionaries.

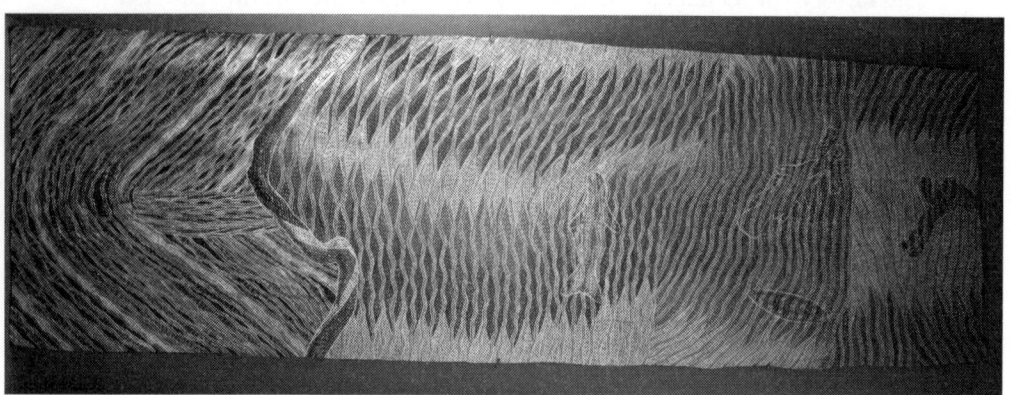

Source of Fire (2014), Djambawa Marawili, earth pigments and sawdust on bark, courtesy of the artist, Buku-Larrŋgay Mulka Centre and the Kaplan & Levi Collection

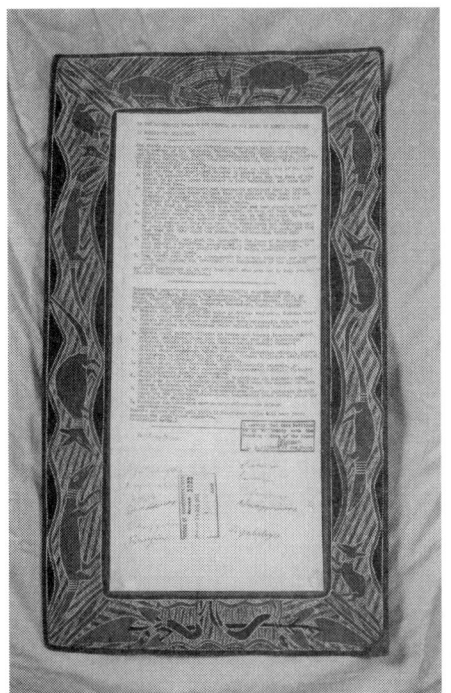 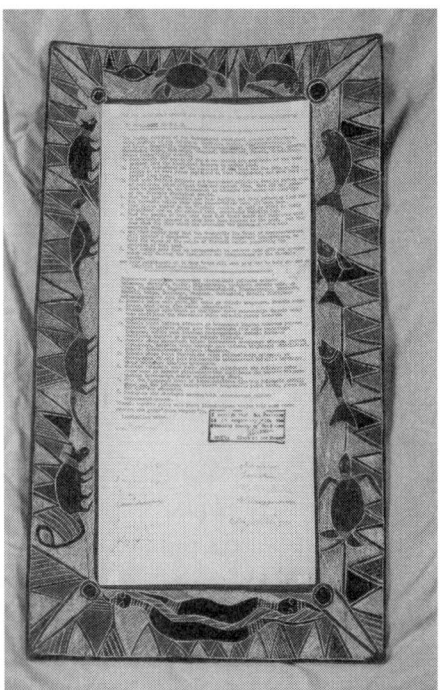

The Yirrkala Bark Petitions presented to Parliament on 14 August (left) and 28 August (right), 1963. Courtesy of the House of Representatives, Commonwealth Parliament of Australia.

Following this, in 1963, in protest at the federal government's decision that bauxite mining could take place on their lands, the Yolŋu clan leaders prepared the famous Yirrkala Bark Petitions. These are sacred paintings that were prepared in ritual fashion, signed in English fashion, and submitted to the Australian Parliament in Canberra. The meetings of Elders to prepare the petitions were the precursor to their litigation in *Milirrpum v Nabalco*. A parliamentary inquiry into the acquisition of the Yolŋu land for mining followed, in 1964. In 1976, the *Aboriginal Land Rights (Northern Territory) Act 1976* was enacted by the federal Parliament to provide inalienable freehold title to Aboriginal land trusts over former Aboriginal reserves and other lands.

In each of the historical events briefly described here, Yolŋu artworks were produced to proclaim the existence of Yolŋu law, particularly land and sea ownership, and the mythological events that resulted in the creation of the land. These paintings represent, in figurative and geometric form, the totemic landscape of eastern Arnhem Land. Naming is perhaps the primary act of representation, and, in the Yolŋu world, it is a tradition of profound importance. Djambawa Marawili explains this in Andrew Blake's book *Saltwater: Yirrkala Bark Paintings of Sea Country*.

> Every individual in this area has a name, small special names, small sacred names, canoe names. Yolŋu have used these names through the ceremonial singing of our ancestors or in the naming of our grandchildren. They are all names in the individual lands; also in the sea. Every small bit of sea has a name ...
>
> There are places there, names there, names that are special, that Yolŋu receive in their heads. And sing and give names to children. Also it explains the country, how they became one, not only the sea but the land too. They became one.[59]

Hence, art serves the purpose of encoding the images that are associated with ancestral names, sacred stories and interpreting people's association with special places and things.

Yolŋu visual representations are intricate and highly structured. The imagery and design of these artworks are rich in metaphor and analogy. If we could read the signs of their culture as they do, a web of the signs of power would emerge from the world around us. Just as the sunset speaks of many sacred elements, so too do flowering plants, which tell us about the seasonality of wild foods; yam leaves, which tell us about an ancestral presence in a clan estate; honey, which tells us about the revolutionary ancestor Ganbulabula; and waterholes, which tell us about souls.

Ethical dealings in First Australians art

It is the special status of art and design in the Aboriginal world that has caused a body of rights to be developed. They are not all recognised by law, but they are observed in the practices of ethical gallery owners and curators. Protection of Aboriginal artists' rights has been the subject of government inquiries, court cases and campaigns over several decades. Crudely manufactured goods made in China or Indonesia, and sold to tourists as 'Aboriginal art', 'boomerangs' and 'didgeridoos', fill souvenir shops and galleries in the tourist precincts of Australia. This trade causes immense harm to Indigenous artists and their families and brings Indigenous art into disrepute.

Establishing the authenticity of an artwork is important for both the Indigenous artists and the people who buy their art. All reputable and ethical commercial galleries and art cooperatives document each piece and the artist and provide certificates of authenticity. Even so, fraudsters have copied works or made works in the style of famous artists and sold

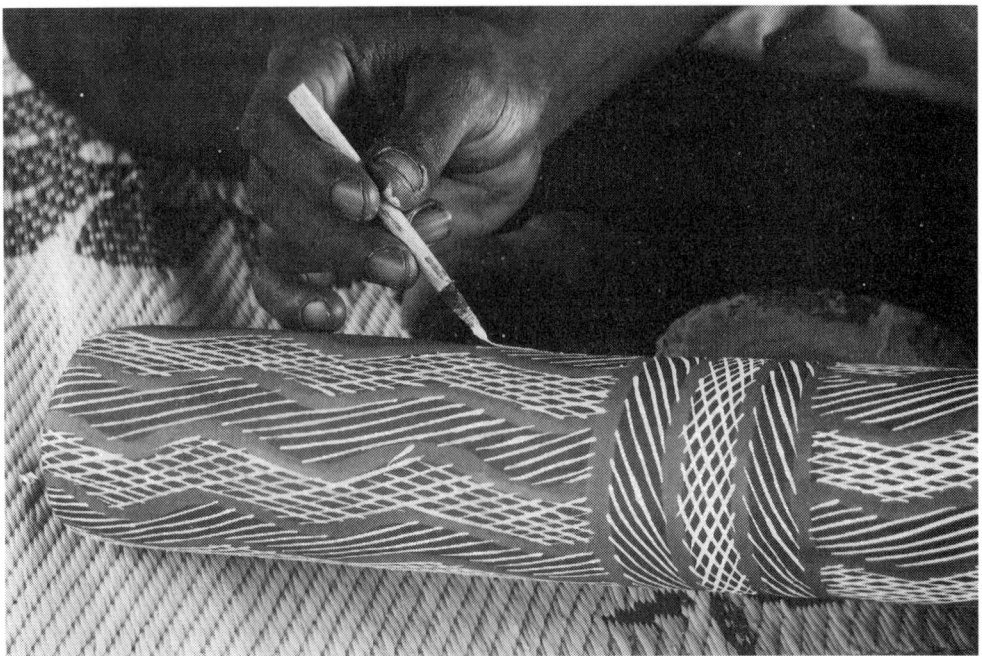

Barayuwa Munuŋgurr painting with marwat (the hair brush used to paint cross-hatching) on a yiḏaki (didgeridoo)

them to naive buyers. The art centres represented at the Indigenous art fairs are backed by groups such as Desart and the Association of Northern, Kimberley and Arnhem Aboriginal Artists. They are governed by elected councils of Aboriginal artists and advocate for their members.

After several copyright cases in the courts, it was a fraud case in Victoria in 2007 that finally delivered justice to Aboriginal artists whose works had been copied. In the first successful prosecution of art fraud, Pamela Yvonne Liberto and her husband Ivan Liberto were found guilty by a county court jury. They had conned the major art auction houses into selling fraudulent copies. It was reported in *The Age* in 2007:

> The Libertos received more than $300,000 after forging and selling four paintings, supposedly by renowned artist Rover Thomas, whose work is keenly sought by collectors across the world and attracted a record price when the National Gallery of Australia purchased *All That Big Rain Coming from Top Side* for $778,000 in 2001.[60]

Scientific examination of the paint and materials to date the works, carried out by the University of Melbourne Centre for Cultural Materials Conservation, provided the evidence of fraud.

Fraud leads to financial losses for the artists and their families, and the artists often feel that their soul has been stolen. Some artists have refused to work again after they discovered copies of their works were sold under their name. Traditional Owners and clans own their traditional designs. Often one person in the group is authorised by their father, mother or grandparent to execute the designs of their people. These designs are inherited, and even though the work of art is intended for the market, the artist feels that they are offering it to the world as a gift with the spirit of their ancestry and special places. The traditional works often depict religious content. In earlier copyright cases in the 1980s and 1990s, aggrieved artists gave evidence to this effect, but these cases did little to protect their rights.

Lawyers Terri Janke and Maiko Sentina have summed up the dilemma succinctly in their work *Indigenous Knowledge*, from 2018:

> Indigenous Knowledge is the heart of Indigenous identity. It connects Indigenous people to the lands and seas that they have lived in, and around, for over 65,000 years ...
>
> Indigenous people assert their rights to their intangible heritage and their Indigenous Knowledge to continue their practice of their culture; and to stop misappropriation of their knowledge without consultation or consent, and to stop debasement and loss of cultural practice.[61]

Understanding the laws, customs and traditions of the First Australians is vitally important. Ethical practices and education about Indigenous art, heritage and cultural traditions will serve to protect them. If you know about our cultures, you will be more likely to respect them.

First Australians art in the global market

Indigenous artists working in non-traditional styles and with contemporary art materials emerged in the nineteenth century, and by the middle of the twentieth century some achieved national fame. Albert Namatjira, an Arrernte man from the Lutheran mission of Hermannsburg, painted exquisite watercolours of his beloved Country in Central Australia. His works were avidly collected and admired, and over time his distinctive style has become recognised as a school of art, with many of his descendants following in his footsteps. The most celebrated today is Vincent Namatjira, who in 2020 became the first Indigenous artist to win the prestigious Archibald Prize for his portrait of champion Australian Rules footballer Adam Goodes. Exhibiting his work both nationally and internationally since 2015, Vincent Namatjira satirises Australia's colonial history in his bold conceptual works 'with recurring references to Captain Cook, the British Royal family and contemporary aspects of Indigenous life'.

Several other Indigenous artists have achieved global fame with their distinctive paintings, motifs, photography and multimedia pieces. Their works often speak back to the highly Eurocentric fine-arts world in Australia. Tracey Moffatt is the first Indigenous artist to have her photographs exhibited in prestigious art galleries in the northern hemisphere. She was chosen to represent Australia at the 2017 Venice Biennale, creating a collection of photographic and video works called *My Horizon*, which was considered a huge success. Moffatt revolutionised the way that Aboriginal art was received and opened the door for the new wave of Indigenous artists experimenting with history, form, media and stereotypes.

Brook Garru Andrew, who claims his Wiradjuri and Celtic ancestors, has similarly achieved global fame. In his own words, his art practice involves deep thinking about the representation of Indigenous people in various media:

> *His interdisciplinary practice harnesses alternative narratives to explore the legacies of colonisation and modernism. His artworks, museum interventions and curatorial projects challenge the limitations imposed by power structures, historical amnesia, stereotyping and complicity to centre Indigenous perspectives. Apart from drawing inspiration from vernacular objects and the archive he travels internationally to work with artists, communities and various private and public collections.*
>
> *The rich, research-based interventions and artworks of Brook Andrew have been presented in exhibitions nationally and internationally since 1996.*[62]

His pieces use media including neon, installation, photomedia, mixed media, performance and video.

Andrew challenges perceptions and history, often manipulating text and images to address colonialism and the racialisation of minority peoples. Andrew was also the first Indigenous Australian to be selected as the artistic director for the Biennale of Sydney, in 2020. He called the event *Nirin*, which is the Wiradjuri word for 'edge' and acknowledges the importance of Indigenous languages. Sadly, this extraordinary exhibition was only available online after the opening week because of COVID-19 restrictions.

These trailblazers have changed the way we think about Australian art, profoundly and permanently. My own view is their art is the most exciting art in Australia, and if their success is a measure, then thousands of people agree with me. Hundreds of Aboriginal artists have followed them. Misinformed art historians call them 'urban artists', but many are not or

VINCENT NAMATJIRA
Stand strong for who you are, 2020
Acrylic on linen
152 × 198 × 3 cm

Image courtesy of the artist, Iwantja Arts & THIS IS NO FANTASY. Collection of Art Gallery of New South Wales.

were not urban dwellers. The late Ian Abdulla was a Ngarrindjeri artist who has been called Australia's greatest 'naïve' artist with his paintings of his early life in the Riverland region in rural South Australia.

Every major and rural gallery has collected some of the works from the multidisciplinary Indigenous artists of the last fifty years and many regularly have major exhibitions. One excellent example was the National Gallery of Victoria's highly successful *From Bark to Neon: Indigenous Art from the NGV Collection*, which exhibited a range of artworks across many media. It is these kinds of exhibitions that illustrate the diversity of Indigenous art. There is no one type of Indigenous art or artist. The richness of our traditions and the genius of our artists speaks to the survival of great human traditions of representing our lives and our worlds.

Advice on buying authentic art

It is the work of the catalogue writers and art historians who meticulously document the art styles and the artists' biographies, that offers the best protection for the buyer. To verify authenticity, it is possible to find examples of artists' works, their representatives, and the explanations of their works in galleries, published in books, and in catalogues online.

The Art Galleries Association of Australia and the Australia Commercial Galleries Association have websites that list their members. Reputable galleries subscribe to the Code of Practice of the National Association for the Visual Arts. The Indigenous Art Code (indigenousartcode.org) was set up in 2010 to preserve and promote ethical trading in Indigenous art. Articles on its website discuss buying art ethically, as outlined below, and the harm caused to artists when people buy fakes.

Major Aboriginal art corporations and associations have long had guidelines for ensuring ethical art purchases. Desart in Central Australia has more than 30 art centres, and ANKA (Arnhem, Northern and Kimberley Artists) Aboriginal Corporation in Australia's north serves Aboriginal artists and 48 art centres. These bodies are governed by their members to represent their interests. 'Working together to keep art, country and culture strong' is ANKA's mission statement. The protection Desart, ANKA and similar Aboriginal art associations and corporations offer is vital to Aboriginal artists' art traditions and their livelihoods, as ANKA attests on its website:

> Aboriginal Art Centres provide economic, cultural and social benefits for some of Australia's most disadvantaged communities, they lead the way in caring for the nation's intangible cultural heritage for all Australians.[63]

Many of these local art centres have websites with the online facilities for secure purchase of art. Not all do, however, so the guidelines provided by ANKA on the organisation's website are important in this very tricky market. As many of the Aboriginal art communities have turned to online sale over the years, so too have the 'carpetbaggers'. You can download guidelines for buying ethically in English, German, French and Japanese from ANKA's website as well as viewing the Indigenous Art Code guidelines, which are summarised further on page 131–132.

Most Australian artists in all of the media, from music to the visual arts, were placed in a precarious financial state when COVID-19 restrictions were imposed to stop the spread of the coronavirus that had taken the lives of hundreds of thousands in other countries, and posed an existential threat to the highly vulnerable Indigenous Peoples who suffer from a range of pre-existing conditions that place them at risk of severe illness and death. The lockdown approach worked, with not only international and state and territory borders shut, but also the borders of Aboriginal and Torres Strait Islander lands and communities. The usual visitors, tourists and art

Walangari Karntawarra with artworks at the Double Bay Library, NSW

collectors were not permitted to go to the Indigenous art centres, and even in some cities, travel outside of the home was radically limited.

The lives of thousands of people were saved but the economic costs of the response to the COVID-19 pandemic were great. For artists who depend on the precarious market of Aboriginal and Torres Strait Islander art, the impacts of the restrictions included a dramatic decline in their incomes as sales stopped, and increased the difficulty of obtaining art materials, which also threatened their livelihoods. Exhibitions were cancelled and airlines cancelled most flights, so the shipping of art sometimes became impossible.

In response to the unethical dealers who flooded the website with fraudulent or substandard Aboriginal works, the Indigenous Art Code set up a campaign to assist artists. *Our Art Is Our Lifeline* was launched by the Indigenous Art Code (IartC) in partnership with Macquarie Group to encourage the ethical purchasing of artwork, especially as audiences embraced online sales. Ethical dealing in Indigenous artwork became the primary consideration for these artists, and they explained how involving them in the sale and licensing of their artwork was fundamental to sustaining their art practice.

Those seeking to purchase Indigenous artworks are advised by IartC to 'look for art centres, galleries and licensed product retailers who are members of the Indigenous Art Code'. The IartC website has a detailed explanation of the things you need to consider to buy ethically. It outlines the questions you should ask an art centre, a gallery, a dealer, auctioneer, or an art fair about the artists and how they are paid; and the importance of provenance, particularly as there are 'some people selling Aboriginal art (and fake Aboriginal art) who respect neither Indigenous culture nor the wellbeing of the artists and their communities':

> *Our experience is of a market in which many, if not most, dealers behave fairly and ethically most of the time. But there are nonetheless too many instances of artists being subject to problematic and exploitative behaviour by some individuals. The common characteristic of problematic behaviour raised with the IartC is coercion by the individual in the perceived position of power. The power imbalance in this sector is real and one which many artists are subject to. Any individual or business engaging in the exhibition, promotion and sale of Aboriginal or Torres Strait Islander art should be cognisant of this. Valuing and appreciating art extends to respecting culture and creating safe environments for the artists to freely engage in and express their own artistic and cultural practice.*

The IartC requires all Code signatories to issue a Code Certificate for any piece of Aboriginal and Torres Strait Islander artwork over AUD$250 sold by a dealer, including art centres and galleries. These certificates 'provide buyers with high levels of confidence in both provenance and fair payment of the artist'. Buyers do need to be aware, though, that 'some unethical dealers have been known to create their own certificates', which are no proof that they have treated Aboriginal and Torres Strait Islander artists ethically or paid a fair price for their work. A buyer can gain certainty by purchasing a piece of art directly from an art centre, but can also gain confidence about purchasing authentic Aboriginal and Torres Strait art when buying from a gallery by asking some questions that 'any reputable dealer will be happy to answer', as the IartC website indicates:

1. Who is the artist?
2. Where is the artist from?
3. How did you get the artwork or product in your gallery or shop?
4. How was the artist paid for their work?
5. If it is a reproduction of an artist's work, how are royalties or licensing fees paid to the artist?
6. How long has your gallery been around?

If it's suddenly appeared from nowhere, where were they before? And where will they be next week?
7. Is your gallery a member of the Indigenous Art Code?
If yes, you know it has agreed to follow the Indigenous Australian Art Commercial Code of Conduct.

As IartC emphasises, ethical galleries and dealers will be willing to answer questions about the artist, their work, the community they come from and the art centre they are connected with. Buyers shouldn't believe galleries or dealers that tell 'stories about the art centre ripping off the artist so they now deal direct' – and, just as the artists do, buyers have a right to know the 'money story' relating to an artwork.

Some warning signs of unethical practices that IartC advises buyers to look out for are:

> A collection of works unconnected by theme, region, language, or culture.
>
> Will the gallery 'do a deal'? Ethical galleries usually work on a fixed price model with a consistent percentage returned to the art centre and artist. Offers of a discount to close the sale can be a cause for concern.
>
> Does the gallery try to prove the provenance of artworks using photos of artists holding the work, rather than official authentication certificates?

IartC also gives this valuable advice to people when buying direct from Aboriginal and Torres Strait Islander artists:

> There are thousands of Aboriginal and Torres Strait Islander artists from across the country. Many are members of Aboriginal and Torres Strait Islander-owned art centres, and many work independently of any art centre structure and support. The Indigenous Art Code does not suggest that purchasing from any single source is superior to another; ethical practice is found in the execution of the associated business model. We encourage buyers to take an active and engaged role in learning about the business model of any dealer you plan to purchase from and how it is applied to the business's relationship with the artist. Different models suit different artists. What is most important is that artists can exercise agency in decision-making regarding commercial agreements and that they can negotiate the market on their terms, whatever they may be.[64]

10
Performance

Singing, dancing, composing and making music are at the core of First Peoples cultures in Australia. Indigenous artists work across the full range of performance art – music, drama, dance and multimedia. They perform in many different styles – traditional styles based on their ancient culture, as well as contemporary ones. Many performers also now mix the two – traditional and modern. Both traditional and contemporary Indigenous performance styles often convey connections to culture and Country. They express the artists' ancient hereditary knowledge.

The traditional ways of making music include singing, clapping and keeping the beat by clapping or playing percussion instruments such as clapsticks. Instruments such as the yidaki (commonly called the didgeridoo) and, in the Torres Strait, various styles of drums are used. Aboriginal and Torres Strait Islander musicians have also adopted musical instruments and techniques from around the world. For non-traditional performances, Indigenous musicians use guitars, including electric guitars, ukuleles, pianos, most of the orchestral instruments, such as brass instruments, modern drums and percussion instruments, and even gum leaves.

Indigenous artists assert their ownership of traditional music and dance as well as of their new works. They have legal protections for their customary rights and ownership of their copyright. The global theft of Aboriginal and Torres Strait Islander cultural heritage, music and performance has presented Indigenous artists and Traditional Owners with huge challenges, including legal cases. This has led to changes in government policies, protocols and patenting initiatives, all designed to protect our performance arts and our performers.

The first Aboriginal songs ever recorded were sung by Fanny Cochrane Smith. She was recorded by Horace Watson at the Royal Society in nipaluna/Hobart, Tasmania, on a wax cylinder device between 1899 and 1903. This was less than a decade after this technology first arrived in Australia. These are the only recordings of Tasmanian Aboriginal songs or of any Tasmanian

Aboriginal language. Singing in both English and her own language, Fanny recorded 'all of the Tasmanian songs she knew, some in Aboriginal languages, others in English'.

In one of the recordings, she talks about being the last of the Tasmanians. Copies are kept in archives, including the National Film and Sound Archive (NFSA) and the Australian Institute of Aboriginal and Torres Strait Islander Studies (AIATSIS) in Ngambri/Ngunnawal/Canberra.

There is a song whose origins are even older than these late nineteenth century recordings of Fanny Cochrane Smith. It is called 'Ngarra Burra Ferra'. Many musicians are fascinated by this song, but it was Daniel Browning, host of the ABC Radio National program *AWAYE!*, who discovered its origins and its story. Browning interviewed Professor Gabriel Solis, a music expert of African American Studies at the University of Illinois, about it. Professor Solis says that the story goes as far back as 1887 and could be older. That was when the world-famous Fisk Jubilee Singers from Fisk

Contemporary dancers perform at an international gathering in Garramilla/Darwin (photo Wayne Quilliam)

University, Nashville, Tennessee, USA, visited the Maloga mission near Moama, in Victoria, in the homelands of the Yorta Yorta People. 'Ngarra Burra Ferra' is a Yorta Yorta version of the song 'Turn Back Pharoah's Army', which the Fisk Jubilee Singers sang during their visit to Australia. Professor Solis explained that 'They left a songbook, and one of their spirituals about the escape of the Israelites from slavery in Egypt became "Ngarra Burra Ferra", translated into Yorta Yorta'.

The song was made famous when it was performed in the 2012 film *The Sapphires*, about the adventures of a Yorta Yorta girl group in the 1960s and 1970s. Four young women formed the group at Cummeragunga in Victoria, and travelled to Naarm/Melbourne and then to Vietnam, where they performed for the Australian soldiers. The version of 'Ngarra Burra Ferra' in *The Sapphires* is sung by cast members Jessica Mauboy, Shari Sebbens, Miranda Tapsell and Deborah Mailman.

The first Torres Strait Islander music and dance ever recorded dates from 1898.

Alfred C. Haddon, a British zoologist and ethnographer from Cambridge University, filmed dances on Mer (Murray Island). Curated at the NFSA, the exhibition *Torres Strait Islanders (1898)* contains the surviving four-and-a-half minutes of footage A.C. Haddon shot. This is the first field footage taken of Indigenous peoples in Australia and was made just three years after the invention of the cinecamera.

Copies of these precious films are archived at the NFSA and can be viewed online. While the film clips are silent, they show the songs and dances that are still performed today. These films were presented as evidence in the famous Mabo case, in the Supreme Court of Queensland. To find out about this case, read the 'Native title' chapter.

Liz McNiven, the NFSA curator, writes in the exhibition catalogue that the 'film shows Torres Strait Islander men performing three dance sequences ... followed by a demonstration of traditional fire-making practices ... The last part of the film shows two short dances performances [*sic*] by young Aboriginal men'.

The first clip, at just over a minute long, shows 'the spectacular Malu-Bomai ceremony performed by the Torres Strait Islander men of Mer at Kiam, in the eastern Torres Strait'. In the other two dance sequences, 'three men wear traditional headdresses and dance in synchronisation', while the 'final sequence shows four young Australian Aboriginal men performing a shake-a-leg dance on the beach, while another beats the rhythm', McNiven writes.

Many Torres Strait Islander communities and families are committed to protecting and performing the various styles of traditional dancing, singing and drumming. They know that their history and culture are important, and they are preserving them through songs and dances. As the late Ephraim Bani, a noted linguist and expert in Torres Strait Islander culture, explained in 1979:

> The importance of dancing and songs in the Torres Strait Islands ... [is not] mere entertainment ... [but] is the most important aspect of Torres Strait lifestyle. The Torres Strait Islanders preserve and present their oral history through songs and dances; in other words, the songs and dances are Torres Strait literature material. Just like any written materials, which are usually illustrations, the dances act as illustrative material and, of course, the dancer himself [sic] is the storyteller.[65]

Mr Bani was the chief of Wagadagam clan, on Mabuyag Island (Jervis Island), and a cultural ambassador for his people.

The Ilan style of music performed by Torres Strait Islanders combines traditional singing with a variety of introduced styles. It is mixed with hymns brought by missionaries and songs shared by sailors whose ships stopped among the islands. The songs, accompanied by drums and other

Christine Anu styling up at the launch of NITV at the base of Uluṟu, Northern Territory (photo Wayne Quilliam)

percussion instruments, guitars and sometimes ukuleles, celebrate living with the sea, love and adventure. Island songs are performed in two- or three-part harmony and are improvised by the singers.

The best example of modern Torres Strait music is that of the late Seaman Dan – Henry Gibson Dan AM (25 August 1929 – 30 December 2020) – whose work is produced by Karl Neuenfeldt. He was seventy years old when he began to sing publicly. Uncle Seaman went on to release five albums of traditional music and his signature Ilan-style blues and jazz. In his biography, *Steady Steady: The Life and Music of Seaman Dan*, Uncle Seaman told stories of his life in the islands as a pearl diver, and his career as a professional singer and musician.

ARIA award–winning singer Christine Anu also hails from the Torres Strait. She has had success with a number of albums and film appearances and sang at the Closing Ceremony of the 2000 Sydney Olympics.

Protecting the traditional styles

Today, the traditional styles of music and performance are at risk of being lost or forgotten. Rescue programs, research projects and festivals are working to collect and preserve these musical forms, which are the oldest in the world. Yolŋu musicians, ethnomusicologists and scholars joined forces to stop their decline, forming the National Recording Project for Indigenous Performance in Australia. The Project's 'Garma Statement on Indigenous Music and Dance' of 2002 tells us:

> *Indigenous songs should also be a deeply valued part of the Australian cultural heritage. They represent the great classical music of this land.*
>
> *These ancient musical traditions were once everywhere in Australia, and now survive as living traditions only in several regions. Many of these are now in danger of being lost forever.*
>
> *Indigenous performances are one of our most rich and beautiful forms of artistic expression, and yet they remain unheard and invisible within the national cultural heritage. Without immediate action many Indigenous music and dance traditions are in danger of extinction with potentially destructive consequences for the fabric of Indigenous society and culture.*
>
> *The recording and documenting of the remaining traditions is a matter of the highest priority both for Indigenous and non-Indigenous Australians. Many of our foremost composers and singers have already passed away leaving little or no record.*[66]

In northern and central Australia, traditional songs are generally sung in cycles. Each song is short but can be combined with others and repeated and performed throughout a ceremony. When men sing their cycles, there are usually two lead singers, a chorus and a yidaki player. In Central Australia, a now rarely seen short wind instrument for ritual purposes was used in the past, and boomerangs, clapsticks and handclapping are the usual accompaniments to singing. Each male singer uses clapsticks to keep the rhythm. Women sing in a variety of styles. For example, following a death, a senior woman will lead the keening or high-pitched singing. In the desert, groups of women sing the cycles, led by one or two lead singers, and clap with cupped hands to keep the beat.

It is not only the traditional styles of Indigenous music that are at risk of being lost forever when each song man or woman passes. It is also the innovations in style and musical and lyrical compositions of Indigenous music that emerged at the end of the frontier wars when most Indigenous people were incarcerated in missions and reserves. Support for our musicians who preserve these new traditions is important as I have pointed out in speaking about the musician Jessie Lloyd and many others.

Danzal Baker, aka Baker Boy, raps in Yolŋu matha languages and English (photo Wayne Quilliam)

TREATY, MUSIC, ART: MANDAWUY YUNUPIŊU AND PAUL KELLY WRITE A NEW ANTHEM

Music and art have been regular companions of politics in our world, and while at least three Australian governments have established formal treaty processes with Indigenous Australians, we should look back into our history to the seminal moment when the demand for treaty was supported by great music and design that drew on ancient traditions.

This is how the song 'Treaty' became a new anthem. As Aaron Corn tells the story in *Reflections and Voices*, in 1988, the bicentennial of Australia as a nation, the late Yunupiŋu carried on the work of his father, Muŋgurrawuy, who in 1962 was involved with the Yirrkala leaders' campaign against the bauxite mine. Yunupiŋu, an elected Chair of the Northern Land Council, collaborated with the late Wenten Rubuntja, Chair of the Central Land Council, to prepare a petition calling on the Australian government 'to enter into a Treaty with Indigenous Australians in recognition of their rights and freedom as Australia's original owners'.

They painted a canvas in which typescript was bordered by sacred designs. On the left were Yolŋu designs for four Yirritja homelands. They were balanced on the right by a Two Sisters Dreaming design common to Central Australia and linked here to Dhuwa ancestors of the Yolŋu. It was called the Barunga Statement and can be viewed at aiatsis.gov.au/explore/barunga-statement. This form was adopted as the model in 2017 for the Uluru Statement from the Heart.

> On 12 June that year, the Barunga Statement was presented to Prime Minister Robert Hawke at the Barunga Sport and Cultural Festival under the most sacred of ceremonial conditions. His initial response was overwhelmingly positive and he promised to start negotiations towards a Treaty with Indigenous Australians within the lifetime of his parliament. But by 1990, no progress had been made and the issue had all but faded from public memory.

In 1990, the late Mandawuy Yunupiŋu, his younger brother and lead singer of the Yothu Yindi band, 'collaborated with Peter Garrett and Paul Kelly to remind everyone of Hawke's well-publicised promise of a treaty at Barunga'. They composed 'Treaty', which endures as Yothu Yindi's best-remembered song. 'Treaty' was remixed in Melbourne by Filthy Lucre and rapidly gained popularity. It became the first song with lyrics in an original Australian language to top the Australian charts.

'Treaty' won many awards, including Best Australian Single from ARIA, Song of the Year from the Australasian Performing Right Association, Song Writing from the Human Rights and Equal Opportunity Commission, Best Australian Video from the Australian Music Awards and Best Australian Video from the MTV International Awards. In 1991, Yothu Yindi performed at the New Music Seminar in New York and signed an international recording contract with Hollywood Records.

Aaron Corn explains the deeper significance of the song for Mandawuy and his people:

> *The song's melody comes through its quotation of an historic Djatpaŋarri item composed by Rrikin Burarrwaŋa and recorded by Richard Waterman at Yirrkala in the early 1950s. With its youthful calls of encouragement to anyone dancing, the exuberance of the Djatpaŋarri style sets the mood and tempo for the entire song and captures Mandawuy's nostalgia for his childhood on the Gove Peninsula before the advent of mining in 1968.*
>
> *Nonetheless, the ideological heart of 'Treaty' lies in the second verse with its bold affirmation that the Yolŋu have never ceded or sold their homelands to the Crown, and that Yolŋu sovereignty was never affected by the British landing at Sydney Cove in 1788. This second verse also employs the* ganma *'converging currents' model for social equity first used by Mandawuy in 'Mainstream'. Here, he describes Indigenous and non-Indigenous Australians as two rivers running their separate courses, and dreams of a brighter day when a Treaty will make those waters one.*

Mandawuy intended that 'Treaty' would 'raise public awareness about this, so that the government would be encouraged to hold to his promise'. He went on to say:

> *The song became a number one hit, the first ever to be sung in a Yolŋu language, and it caught the public's imagination.*
>
> *Though it borrows from rock'n'roll, the whole structure of 'Treaty' is driven by the beat of the Djatpaŋarri that I worked into it. It was an old recording of this Djatpaŋarri that triggered the song. The man who originally created it passed away a long time ago in 1978. He was a real master of the Djatpaŋarri style.*[67]

Indigenous music today: Indigenous musical innovations

In the cities and towns of Australia, balladeers had long turned the conditions of Aboriginal life – the hunger, poverty, racism and cruelty, whether on the missions and administered reserves or as victims of the Stolen Generations – singing a melancholic style of resistance in the tunes of Christian hymns, country and western and other popular western songs.

The late Archie Roach was one of Australia's most treasured singers. He passed away on 30 July 2022 at the age of 66. His debut and award-winning album, *Charcoal Lane*, was released in 1990. It was his song 'Took the Children Away' about the Stolen Generations that catapulted Roach to fame in the Indigenous world. Roach was a member of the Stolen Generations. He toured and sang with his late wife, Ruby Hunter, for more than three decades, until she passed away in 2010.

In 2012, Archie returned to performing and touring, and released a box set of live recordings called *The Concert Collection 2012–2018* in 2019. His tour in 2018 featured a new song 'Dancing with My Spirit'. His most popular book is his autobiography *Tell Me Why: The Story of My Life and My Music* (Simon & Schuster, 2019). A State Memorial Service to commemorate his remarkable lifetime of music and cultural contributions was held in Melbourne on 20 December 2022.[68]

The late Archie Roach led the way for Aboriginal musicians to experiment with different styles, fusing traditional Aboriginal music with contemporary sounds, particularly rock music.

The gospel and country band Soft Sands, from Arnhem Land, started in the 1970s. The singing style made popular by bands such as Soft Sands, Yothu Yindi, East Journey and many others from Arnhem Land is called Manikay. Ethnomusicologist Aaron Corn explains the powerful force of Manikay in Yolŋu society: 'whenever people sing Manikay, their voices are not their own, but rather mingle with those of the ancestors themselves – all those who have gone before and all those who are yet to be.'

Yothu Yindi was formed in 1986 and became the most successful and internationally recognised Aboriginal band in that decade. Warumpi Band, with its mix of rock with Arnhem Land and Warlpiri style, also became successful, touring with Midnight Oil. In South Australia, Us Mob and No Fixed Address became popular and toured with several hit songs in Australia and the Pacific region. There are many other bands that have started playing in their communities and tour locally in their regions.

MISSION SONGS PROJECT

Jessie Lloyd is a musician and singer whose cultural connections from family who lived on Palm Island are both Aboriginal and Torres Strait Islander. She has researched the song compositions of Indigenous Australians on Christian missions and state-run settlements in the early to mid-twentieth century. Jessie explains that she 'first became curious about the songs from the Aboriginal reserves or the mission days when she heard her Aunties singing an old tune from Palm Island'.

Jessie Lloyd of the Mission Songs Project

For many decades, the reserve on Palm Island in Queensland was a prison camp for rebellious or non-compliant Aboriginal and Torres Strait Islander people. Indigenous people from across the state and the Torres Strait Islands were forced together under a brutal regime implemented by the Department of Native Affairs.

Jessie's Mission Songs Project is a collection of songs composed by Indigenous people during that time – the assimilation era. 'We're looking at four to five generations of unrecorded song traditions,' Jessie said, when talking about the Project. The song lyrics show what daily life was like for the people herded into these settlements and their concerns about their dispossession and treatment.

Jessie has found rare secular songs that were sung after church. In many cases the descendants of the songs' composers shared the songs with her. Jessie and the singers of the Mission Songs Project perform the songs at music festivals and events in Australia and internationally. Jessie's aim is for audiences to gain 'a deeper understanding about the history of Elders, families and communities, from cultural identity to love and loss'.

During her research, Jessie heard the song 'The Irex'. It is about the boat of the same name that was used to transport children and adults who'd been forcibly removed from their families in the early to mid-twentieth century because of policies related to the *Aboriginals Protection and Restriction of the Sale of Opium Act 1897*. She discovered that it was sung as a lament and farewell song: 'This song was what the families used to sing as they didn't know if they would see their loved ones again'. You can watch a video of this song and others at missionsongsproject.com.

Appendix A

Marriage rules in the Yolŋu kinship and classification system. The top diagram shows that a person born into a Dhuwa clan must marry a spouse from a Yirritja clan, and vice versa. The bottom diagram shows that in addition to being born into one's father's clan (0), Yolŋu People, whether Dhuwa or Yirritja, also use the gurruṯu system to trace their relationships to other clans through the mother's lineage (based on an original painting by Joe Gumbula).

Appendix B

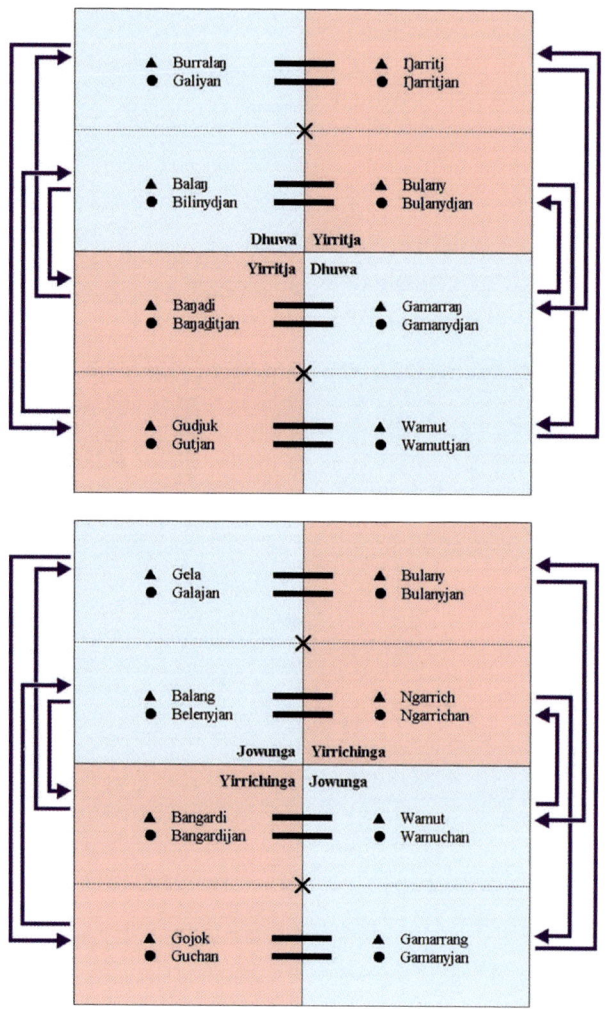

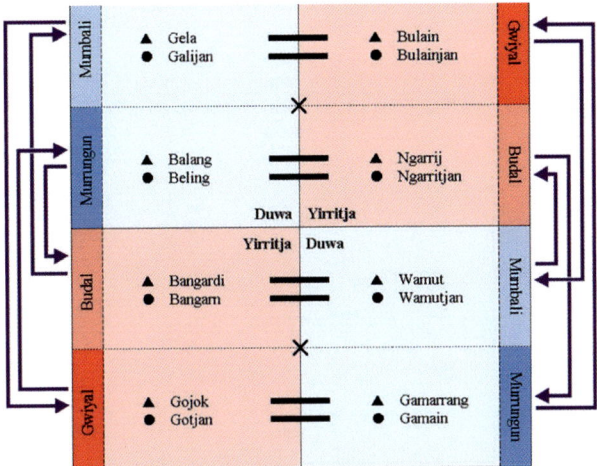

Key

▲ Male
● Female, Mother
→ Child descent
= First-choice marriage
✕ Second-choice marriages

These diagrams show the ideal Yolŋu mälk (skin name) system for relationships through marriage and descent and equivalent expressions in Kriol and Burarra. (Aaron Corn)

Appendix C

Appendix D

'Dangerous Fictions' graphic by Sarah Firth (Festival of Dangerous Ideas, presented by The Ethics Centre)

Appendix E

	Count of persons (no.)	Intercensal change (no.)	Intercensal change (%)
2006	455,028	45,025	11.0
2011	548,368	93,340	20.5
2016	649,171	100,803	18.4
2021	812,728	163,557	25.2

Data is based on place of usual residence. Excludes overseas visitors.
Source: Census of Population and Housing, 2005, 2011, 2016 and 2021.

Census counts and intercensal change, Aboriginal and Torres Strait Islander persons, 2006–2021

Australian Bureau of Statistics (2023), 'Table 1. Census counts and intercensal change, Aboriginal and Torres Strait Islander persons, 2006-2021', *Understanding change in counts of Aboriginal and Torres Strait Islander Australians: Census* [https://www.abs.gov.au/statistics/people/aboriginal-and-torres-strait-islander-peoples/understanding-change-counts-aboriginal-and-torres-strait-islander-australians-census/latest-release], ABS Website, accessed 19 April 2023.

The National Indigenous Music Awards, held annually in Garramilla/Darwin, celebrate the work of Indigenous performers. Musicians, many of whom sing in their Indigenous languages as well as English, compete for the honour of being named the best in their category or genre, from traditional to heavy metal. Emerging artists such as Gawurra, Apakatjah, Electric Fields, Emily Wurramara, Tia Gostelow and Yirrmal have had their careers launched at this prestigious event.

Many musical artists today bring their traditions into modern genres, such as folk, rock, electronic and rap styles. Danzal Baker, aka Baker Boy, is a Yolŋu artist from Miliŋimbi and Maningrida in the Northern Territory. His talents span rap, dance, acting and visual art, and include multilingual rapping in Yolŋu matha languages and English. He rose to prominence in 2017 when his work was showcased on Triple J's Hottest 100. Since then, he has been a winner at the National Indigenous Music Awards, received the prestigious Charles Darwin University Art Award at the Northern Territory Young Achievers Awards, and was named 2019 Young Australian of the Year.

Another singer of emerging renown, Barkaa, was tapped on the shoulder to sign on to Briggs's prolific Bad Apples music label, who released her songs 'Our Lives Matter' and 'I Can't Breathe' (with Dobby); these became prominent during the 2020 Black Lives Matter protests in Australia. Barkaa's artist name comes from the Barkindji Nation where she is from – 'Barkindji means "river people" and we name our river the Barkaa'.[69] The rapper uses her craft to resist, educate and connect with culture. Some of Barkaa's songs include Barkindji language, and the video clip of her hit song 'For My Tittas' shows Barkaa teaching ceremony and language to her young daughter.

Sydney-based rapper Ziggy Ramo recently collaborated with Australia's celebrated singer-songwriter Paul Kelly on the song 'Little Things', an update of the classic song 'From Little Things, Big Things Grow', written by Kelly and Kev Carmody about Vincent Lingiari and the Gurindji Strike.[70]

Dan Sultan is an alternative rock singer-songwriter and guitarist, and winner of three ARIA awards for his 2010 album *Get Out While You Can* and 2014 album *Blackbird*. In 2009, Sultan appeared in the feature film *Bran Nue Dae*, directed by Rachel Perkins and starring Jessica Mauboy, Geoffrey Rush and Missy Higgins. Like many of the other musicians mentioned in this chapter, Sultan is a member of Black Arm Band, a collection of various Indigenous musicians and performers. He also sings with Paul Kelly, including for the song 'Every Day My Mother's Voice', which featured in *The Final Quarter*, the documentary about the sustained campaign against Indigenous AFL footy star Adam Goodes.

A TRIBUTE TO GURRUMUL YUNUPIŊU

The late Gurrumul Yunupiŋu won the hearts of music lovers in Australia and around the world. He was born on Elcho Island on 22 January 1971, the eldest of four children. It was said that his hearing was so acute that it took his family some time to realise he was blind at birth. Despite this, his childhood was much the same as other Gumatj children on Elcho Island, spent running barefoot, playing on the beach and riding bicycles at breakneck speeds. Beyond instructing the other kids to 'keep an eye on him', it was not the Yolŋu way to regard his blindness as a significant limit on his capacity to participate in the life of the island. Therefore, Yunupiŋu did not grow up regarding himself as someone who was disabled. He never used a white cane or had a guide dog. He never learned braille. He was a self-taught musician from a young age playing on a toy piano and accordion. His first drum kit was tin cans balanced on sticks.

In his late teens, Yunupiŋu traded in his tin cans for keyboards and a guitar, and embarked on a rock apprenticeship with Yothu Yindi, playing on their worldwide hit 'Treaty'. But Yunupiŋu's time with Yothu Yindi was short-lived – the Elders on Elcho Island were concerned about the impact of a rock 'n' roll lifestyle, so requested his return home. A few years later he would

---

The most famous Aboriginal rapper is Briggs. A Yorta Yorta man, Adam Briggs owns record label Bad Apples Music, he also writes comedy and acts. He's appeared in various TV shows on the ABC including *Black Comedy* and is a regular cast member on *The Weekly with Charlie Pickering*. Under the name A.B. Original (which stands for Always Black, Original), Briggs also creates music with Ngarrindjeri man Trials, and together their work might be characterised as explosive political rap.

Aboriginal women singers and musicians often don't get the recognition they deserve, despite their long history in the music industry and their stellar performances across all genres. Casey Donovan, Thelma Plum and Gina Williams are all headline acts, while emerging talents include Emily Wurramara and Alice Skye. Emma Donovan of the famous Donovan family began singing when she was seven years old. She went on to form the singing group Stiff Gins, and more recently has become famous for her soul music. Dr Lou Bennett, a Yorta Yorta Dja Dja Wurrung woman from

meet long-time collaborator Michael Hohnen. In 2008, Yunupiŋu embarked on his first solo album. While this self-titled recording continued the earlier vein of songs in Yolŋu matha languages backed by contemporary western instruments, the songs highlighted the ethereal beauty of Yunupiŋu's voice. This album would go on to be triple platinum, making him the most commercially successful Indigenous recording artist in history. Yunupiŋu released three more studio albums, *Rrakala* (2011), *The Gospel Album* (2015) and the posthumously released *Djarrimirri* (Child of the Rainbow, 2018), and a live collaboration with the Sydney Symphony Orchestra, *His Life and Music* (2013). These recordings all won multiple ARIA awards.

In July 2017, Yunupiŋu died after a long bout of illness brought on by liver and kidney disease. During a career that included high-profile international collaborators such as Sting, A.B. Original and Delta Goodrem, perhaps the most notable aspect of Yunupiŋu's career has been a commitment to Yolŋu culture. When culture and a commercial career came into conflict, it was always culture that won out. Royalties and appearance fees were often shared among extended Elcho Island family in the Yolŋu manner. In a continuation of these principles, royalties from the sales of his last album will, in part, be directed towards a foundation that aims to create greater opportunities for remote Indigenous young people.

Echuca, was one of the three founders of Tiddas, a folk and acapella group with Gunditjmara woman Amy Saunders from Portland, and Sally Dastey from West Heidelberg in Melbourne. They disbanded in 2000 and won a Deadly Award that year. They returned in 2018, touring across Australia with Archie Roach to celebrate his album *Dancing with My Spirit*.

A young woman who will join the stars is Miiesha whose works are available on YouTube. She writes original ballads such as 'Damaged,' 'Drowning' and 'Black Privilege' with a velvet voice and steely lyrics.

Aboriginal and Torres Strait Islander dance traditions

Traditional ceremonies are great spectacles that appeal to Indigenous and non-Indigenous audiences. They are also an important part of traditional Aboriginal life and beliefs. They usually involve dance performances and singing that brings the ancestors to life, and the ancestral stories into the lives of Aboriginal families. Some ceremonies are for the purpose of man-making, or initiation, while others celebrate ancestors.

Funeral ceremonies are often celebrations of the ancestral connections of the deceased. These ceremonies are often now mixed with Christian traditions, and sometimes incorporate other cultural influences as well. There are ceremonial dance performances that involve men and women, and others that are performed by men only, or by women only. Children often join in public forms of ceremony. Dance performances are also staged for storytelling and for pure entertainment.

Dancers are allowed a great deal of freedom of expression. The movements vary according to the dance style. The performers are barefoot and kick up the sand they are dancing on as a part of the performance. In some styles, dancers keep their feet close to the ground to symbolise their connection with the earth or emotional states of being. Other movements and gestures communicate specific ancestral beings and emotions. Pounding the earth in unison, leaping into the air and imitations of animals are some of the movements most Australians will have seen.

In traditional ceremonies, male dancers often adorn themselves in colourful cloths and ochres to indicate their clan and various affiliations (photo Wayne Quilliam)

Performers in a contemporary dance style (photo Wayne Quilliam)

Dancers also call out in response to the singers and musicians. This is to express the ancestral events that are part of the performance, and to mark the end of a dance. Male dancers adorn themselves with colourful cloth wrapped around their bodies, feather headdresses, gum-leaf anklets, and other decorations to indicate their clan and various affiliations. Women wear swaying skirts and, when dancing topless, they paint their bodies with ochre. Both men and women paint their faces with clan emblems. Body painting is a spectacular feature of Aboriginal dances at ceremonies. Each of the designs painted on the skin has a meaning, and they all tell a story; often it is about Country and ancestral beings. The same or similar designs are used on objects, especially for ceremonies, but also on everyday objects.

Stephen Page, Aboriginal choreographer and founding Artistic Director of the Bangarra Dance Theatre, explains his own experience with body paint in dance:

> For Indigenous Australians, spirituality centres around the land. The nurturing and life-giving capacity of even our hardest terrains has been the mainstay of Indigenous religious beliefs. Incorporating the earth into spiritual ceremonies is done by many tribes using various ochres. Different coloured ochre is applied to various designs according to your totem so that spirituality is awakened during the paint-up. There are no time constraints, no boundaries; there's an apparent timelessness about the ritual.

Festivals and performances of Aboriginal and Torres Strait Islander dancing are held regularly in most cities and in some remote areas. The longest running Indigenous dance festival in Australia is the Laura Quinkan Dance Festival. It began in the early 1980s near Laura, a tiny town in central Cape York and an important meeting place for people from the area. It is the

Country of the Kuku Thaypan and other Peoples and the location of one of Australia's most significant collections of rock art.

Hosted by the Ang-Gnarra Aboriginal Corporation, the festival is held in July every second year. As explained on the website anggnarra.org.au, it is held on 'the site of a very old, traditional Bora ground. It's a respected and sacred site. Here, people from about twenty different communities located across the Cape come together to celebrate with music, dance, singing and cultural performances'. Visitors from other parts of Australia and overseas sometimes present their own dance traditions at the festival.

One of the leading Indigenous performance groups is the Bangarra Dance Theatre. The company was formed in 1989 and is still thriving. American dancer Carole J. Johnson was a founding director of NAISDA (National Aboriginal Islander Skills Development Association) Dance College, and she founded Bangarra with NAISDA graduates Rob Bryant and Cheryl Stone.

Artistic Director Stephen Page led Bangarra for many years until his retirement in 2022. Over this time it has become one of the most successful performing arts companies in Australian history. Its founding story is captured in two documentaries, *Firestarter: The Story of Bangarra*, and *Dubboo: Life of a Songman*. Performing nationally and internationally, the company's dancers are professionally trained, and each has an Aboriginal and/or Torres Strait Islander background. Indigenous choreographers and musicians collaborate with the dancers to create works that are both contemporary and draw on at least 65,000 years of stories and culture. Stephen Page has referred to the traditional aspects of Bangarra in this way:

> [It's] 'grass roots' in that traditional Aboriginal dance ... is about building a bridge between urban blacks and remote blacks, it's a wonderful marriage for rekindling one's culture and inspiring urban energy ... Without these traditional aspects, Bangarra would not exist in terms of its creative development.[71]

Traditional Indigenous dance draws on songs and storytelling as well as movement. It is part of the First Peoples' language and is essential to our culture and our daily lives. Aboriginal and Torres Strait Islander performers are committed to keeping alive the traditional styles of music, dance and storytelling, and to creating new forms of performance. The peoples whose traditions were all but destroyed by colonisation and assimilation see the traditional forms of dance, singing and music as a precious legacy inherited from their ancestors.

The terrible history of oppression has not stopped the flow of cultural energy and creativity. Events, ceremonies and festivals featuring Indigenous performance styles are held all around Australia. Storytelling through performance is a distinctive part of our cultures. Many Indigenous performers work to maintain and revitalise our culture, offering our young people the opportunity to learn our stories, identify with their traditions and develop their identities and self-respect. Bringing the sacred past and ancestral events to life through performance lies at the heart of our cultures.

THE FIRST ABORIGINAL OPERA, *PECAN SUMMER*

Deborah Cheetham Fraillon AO is a Yorta Yorta woman who trained in opera and has become one of Australia's most loved sopranos. She wrote and composed the first Aboriginal opera, *Pecan Summer*. In the opera, Deborah performed the role of Ella, the mother of Alice, who is forcibly separated from her family by a police officer under instructions from the Aboriginal Protection Board. This story reflects Cheetham Fraillon's own life history.

Deborah Cheetham Fraillon was taken from her family at a young age under the government's assimilation policies. This happened during the time when there were efforts 'to breed out the Aborigines' by removing their children and sending them to institutions and white families as domestic servants. In an event that became known as the 'walk-off from Cummeragunga Mission', one group of Indigenous people could no longer stand the white manager's cruelty and so they left, crossing the river into

Deborah Cheetham Fraillon in the role of Ella in *Pecan Summer*

Victoria from the New South Wales side of the Dhungala (Murray River) on 4 February 1939.

Pecan Summer brings this important historical event to life on stage. It weaves together the stories of those people who refused to live under the administration of the Aboriginal Protection Board and led their people to a kind of freedom. Events such as the forced separation of children from their families, and the suffering this caused, led to Cummeragunga. The walk-off and the strong protest movement led by Yorta Yorta leaders are recounted in many books, plays and songs.

The late Margaret Tucker (nee Clements) was one of those leaders. A Yorta Yorta (Dhulinyagan) woman born at Warangesda Mission on the Murrumbidgee River, she was removed at the age of twelve. She told her story in 1983, in the book *If Everyone Cared*.

Realising Cheetham Fraillon's long-held dream, *Pecan Summer* was performed at the Sydney Opera House in 2016. It has also been performed in Shepparton and Melbourne in Victoria, in Adelaide in South Australia and in Perth in Western Australia, and excerpts have been performed in Europe, the United Kingdom, the USA and around Australia.

Cheetham Fraillon has established an opera company, Short Black Opera, to develop her distinctive approach to music and Aboriginal culture. She and her team have also worked with children's groups in many rural and urban settings. One of the outcomes of her work to strengthen and express Aboriginal cultures is the Dhungala Children's Choir. Most of the choir's members are Yorta Yorta children. They are often joined by children from other communities from around Australia when they come together to take part in music workshops.

Cheetham Fraillon's work *Eumeralla: A War Requiem for Peace* is based on the twenty-three-year Eumeralla Resistance Wars (mid-1840s–1860s) that occurred between the Indigenous people and European settlers along the Eumarella River in Gunditjmara Country in south-west Victoria. In this work, Cheetham Fraillon adapts the movements and the text of the traditional Requiem Mass. The result is a stirring nineteen-movement work that blends the traditional Latin text, translated by Gunditjmara language custodian Vicki Couzens and linguist Travers Eira into the dialects of the Gunditjmara People. Rather than detailing the atrocities, the text offers poetic references to the violent loss of the people who belonged to the land of the Eumeralla. Cheetham chose to write about the feelings and emotions of the Gunditjmara who were murdered, their unanswered questions, and a hope that they might find eternal rest.

11
Storytelling

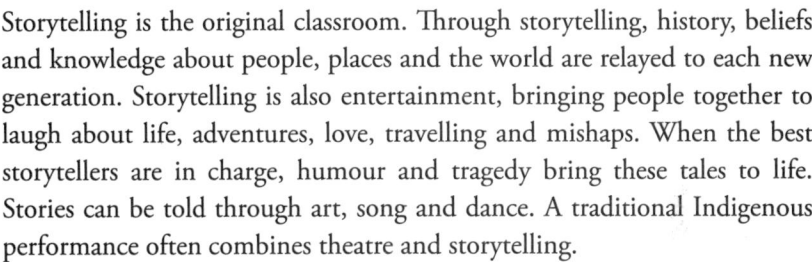

Storytelling is the original classroom. Through storytelling, history, beliefs and knowledge about people, places and the world are relayed to each new generation. Storytelling is also entertainment, bringing people together to laugh about life, adventures, love, travelling and mishaps. When the best storytellers are in charge, humour and tragedy bring these tales to life. Stories can be told through art, song and dance. A traditional Indigenous performance often combines theatre and storytelling.

For a people on the verge of extinction in the early twentieth century due to the frontier wars and introduced diseases, the Indigenous people have shown great resilience. Many of them are cultural warriors who paint, sing, write and tell stories. This is a testament to the power of our culture. Storytelling continues in the same form as before European contact (e.g. oral history), as well as in introduced forms (e.g. literature). Our storytellers can be heard at Indigenous festivals and writers' festivals around the country.

Many collectors of Aboriginal stories are surprised at how little the traditional stories have changed over the generations. There are stories that tell of the rising of the oceans around 7000 years ago, erupting volcanoes 30,000 years ago, and the very different climate, landscapes and animals of the long-distant past.

Aboriginal poets, playwrights, scriptwriters and authors of novels, histories and memoirs continue the tradition of storytelling that has preserved the history and myths of our peoples for thousands of years. Their works have won national and international awards and hold a highly respected place in Australian literature.

Indigenous writers have not always been praised and awarded for their contributions, and they have not always been respected. In fact, it took an outsider to recognise the significance of Aboriginal writing to the world. Adam Shoemaker came to Australia from Canada in the 1980s to undertake his doctorate at the Australian National University. His award-winning doctoral research on Aboriginal literature, *Black Words, White Page*, was first published in 1989. He has published more works on Indigenous literature and writers since then, including as co-editor of the first national anthology of Black Australian writings, *Paperbark* (University of Queensland Press [UQP], 1990) and editor of *Oodgeroo: A Tribute* in *Australian Literary Studies* (UQP, 1994).

Much has been written and published since then. And Aboriginal authors have been recognised in the awarding of major national prizes for literature: Kim Scott, Alexis Wright, Tara June Winch and Melissa Lucashenko have won the prestigious Miles Franklin Award; Alexis, Melissa and Evelyn Araluen have won the Stella Award for women writers; and Ali Cobby Eckermann was recognised with the prestigious international Windham Campbell Prize for her poetry. It is time for a scholar of Australian Aboriginal and Torres Strait Islander literature to write another book about the many oral histories and biographies, novels, short stories, poems and plays that Indigenous people have written. Those stories are our history.

Indigenous storytellers are also making their mark in traditionally non-Indigenous spaces, within art galleries and museums. Nathan Sentance, a Wiradjuri man, is currently the Head of Collections, First Nations at the Powerhouse Museum in Sydney. Nathan argues that museums and other 'memory institutions' have contributed to the many biases and misinterpretations of Aboriginal culture and people.

> *Galleries, libraries, archives and museums are considered sites of memory, spaces to engage with history and identity, but for me these places are sites of forgetting, erasure and distortion. They are built on stolen land. Their names validate the place names that colonisers used to confirm their occupation of stolen land and to nullify the history that took place before colonial invasion.*
>
> *My ancestors are in these memory institutions, but their voices are missing from the words written, the art created and the cultural objects taken. All of their cultural knowledge and their history is recorded and interpreted through the colonisers' lens.*
>
> *We are part of the memory conveyed by galleries, libraries, archives and museums, but we have had no say or agency in construction of it.*[72]

To help challenge and correct this impact, Nathan attempts to decolonise the museum's exhibitions and demonstrate the complexity and diversity of Aboriginal and Torres Strait Islander cultures. 'This will help us take control of the narrative that surrounds them.'

David Unaipon

The impact of the denial of Indigenous writing and writers over many decades is best told in the true story of writer David Unaipon. A Ngarrindjeri man from the Coorong region of South Australia, Unaipon was born on 28 September 1872, at Point McLeay Mission, and was sent to work as a house boy, unusually, for a man who encouraged him to read and write. He returned to Point McLeay and became a writer, inventor and philosopher; a forceful advocate for his people. The Australian $50 note features a portrait of him in an acknowledgement of his contribution to Australian life.

Unaipon's work was stolen by the publisher George Robertson in 1925 when he sold the complete manuscript to 'the amateur anthropologist and principal medical officer of South Australia, William Ramsay Smith'. In 1930, Smith published the collection under his own name and with a new title: *Myths & Legends of the Australian Aboriginals*. As a result, Unaipon's authorship was not recognised until Australian literature experts, Stephen Muecke and Adam Shoemaker, learnt about this theft and republished the original work under Unaipon's name in 2001. In their introduction to Unaipon's book, *Legendary Tales of the Australian Aborigines*, Muecke and Shoemaker tell the story of this literary theft. Billy Griffiths, author of *Deep Time Dreaming*, a history of archaeology in Australia, provides a good summary of the underhanded treatment of Unaipon in his article in *Australian Book Review* from August 2016:

> In appropriating the book, Smith not only denied Unaipon's authorship, he also systematically removed his interpretations and narrative voice from the text. Smith's plagiarism and selective editing speaks volumes for the way Indigenous people were marginalised and oppressed in the early twentieth century.[73]

'Our legends and traditions are all the same tales, or myths, told slightly differently, with local colouring,' Unaipon wrote in his book. From 1924 to 1925, he collected the stories for his proposed collection from his own Ngarrindjeri People, on a tour of southern and Central Australia with an Aboriginal translator, and in Queensland. He found many different languages and customs but also, as Billy Griffiths writes, 'a great common understanding running through us all'. According to Griffiths, Unaipon 'infused the stories he collected with his own personal philosophy, and wrote them up in the formal, ornate literary style of the era, overlaid with biblical references and classical tropes'.

The Australian $50 note shows writer, inventor and philosopher David Unaipon in an acknowledgement of his contribution to Australian life

Although it has taken a long time, today Indigenous literature is acknowledged as Australian literature. The many awards won by Indigenous writers is evidence of this new attitude.

Many of the recommendations over the following pages are my own personal favourites, in addition to being widely read and awarded nationally and internationally.

Luke Pearson has also made several recommendations to this chapter. Luke founded and runs the online company IndigenousX Pty Ltd. It has given a voice to many young Indigenous writers, scientists and intellectuals. We have suggested here some works that may be challenging, but all are outstanding works by Indigenous writers and creators.

Tara June Winch

A prize-winning author since the publication of her critically acclaimed first novel *Swallow the Air* (UQP, 2006) and then her collection of short stories *After the Carnage* (UQP, 2016), Tara June Winch was recognised in 2020 as one of Australia's best writers, winning several major literature awards with the publication of *The Yield* (Penguin Random House, 2019), which has also been optioned for production for the screen. Tara was born in Australia in 1983 and has been based in France for many years. In 2008, as part of the prestigious Rolex Mentor and Protégé Arts Initiative, Tara was mentored by Nigerian playwright and Nobel Prize winner Wole Soyinka.

In addition to her works of fiction, she wrote the script for the Indigenous dance documentary *Carriberrie*, which screened at the 71st Cannes Film

Festival in 2018 and toured internationally. She won the following awards for *The Yield*:

- 2020 Miles Franklin Literary Award, Australia's foremost literary prize
- 2020 NSW Premier's Literary Awards Christina Stead Prize for Fiction
- 2020 NSW Premier's Literary Awards People's Choice Award
- 2020 NSW Premier's Literary Awards Book of the Year
- 2020 Prime Minister's Literary Awards Fiction
- The book was also shortlisted for the 2020 Stella Prize.

The Yield is a profoundly moving and important work of fiction based on Tara June Winch's ancestors who lived on Wiradjuri Country. A lamentation for her father's language, it is also a story about Wiradjuri People's victory over the traumatic burden of history as her character, August Gondiwindi, returns home from overseas for her grandfather's burial, consumed with guilt that she has not learnt the language. This is a parable for thousands of Aboriginal people whose past involves such painful cultural dispossession.

The publisher has provided teachers' resources[74] for this book and I highly recommend them to our teachers throughout Australia.

Kim Scott

Works by Indigenous writers regularly appear on the short and long lists for major literary prizes, and they are reviewed in newspapers and literary journals. These reviews show us the critics' and readers' appreciation for writing by Indigenous authors. Noongar writer Kim Scott is a case in point. Rohan Wilson, in *The Australian* newspaper on 5 August 2017, wrote of Kim Scott's novel *That Deadman Dance* (Picador, 2010), 'Scott announced himself as the country's most important novelist.'

His novel *Benang* (Fremantle Arts Centre Press, 1999) was the first by an Indigenous writer to win Australia's most prestigious literary prize, the Miles Franklin Award. *That Deadman Dance* also won the Miles Franklin Award, among many other literary prizes.

His fifth novel, *Taboo* (Picador, 2017), won four major awards and was reviewed in several journals.

A Companion to the Works of Kim Scott, edited by Belinda Wheeler (Camden House, 2016), deals with aspects of Scott's career in education and literature; and *Kim Scott: Readers, Language, Interpretation*, edited by Philip Morrissey, Ruby Lowe and Marion Campbell (UWAP, 2019) is another useful resource.

Scott's other works include a children's book, short stories and an oral-history account of his family, of the Noongar People from the south coast of Western Australia, *Kayang and Me* (Fremantle Arts Centre Press, 2005). Scott wrote this in collaboration with his aunt, Noongar Elder Hazel Brown.

Scott also founded and is the current chair of Wirlomin Noongar Language and Stories, which has produced six bilingual (Noongar and English) community-authored picture books.

Melissa Lucashenko

Melissa Lucashenko is a Goorie writer of fiction, journalism and non-fiction. She lives between Meanjin/Brisbane and the Bundjalung Nation in northern New South Wales.

With the publication of her sixth novel, the acclaimed *Too Much Lip* (UQP, 2020), Melissa joined eminent writers Kim Scott and Alexis Wright in winning the prestigious Miles Franklin Award in 2019. *Too Much Lip* also won the Queensland Premier's Award for a Work of State Significance and was shortlisted for the Prime Minister's Literary Award for Fiction, the Stella Prize, two Victorian Premier's Literary Awards, two Queensland Literary Awards and two NSW Premier's Literary Awards. It was widely reviewed and the article by fellow writer Maxine Beneba Clarke is memorable for its grasp of Lucashenko's subjects, 'sharp defiance' and the power of writing. Having met Lucashenko at writers retreats and events, Clarke observes:

> Lucashenko works with Sisters Inside, a Queensland-based organisation that advocates the human rights of girls and women in prison. She is no stranger, personally or in witness, to the scars stories leave. Yet the emotional weight of writing Too Much Lip was an unexpected drag into the darkness.[75]

Lucashenko is a founding member of Sisters Inside, and it was fitting that she should have this recognition in the year before the Black Lives Matter protests exploded, and the sky-rocketing rates of Indigenous incarceration became the subject of public debate after years of being ignored.

Melissa is a Walkley Award winner for her non-fiction, the essay 'Sinking below sight: Down and Out in Brisbane and Logan' in *Griffith REVIEW 41: Now We Are Ten*.

Her previous novel, the award-winning *Mullumbimby* (2013), was described by her publisher, University of Queensland Press, as 'a darkly funny novel of romantic love and cultural warfare'. For a more serious understanding of this novel, read the review in *The Sydney Review of Books* by Eve Vincent in which the author's handling of Aboriginal language code-switching, the debilitating nature of native title processes, and the experience of being on Country are drawn out.⁷⁶ It won the Queensland Literary Awards for Best Fiction in 2013.

She has also published fiction for younger readers, *Too Flash* (IAD Press, 2002) and *Killing Darcy* (UQP, 1998), and short works of fiction, such as 'A saltwater to watch', published in *The Saturday Paper* (22 Jan 2021).

Bruce Pascoe

Acclaimed writer and Yuin, Bunurong and Tasmanian man Bruce Pascoe started a major national debate with his publication of *Dark Emu: Black Seeds: Agriculture or Accident?* (Magabala Books, 2014). *Dark Emu* won both Book of the Year and the Indigenous Writer's Prize in the 2016 NSW Premier's Literary Awards and was shortlisted for the 2014 Victorian Premier's Award and the History Book Award in the Queensland Literary Awards. In 2019, we welcomed Pascoe's collected essays and stories, *Salt*. His 2020 book, *Loving Country: A Guide to Sacred Australia* (Hardie Grant Explore), co-written with Vicky Shukuroglou, offers a deeper understanding of Australia from an Indigenous perspective. Pascoe received the Fellowship of Australian Writers' Literature Award in 1999 and the Australia Council Award for Lifetime Achievement in Literature in 2018. His novel *Fog a Dox* (Magabala Books, 2014) won the Prime Minister's Award for Young Adult Fiction in 2013. His stories have won ten national competitions and have been published in six languages and nine countries.

Bruce Pascoe has worked as a teacher, farmer, fisherman and an Aboriginal language researcher. In the many books he has written, Pascoe incorporates Aboriginal knowledge and cultural aspects into his storytelling. He believes it is in this way that he can educate people about the factual history of Australian colonialism. In addition to his published works, he is also the Director of the Commonwealth Australian Studies Project. Other books by Bruce Pascoe include:

- *Fox* (McPhee Gribble/Penguin Books, 1988)
- *Shark* (Magabala Books, 1999)
- *Nightjar* (Seaglass Books, 2000)
- *Convincing Ground* (Aboriginal Studies Press, 2007)
- *Bloke* (Penguin Books 2009)
- *Country*, co-authored with Bill Gammage (Thames & Hudson, 2021).

Alexis Wright

Alexis Wright is an award-winning novelist and writer, and member of the Waanyi Nation of the Gulf of Carpentaria. She has written widely on Indigenous rights. Her major novels are:

- *Plains of Promise* (UQP, 1997): shortlisted for the Commonwealth Prize and published in France as *Les Plaines de L'Espoir*.
- *Carpentaria* (Giramondo Publishing, 2006): won five national literary awards in 2007, including the ASAL Gold Medal and the Miles Franklin Award.
- *The Swan Book* (Giramondo Publishing, 2013): won the ASAL Gold Medal.

Her book *Tracker: Stories of Tracker Tilmouth* (Giramondo Publishing, 2017), about Indigenous activist Tracker Tilmouth, won the 2018 Stella Prize. In their award statement, the judges called it 'a new way of writing memoir' and observed:

> It is fitting that a book written in the mode and genre of Aboriginal storytelling should win a prize that encompasses both non-fiction and fiction. It is a work, epic in scope and size, that will ensure that a legend of Central Australian politics is preserved in myth.

At around 600 pages, the book features interviews that Wright conducted with people Tracker chose himself before he passed away in 2015. Ben Etherington in his review in *The Conversation*, in April 2018, wrote:

> It is simply remarkable to hear Tracker's genuinely funny jokes and stories told repeatedly, often word for word and channelling Tracker's unmistakable style, by such a range of different speakers.

Wright is also editor of *Take Power, Like This Old Man Here* (IAD, 1998), a collection of essays and stories celebrating twenty years of land rights in Central Australia, and wrote *Grog War* (Magabala Books, 1997), a study of alcohol abuse in Tennant Creek.

Claire G. Coleman

Claire G. Coleman is a Noongar woman who has travelled extensively across Australia. Her novel *The Old Lie* (Hachette) was published in 2019. She has received much-deserved accolades for her book *Terra Nullius* (Hachette, 2019), including the 2016 black&write! Fellowship and the

2018 Norma K. Hemming Award. The book was also shortlisted for the 2018 Stella Prize.

Terra Nullius is a speculative fiction that tells the story of the Australian 'natives' as they fight for survival against the 'settlers', but not in the way you would expect. It creates a picture of an apocalyptic dystopia which forces the reader to confront the idea that what is created as fiction is in fact a reality for all Indigenous Peoples who have survived massive upheaval and devastation, and the journey to reclaim culture and identity and have their humanity recognised in the wake of colonisation.

Tony Birch

Tony Birch, a Naarm/Melbourne Koori man, is an award-winning writer, academic and activist. In 2003, his PhD thesis won the Chancellor's Prize for Excellence at the University of Melbourne, where he lectured for many years. Birch is the inaugural recipient of the Dr Bruce McGuinness Indigenous Research Fellowship at Victoria University and in 2017 he was awarded the Patrick White Literary Award. His recent novel *The White Girl* (UQP, 2019) won the 2020 NSW Premier's Award for Indigenous Writing and was shortlisted for the 2020 Miles Franklin Literary Prize. His other novels and short-story collections include:

- *Common People* (UQP, 2017), shortlisted for the 2018 NSW Premier's Literary Awards Christina Stead Prize for Fiction and the 2019 Victorian Premier's Literary Awards Prize for Indigenous Writing
- *Ghost River* (UQP, 2015), winner of the 2016 Victorian Premier's Literary Award for Indigenous Writing
- *Blood* (UQP, 2011), shortlisted for the 2012 Miles Franklin Award
- *Shadowboxing* (Scribe Publications, 2006)
- *Father's Day* (Hunter Publishers, 2009)
- *The Promise: Stories* (UQP, 2014)

Leah Purcell

Leah Purcell is an award-winning author, playwright and actor. In 2017, her play *The Drover's Wife* (Penguin, 2021), a radical re-interpretation of Henry Lawson's short story of the same name, won the Victorian Prize for Literature and the Victorian Premier's Literary Award for Drama, the Book of the Year Award and the Nick Enright Prize for Playwriting in the NSW Premier's Literary Prize, and associated film and theatre awards. Her other works include:

- *Box the Pony* (playscript) (Hodder Headline, 1999)
- *Black Chicks Talking* (Hodder Headline, 2002)

Purcell appears in the TV series *Wentworth* in the lead role of Rita Connors. In 2019, she received a Logie nomination in the Outstanding Actress category.

Ellen van Neerven

Winner of three NSW Premier's Literary Awards and the inaugural Quentin Bryce Award for their latest poetry collection *Throat* (UQP, 2020), Ellen van Neerven is of Mununjali Yugambeh (south-east Queensland) and Dutch heritage. *Heat and Light* (UQP, 2014), their first book, is a highly praised short-story collection and received the David Unaipon Award, the Dobbie Literary Award and the NSW Premier's Literary Awards Indigenous Writers Prize, and was shortlisted for the Stella Prize, the Queensland Literary Award for State Significance and the Readings Prize. Ellen van Neerven also writes plays and non-fiction. Their second book, *Comfort Food* (UQP, 2016), a collection of poetry, won the Tina Kane Emergent Award and was shortlisted for the NSW Premier's Literary Awards Kenneth Slessor Prize and Highly Commended for the 2016 Wesley Michel Wright Prize. Their play *Swim* featured at the Yellamundie First Peoples Playwriting Festival in January 2019.

Anita Heiss

Dr Anita Heiss is a prolific Wiradjuri author of poetry, non-fiction and fiction, including chick lit (commercial women's fiction) and children's novels. Her recent work has brought her to greater prominence and includes the novel *Bila Yarrudhanggalangdhuray* and a stage play based on her book *Tiddas*. A collection she edited, *Growing Up Aboriginal in Australia*, was published by Black Inc. in 2018 and her memoir on identity, *Am I Black Enough for You?* (Random House, 2011), won the Victorian Premier's Literary Award for Indigenous Writing and was a finalist in the Human Rights Awards Media (non-fiction). She lists her other works and prizes on her website.

Her children's literature includes *Kicking Goals with Goodesy and Magic*, co-written with Adam Goodes and Michael O'Loughlin. She also wrote two kids' novels with students from La Perouse Public School – *Yirra and Her Deadly Dog, Demon* and *Demon Guards the School Yard*.

She has been an advocate for Indigenous literacy, working in remote communities as a role model and encouraging young Indigenous Australians to write their own stories.

A selection of the awards she has won includes:

- 2012 Victorian Premier's Literary Award for Indigenous Writing, for *Am I Black Enough for You?*
- 2011 Deadly Award for Most Outstanding Contribution to Literature, for *Paris Dreaming*
- 2010 Deadly Award for Most Outstanding Contribution to Literature, for *Manhattan Dreaming*
- 2008 Deadly Award for Most Outstanding Contribution to Literature, with Peter Minter, for the *Macquarie PEN Anthology of Aboriginal Literature*
- 2007 Deadly Award for Most Outstanding Contribution to Literature, for *Not Meeting Mr Right*
- 2003 Inaugural Australian Society of Authors Medal (Under 35) for contribution to Australian community and life
- 2002 NSW Premier's History Award (Audio Visual) for *Barani: The Aboriginal History of the City of Sydney*
- Shortlisted for the 2002 NSW Premier's History Award (Young People's History) for *Who Am I? The Diary of Mary Talence, Sydney 1937*.

Stan Grant

Stan Grant is a Wiradjuri journalist and international relations specialist who has covered events in several war zones throughout his career. He has anchored television radio programs and writes prolifically in newspapers and other media. Since his return to Australia his books have mounted up and he brings an acute compassion combined with a sense of the deep wound that the treatment of his own family has caused. His commonsense balancing of the need to correct the injustices and find a better Australia is his great contribution to the debate about Indigenous history and current affairs. I recommend his latest books:

- *Talking to My Country* (HarperCollins, 2016)
- *Australia Day* (HarperCollins, 2019)
- *On Identity* (Hachette, 2020)
- *With the Falling of the Dusk* (HarperCollins, 2021)

Larissa Behrendt

Indigenous academics such as Professor Larissa Behrendt have made a significant contribution as well. Behrendt's books, which span a range of genres, have won awards, and she produces programs across other media including radio and television. She is the author of three novels:

- *Home* (UQP, 2004), which won the 2002 David Unaipon Award and the regional Commonwealth Writers' Prize for Best First Book
- *Legacy* (UQP, 2009), which won the 2010 Victorian Premier's Literary Award for Indigenous Writing
- *After Story* (UQP, 2021), shortlisted for several awards.

In the non-fiction genre, *Finding Eliza: Power and Colonial Storytelling* (UQP, 2016) is well regarded.

She has also published books on Indigenous legal issues.

Poetry

The Aboriginal bent for the poetic and rhythmic is evident in recent anthologies that provide samplings from award-winners and new poets. *Homeland Calling: Words from a New Generation of Aboriginal and Torres Strait Islander Voices* (Hardie Grant Explore, 2020), edited by Ellen van Neerven with a foreword by rapper Baker Boy, brings together poems created from hip-hop song lyrics in collaboration with Desert Pea Media.

Fire Front: First Nations Poetry and Power Today (UQP, 2020), edited by Alison Whittaker, is challenging in reach and message. Curated under five themes, each introduced in short, powerful essays by Bruce Pascoe, Ali Cobby Eckermann, Chelsea Bond, Evelyn Araluen and Steven Oliver, this book makes available the poetry of our most famous and best writers, some of it half-remembered and no longer in print.

Alison includes great poets published in the twentieth century and who have passed: the late Oodgeroo Noonuccal, Jack Davis, Kevin Gilbert and Ruby Langford Ginibi. She also presents us with a clever sampling of present-day stars: Ellen van Neerven, Lionel Fogarty, Ali Cobby Eckermann, Sam Wagan Watson and Evelyn Araluen, while those better known for their novels, biographies, short stories and songs are here also: Archie Roach, Alexis Wright, Tony Birch and Claire G. Coleman.

Less well known as poets – and deserving of a wider audience – are Mojo Ruiz de Luzuriaga, Joel Davison, Declan Furber Gillick, Provocalz, Ancestress and Dylan Voller. Declan Fry in his review of this breathtaking collection writes that it is 'not so much an anthology as a reckoning'.[77] See a video of Alison and Evelyn speaking and readings of the poems in Naarm/Melbourne on the Wheeler Centre website.[78]

Another anthology, *Guwayu – For All Times* (Magabala Books, 2020), edited by Jeanine Leane, is a collection of First Nations poetry commissioned by Red Room Poetry and produced in a series of workshops. This collection too is curated in sections and includes works in Indigenous languages, including Aboriginal English.

First Australian poets are being supported by the Poetry in First Languages (PIFL) program, developed by Red Room Poetry. During the UN International Year of Indigenous Languages in 2019, the Copyright Agency funded PIFL to expand the teaching of poetry in First Australian languages. This is to ensure that our cultures and languages are strengthened. Published online on the Red Room Poetry website, the contributing poets are Alison Whittaker (Gomeroi), Ellen van Neerven (Mununjali Yugambeh), Matthew Heffernan (Pintupi–Luritja), Melanie Mununggurr-Williams (Djapu), Declan Furber Gillick (Arrernte), Nicholas Paton (Ngunawal), Ethan Bell (Ngunawal), Nicole Smede (Worimi), Jacob Morris (Gumea Dharawal), Paul Collis (Barkindji) and Joel Davison (Gadigal). They are supported by contributing artists and educators including David Cragg (Bundjalung) and Allan Giddy, as well as Elders and cultural knowledge holders Aunty Sharyn Halls (Gundungurra), Aunty Trish Levett (Gundungurra), Jacob Morris (Gumea Dharawal), Aunty Jodi Edwards (Yuin), Uncle Richard Campbell (Yuin) and Joel Davison (Gadigal).

The following poems and collections are also recommended:

- Bobby McLeod, *Ngudjung Yugarang 'Mother's Heartbeat'* (BMAC Publishing, 2008)
- Alexis Wright, 'Hey Ancestor!' (on the IndigenousX website)
- Matthew Heffernan, 'Ngurrparringu (forgotten)' (on the IndigenousX website)
- Yvette Holt, *Anonymous Premonition* (UQP, 2008)
- Lionel Fogarty, *Yerrabilela Jimbelung: Poems about Friends and Family* (Keeaira Press, 2008)

Theatre, scriptwriting, plays and stage production

I was not surprised to learn in 2020 when the Archibald Prize for portraiture prize winners were announced that the self-portrait by Meyne Wyatt, better known as an actor and writer than as an artist, won the Packing Room Prize by popular vote. It is a stunning self-portrait that captures much of Meyne's demeanour and personality.

Meyne is a Wongutha-Yamatji actor and writer, born in 1989 in Subiaco, Western Australia. He grew up in Kalgoorlie, the famous gold-mining town, on Wongutha Country, inland from Boorloo/Perth. He now lives in Warrane/Sydney. This was the first time he had entered the Archibald Prize. Simply titled *Meyne*, and painted in acrylic on canvas, it has many of the hallmarks of a mature and technically proficient artist. Painting is a well-hidden talent in this case, obviously learnt from his mother, who is an artist, but few knew of his art practice. He explained more when interviewed by the Archibald Prize staff at the Art Gallery of New South Wales:

> My self-portrait is the first painting I've done in over ten years and I decided to enter it at the behest of my artist mother, Sue Wyatt, an Archibald Prize finalist in 2003 for her portrait of writer Doris Pilkington.
>
> I began painting again because I wanted to get back into it at some point, then we went into lockdown [due to COVID-19] and I thought there was no better time than now. Over a span of about four months it took me about five days in total to complete it and I used good old acrylic because it's what I know. I decided to paint myself because there would be no one to offend if the painting wasn't any good.
>
> I've had no formal art training, just tips from my mum. In 2007 I won an award as part of the Year 12 Perspectives exhibition at the Art Gallery of Western Australia and travelled to Japan, where my painting was on exhibit.[79]

Meyne has achieved critical praise and fame as a playwright for his debut work *City of Gold* in 2019. He performed in the play as the main character at the highly successful world premiere at Queensland Theatre. It was transferred to Griffin Theatre Company, where it also sold out. The notes published by the Griffin Theatre Company describe the play as 'a howl of rage at the injustice, inequality and wilful amnesia of this country's 21st century. It's an urgent play for our moment from a vital new voice. As Childish Gambino sings across the Pacific "This is America," Meyne Wyatt calls back loudly "This is Australia."' [80]

City of Gold was shortlisted for the 2020 Victorian Premier's Prize for Drama and for the NSW Premier's Literary Award. At the Sydney Theatre Awards, it was nominated for Best New Australian Work. Wyatt won Best Male Actor in a Leading Role and Shari Sebbens won Best Female Actor in a Supporting Role for their performances in *City Of Gold*. The Judges Report of the Victorian Premier's Literary Awards, for which City of Gold was shortlisted for the unpublished manuscript prize, said:

> City of Gold *is an extraordinary cri de coeur; a scream of rage and despair from the heart of First Nations people, it's a work of often breathtaking rhetorical force. Energised by the crisis at the heart of our country, it paints a picture of dire societal pressure and galvanising personal courage.*
>
> *Uncompromising, raw and shocking, it is a play that cries 'Enough! Our people are dying'. Necessary and unforgettable.*[81]

Meyne's career successes since graduating from NIDA in 2010 are astonishing: as the Victorian Premier's Literary Awards notes acknowledge, he was 'just 18 when he was accepted into the National Institute of Dramatic Art and has created a buzz in the industry with non-stop theatre, television and film work since graduating in 2010'.[82]

Meyne's performance in Lachlan Philpott's *Silent Disco* (Griffin Theatre Company) earned him an award for Best Newcomer at Sydney Theatre Awards. Other theatre performances have included *King Lear*, *Bloodland* (Sydney Theatre Company), *Peter Pan, Buried City* (Belvoir) and *Gloria* (Griffin Theatre Company). With a sound theatre background, it was inevitable that he would become a star in television and film productions, which include:

- ABC tele-movie *The Broken Shore* (2013)
- *Redfern Now* (2013), for which he earned nominations for Most Outstanding Newcomer at the 2014 Logie Awards and Best Lead Actor in a Television Drama at the 3rd AACTA Awards
- From 2014 to 2016 he also appeared in *Neighbours*, making history as the first Indigenous actor to join the main cast
- *Black Comedy* (ABC, 2016)
- *The Leftovers* (HBO, 2017)
- The AACTA award winning series *Mystery Road* (SBS, 2018) and *Les Norton* (ABC, 2019)

And the feature films:

- *The Sapphires* (2012)
- *The Turning* (2013)
- *Strangerland* (2015), opposite Nicole Kidman and Hugo Weaving

In 2020, he appeared on the ABC television program *Q&A* and delivered a monologue from *City of Gold* that shocked and thrilled audiences at the height of the Black Lives Matter global protests. It is a powerful statement on racism and his own victory over it, with all the damage it causes to its victims laid bare.[83] (Advisory note: It contains strong language.)

Nakkiah Lui

A Gamilaroi and Torres Strait Islander woman, Nakkiah Lui is a celebrated playwright, television screenwriter, author, actor, performer, comedian and satirist. She is best known in the Indigenous world for her performances in the ABC's *Black Comedy* and *Kiki and Kitty* (2017), the latter which Lui wrote and stars in. Her theatre pieces include *How to Rule the World* (2019), *Black is the New White* (2017), *Power Plays* (2016), *Kill the Messenger* (2015), *Blackie Blackie Brown: The Traditional Owners of Death* (2013), *I Should Have Told You Before We Made Love (That I'm Black)* (2012) and *This Heaven* (2013). With Indigenous Australian actress Miranda Tapsell, Lui hosts the podcast *Debutante: Race, Resistance and Girl Power* (2020) and the Buzzfeed podcast *Pretty for an Aboriginal* (2017). She now heads up her own book publishing imprint, JOAN, with Allen & Unwin.

Lui was the inaugural recipient of the 2012 Dreaming Award, presented by the Aboriginal and Torres Strait Island Arts Board of the Australia Council, and the 2013 Balnaves Foundation Indigenous Playwright award. Her other awards include the Malcolm Robertson Prize, the Green Room Award for Best Independent Production, the Nick Enright Prize for playwriting and a 2018 NSW Premier's Literary Award for *Black is the New White*.

She is a regular columnist for the *Australian Women's Weekly* and has also hosted Radio National's *AWAYE!* and *NAIDOC Evenings* for ABC Local Radio. She has been a guest on the ABC's panel shows *Q&A* and *The Drum*, a keynote speaker at writers' festivals and has big social media followings.

Jada Alberts

Brothers Wreck by Jada Alberts was staged at Sydney's Belvoir Street Theatre in 2014 and Melbourne's Malthouse Theatre and Adelaide's State Theatre Company of South Australia in 2018 to great acclaim. The play centres on Ruben, and the impact on him and his family following the suicide of his cousin. Ruben's family members grapple with this shocking death and work together to bring Ruben back from the feelings of loneliness and anger through compassion and care. The script and staging capture the tension of the wet season in Garramilla/Darwin, where the story unfolds. This insightful writing reflects Alberts's experiences as a Larrakia, Bardi, Wadaman and Yanuwa person from the Top End of Australia.

In addition to being a playwright, Jada Alberts is also an accomplished actor, musician and painter. They have appeared on stage in *Frost/Nixon*, *The Birthday Party, Second to None, Yibiyung* and on the national tour of *The Shadow King*. Alberts also appeared in the feature film *Red Hill* and is widely known for their roles in *Redfern Now, Wentworth, Rush* and *Cleverman*; they also wrote two episodes for the latter show in season 2. Alongside Aaron Pederson, Alberts starred in the leading role of season 2 of *Mystery Road*. They graduated in 2006 from the Adelaide Centre for the Arts, and in 2007, won the Adelaide Critics' Circle Award for Best Emerging Artist.

In 2013, Alberts won the Balnaves Foundation Indigenous Playwrights Award, and in 2014 they were nominated for Best New Australian Work at the Sydney Theatre Awards for *Brothers Wreck*. In 2015, Alberts was nominated for the Nick Enright Prize for Playwriting, the NSW Literary Awards, and for Best Stage Play in the AWGIE Awards for *Brother's Wreck*. They were a Writers Fellow at Bell Shakespeare from 2016 to 2017.

Beautiful One Day

Beautiful One Day is a theatrical documentary about the death of an Aboriginal man in police custody on Palm Island, Queensland, in 2004. It also explores the aftermath of his death and the demands for justice from the community's residents. The details are told by weaving reports, interviews, transcripts of court hearings and other documents into the script, as well as incorporating audio and video stage elements into the stage performance. It was devised and performed by Sean Bacon, Magdalena Blackley, several Palm Island residents and the Ilbijerri Theatre Company. Much of the play is performed by three people from Palm Island who lived through these events.

Children's literature

Indigenous literature written for children deals with matters of great importance to children and adults alike: freedom, finding oneself and the legacy of the ancestors. *Finding Our Heart* by Thomas Mayo (Hardie Grant Explore, 2020), *The First Scientists* by Corey Tutt (Hardie Grant Explore, 2021) and Adam Briggs's *Our Home, Our Heartbeat* (Hardie Grant Children's Publishing, 2020) explore both Aboriginal and Torres Strait Islanders' place in Australia today and our past.

Once there was a Boy by Dub Lefler (Magabala Books, 2011) was a finalist in the 2012 Deadly Awards, in the Outstanding Achievement in Literature category, and was shortlisted in the Speech Pathology Australia Book of the Year Awards (Indigenous Children category) in 2012.

Stolen Girl, written by Trina Saffioti and illustrated by Norma MacDonald (Magabala Books, 2011), tells the story of a young Aboriginal girl removed from her family and taken to an institution, where 'one day she unlocks the door and takes her first step toward home'.

The following children's books are also recommended:

- Amy McQuire, *Day Break* (Hardie Grant Children's Publishing, 2021)
- Bruce Pascoe, *Found* (Magabala Books, 2020) and *Young Dark Emu* (Magabala Books, 2019)

- Aunty Joy Murphy, *Welcome to Country* (Walker Books, 2016)
- Aunty Fay Muir & Sue Lawson, *Family* and *Respect* (Magabala Books, 2020)
- Kirli Saunders, *Bindi* (Magabala Books, 2020)

Graphic novels

Brenton McKenna's series of graphic novels bring together oral history and stories about life for a young Aboriginal girl in Broome in the late 1940s. Published by Aboriginal publishing house Magabala Books, the Ubby series shows the Aboriginal and multicultural history of Broome after World War II and describes 'adventures full of myths and legends'. Ubby is a smart, streetwise leader of a small gang known as the 'Underdogs'. The first book, *Ubby's Underdogs: The Legend of the Phoenix Dragon* (2011), was followed by *Ubby's Underdogs: Heroes Beginnings* (2013). The publisher's notes tell us that this 'is storytelling on a remarkable scale. It continues with established characters that have links to other worlds amidst an intricate backdrop of Aboriginal and Chinese mythology.' *Ubby's Underdogs: Return of the Dragons*, the final book in the series, was published in 2019.

Digital writing

We are witnessing a generational shift in Indigenous writing and thinking. This is largely brought about by the digital writers in our population who have turned to more immediate styles of storytelling.

Anyone can have a blog these days, but the most important online writing from Indigenous Australia comes from IndigenousX Pty Ltd. I have mentioned that my colleague Luke Pearson founded and runs the company with a mission to publish original content from emerging and established Indigenous writers across Australia online and on several social media platforms, such as Twitter, Facebook and Instagram. The company specialises in analysis, commentary and public interest journalism. It has given a voice to many young Indigenous writers, scientists and intellectuals.

Associate Professor Chelsea Watego's essay 'The irony of the Aboriginal academic' is a defence of Indigenous intellectual work and writing, and was published by IndigenousX. As a senior academic at the prestigious University of Queensland, she felt compelled to write:

> The foundations of our most learned institutions were built upon the premise that the Aborigine was not human, and thus incapable of learning or knowing. Our presence was merely an accessory adding to

the aesthetic of white knowing, and to this day as a Black academic, I'm still forced to contest this ideology as an everyday practice.[84]

She concludes her essay about the continual production of racist knowledge in universities with these words: 'there remains both real work and a real war to be waged in the academy; it just requires a few more warriors to serve'. Her book, *Another Day in the Colony* (UQP, 2021), won major awards.

Competing strongly with IndigenousX is Blackfulla Bookclub with the maxim, 'Our Ancestors are the original storytellers'. It is an initiative of Teela Reid, who describes herself as a Wiradjuri and Wailwan woman, lawyer and storyteller, and Merinda Dutton, also an Indigenous lawyer. They are 'Sharing stories to heal our nation' on Instagram @blackfulla_bookclub and Twitter #blackfullabookclub.

Film and television storytellers

The new storytellers include the film and television makers who are bringing ancient and contemporary stories to the screen. Despite the COVID-19 restrictions keeping us away from cinemas for most of the year, 2020 was a great year for Australian Indigenous films. I gave five stars to *High Ground* and *The Furnace*. In 2021, Leah Purcell's *The Drover's Wife: The Legend of Molly Johnson* was screened at its world premiere at Texas' South By Southwest film festival and was available to Australian audiences after its premiere at the Melbourne International Film Festival in August.

High Ground, set in the magnificent Kakadu National Park region where the Church Missionary Society established the Anglican mission in 1925, melds the oral and documented history of the wars in Arnhem Land, the savagery of the police and vigilantes who massacred Aboriginal people and the resistance by those who refused to surrender. Travis, a former soldier turned bounty hunter with a moral compass, played by Simon Baker of *The Mentalist* fame, joins Jacob Junior Nayinggul as Gutjuk, a young man from the Christian mission, to hunt the renegade warrior (and Gutjuk's uncle) Baywara, played by Sean Mununggurr. It emerges that Gutjuk is the only survivor of a massacre committed by Travis when Gutjuk was a child, when his father, Dharrpa, played by Rirratjiŋu songman and cultural leader Witiyana Marika, was absent from the family group. Redemption and revenge are the twin themes of this frontier war story. Esmerelda Marimowa is utterly captivating as the rape victim turned guerrilla who joins Gutjuk in the resistance.

The film's title is a double entrendre on Travis's moral epiphany as he confronts his terrible guilt and his mastery of the sniper's high point. It may also refer ironically to the moral failure of the Australians who sought to suppress and control Aboriginal people by brutal means.

As well as his key role as Dharrpa, Witiyana is the producer. He worked with director Steven Maxwell Johnson when he was a member of the band Yothu Yindi, led by the late Mandawuy Yunupiŋu. Johnson directed Yothu Yindi's ARIA award–winning music video 'Djäpana'. *High Ground*'s script was written by Chris Anastassiades who also wrote Johnson's 2001 film *Yolngu Boy*. The idea for the film formed when Witiyana was a young man. He told Belinda Quinn of *NME*:

> He first learnt about the white 'horsemen' who massacred his grandmother's clan, Dhalwaŋu, when as a teenager he journeyed to do ceremony with his grandfather, Birrikitji Gumana, on their homeland Gängän. 'I didn't learn it from the school,' he says. 'My grandfather brought all the nephews, sons and daughters to Gängän. There were over 100 people that had passed away.' Marika and his dear friend, relative and Yothu Yindi co-founder Dr. M. Yunupingu later returned to Gängän to visit their grandmother, hoping to learn more about the massacre that took place in the early 20th century. 'In the ... early days we were walking and we were searching, researching.' [85]

The police chief Moran – a character based on the vicious first Police Commissioner of the Northern Territory, Paul Foelsche – is played by Jack Thompson, whose Yolŋu name Gulkula was given to him by Mandawuy's eldest brother, the late Gumatj leader and chairman of the Yothu Yindi Foundation Yunupiŋu. The mesmerising Aaron Pedersen from Central Australia plays the role of a native police tracker from Queensland, the feared and hated assassins that wiped out thousands of their own people.

The cast includes people from many tribes across Arnhem Land, all of whom are acknowledged in the lengthy credits, worth watching to see the list of clans, languages and cultural leaders who gave their permission for the stories to be told and the film locations.

The Furnace by writer-director Roderick MacKay was called a 'brutish western'[86] by a reviewer, but this is an entirely glib and incorrect way to describe it. This is a distinctively Australian film that will hold you in its grip with a story that surprises at every turn. It is based on historical events that have been kept largely secret for decades.

Why have so few historians told the stories of these events? I knew about some of them because of my friends who have Aboriginal and Afghan ancestry from the days when Muslim cameleers 'moved cargo throughout the vast desert interior' with their camel caravans.[87] Although not the first people of the Islamic faith to come to our country, they left a remarkable imprint. They made friends with Aboriginal people they came to know on the great Aboriginal trade routes criss-crossing the continent and sometimes married Aboriginal women. Set in Yamatji Badimaya Country around Mount Magnet in Western Australia, and with its main characters played by Egyptian star Ahmed Malek, Australian star David Wenham and emerging Yolŋu star Baykali Ganambarr, the story unfolds across the arid lands in a hunt by a young cameleer and a mysterious 'bushman' for stolen gold. For its world premiere at the 2020 Venice Film Festival, the director's notes are illuminating:

> Today, Australia has the world's largest wild camel population. Yet, most Australians do not know that, from the 1860s, The British Empire imported camels and handlers from Afghanistan, India and Persia to open up Australia's desert interior. These Islamic, Sikh and Hindu men provided the main form of exploration and freight transport between colonies and gold mining camps. They were vital to the nation's formation, yet experienced much prejudice and were often coerced into indentured labour. The Furnace *is a revisionist frontier mythology that weaves this forgotten history into the tapestry of the Outback. It is my hope that this film enacts a more inclusive sense of Australian identity.* [88]

Rachel Perkins and Warwick Thornton are two of Australia's greatest filmmakers. Both Indigenous, they use the power of cinema and television to tell their stories. They are prolific writers, directors and producers, and have won scores of awards in Australia and around the globe.

Rachel Perkins

Rachel Perkins is an Arrernte and Kalkadoon woman from Alice Springs, who has been making television programs and films since 1992. She has established her own company, Blackfella Films, and has been a prolific producer of award-winning television series and documentaries, such as *The Tall Man*. Based on a book by Chloe Hooper, *The Tall Man* is the true story of the death of Indigenous man Cameron Doomadgee in police custody in Queensland (which is also the topic of play *Beautiful One Day* discussed earlier in this chapter).

Perkins has directed four feature films: *Jasper Jones* (nominated for Best Film at the 2017 AACTA Awards), *Radiance, One Night the Moon* (which received five Australian Film Institute Awards) and the musical *Bran Nue Dae*, which screened at the Sundance, Berlin and Toronto film festivals. Released in 2009, *Bran Nue Dae* tells the story of a young man in the 1960s who runs away from the mission school, back to his home in Broome and to his love, Rosie.

In 2012, Perkins directed the telemovie *Mabo*, which screened on ABC1 to mark the twentieth anniversary of the historic High Court decision (of the same name). *Mabo* was nominated for Most Outstanding Mini-Series or Telemovie at the 2013 TV Week Logie Awards. Perkins directed three episodes of the landmark television drama series *Redfern Now*, the first Australian drama series written, directed and produced by Indigenous Australians. In 2015, she received the Australian Directors Guild (ADG) Award for Best Direction in a TV Drama Series for *Redfern Now: Promise Me*.

Perkins directed *Total Control* and season one of *Mystery Road* for the ABC. This show premiered in 2018 as a critical and ratings hit. She also wrote, directed and co-produced the seven-hour documentary series *First Australians* (2009), which received Australia's top honours including AFI and IF Awards, the UN Media Peace Prize, TV Week Logie, and the Writers and Directors Guild of Australia Awards. The second and third series of *Mystery Road* have become addictive television programs, winning yet more awards and starring yet more young actors and production crew.

In addition to all of this, Perkins has worked with Arrernte women who sing the ancient song series and recorded them with linguist Myfany Turpin. Through the Arrernte Women's Project, hundreds of traditional songs were methodically recorded and catalogued, creating an important resource and a national treasure.

Warwick Thornton

The extraordinary filmmaker Warwick Thornton, who hails from Alice Springs, has made several award-winning films. The film that catapulted him to global fame, *Samson and Delilah*, won more than twenty awards, including the coveted *Camera d'Or* at the 2009 Cannes Film Festival.

Samson and Delilah and his other most famous and most awarded film, *Sweet Country*, are not easy to watch but they address truths about life and history in Central Australia in a way that no other Australian filmmaker has ever achieved. In *Sweet Country*, as in Thornton's earlier works, the characters and landscapes are beyond realistic; these films resemble great parables. Inspired by real events, *Sweet Country* is a period western set in 1929 in the outback of the Northern Territory. At its world premiere screening at the 2017 Venice Film Festival, it received a standing ovation, great acclaim from critics and won the Special Jury Prize. It was also the prestigious Platform winner at the 2017 Toronto Film Festival, Best Feature Film at the 2017

Asia Pacific Screen Awards, Best Dramatic Feature at the ImagineNATIVE Festival 2017, the Audience Award at the Adelaide Film Festival, Best Feature Screenplay at Australian Writers Guild, and received Critics' Awards at Camerimage, Luxembourg, Venice and Dublin film festivals.

Tony Briggs

A great example of a modern Aboriginal story is told in the film *The Sapphires*, written by Yorta Yorta and Wurundjeri man Tony Briggs and based on the experiences of his mother, Laurel Robinson. It received standing ovations at its premiere at the Cannes Film Festival in 2012. The British newspaper *The Times* described it as 'the kind of film that makes you want to leap from your seat and shout for joy'. This feature-length film, directed by Indigenous director and actor Wayne Blair, tells the story of four young Yorta Yorta women who took their soul music act to Vietnam in 1968 to entertain the troops. Its cast includes strong Aboriginal leading women Deb Mailman, Miranda Tapsell, Shari Sebbens and Jessica Mauboy. It is an adventure story, a love story and a musical. Its historical setting is the Aboriginal community at Cummeragunga on the Murray River, which forms the border of Victoria and New South Wales. Tony is also the curator of the recently established film festival Birrarangga, which runs at ACMI in Naarm/Melbourne and showcases Indigenous films on strength, resilience and the environment from filmmakers around the globe.

Ryan Griffen

The gripping television series *Cleverman* was based on an original concept by Ryan Griffen. He created the story idea so that his son would have a superhero that he could relate to. It is a powerful drama depicting a dystopian future in which the Hairy People, a superhuman species based on mythical beings in Aboriginal lore, are persecuted by humans. They are hunted and, when captured, confined in laboratories to change their nature and 'humanise' them.

As a parable of racial politics and policing, it excels in dramatically depicting dangerous myths about science and progress. It also shows the human tendency to dominate other beings. It pits brother against brother in the struggle between the Hairy People and the Containment Authority, recalling the terror inflicted on First Australians during the assimilation period when children were torn from their families.

Doris Pilkington Garimara

The book *Follow the Rabbit-Proof Fence* (1996), written by Doris Pilkington Garimara, was made into a film, *Rabbit-Proof Fence*, in 2002. It is a true, powerful and heart-breaking account of how Doris's mother Molly, Doris's aunt Daisy, and Molly's cousin Gracie – all Martutjarra girls – were forcibly removed from their families in the East Pilbara in Western Australia in 1931, under the 'assimilation' policy. Molly (aged fourteen), Daisy (eleven) and Gracie (eight) escaped from the Moore River Native Settlement, where they had been taken, and were pursued by an Aboriginal tracker. The girls walked for some 1600 kilometres using the rabbit-proof fence that runs north–south through Western Australia as their guide. Historian Doris Pilkington Garimara used archival evidence and interviews with her mother and her Aunty Daisy to write the story.

The film is gripping viewing, with David Gulpilil in the role of the tracker and Kenneth Branagh in the role of A.O. Neville, the 'Chief Protector of Aborigines', who ordered the forced removal of Aboriginal children in Western Australia. The film won many awards and was screened worldwide.

This story about members of the Stolen Generations helped Australians to understand the suffering that has been caused to thousands of families. Eventually the sentiment around the country led to the National Apology to the Stolen Generations, delivered by then prime minister Kevin Rudd in 2008.

Storytelling is culture

There are Aboriginal and Torres Strait Islander storytellers working across most genres and formats. They are continuing ancient traditions of sharing culture, knowledge, ideas, wisdom and understanding about people and our world, and, above all, entertaining audiences.

Now our creators have access to global publication and the broadcast potential of film, television and, increasingly, the worldwide web.

As Indigenous storytelling adapted to new ways of communicating in the twentieth and twenty-first centuries, the positive reception to this creative outpouring has been encouraging. Best of all, our most accomplished storytellers keep our cultures alive and make a living from their talents.

Our children and youth – indeed all children and youth – have a right to read and hear these great stories. They will help them to learn about themselves and about the Aboriginal and Torres Strait Islander worlds, and to enjoy them.

12
Native title

Eddie Koiki Mabo had an impact on Australian life that was profound and life-changing for thousands of Torres Strait Islanders and Aboriginal people across the nation. He was born on the island of Mer (Murray Island) in the Torres Strait, in 1935. In 1974, while working as a gardener at James Cook University in Townsville, he met historians Henry Reynolds and Noel Loos. The three men became friends. For so long, writers and historians had ignored the history of Indigenous Australia, but both Reynolds and Loos wrote groundbreaking books about the Aboriginal resistance to the frontier war in North Queensland that placed Indigenous people at the centre of Australian history.

Through Reynolds and Loos, Koiki found out that he did not own his traditional land – that it was owned by the state of Queensland. Koiki began teaching, lecturing at the university and writing about his culture and his ties to his land. He wrote about the land ownership and inheritance system on Mer.

He did not accept that the land his grandfather had bequeathed to him did not belong to him by law. In 1982, he met with a group of lawyers in Townsville to begin his legal challenge to the Queensland land laws. That year the case was lodged in the High Court. Koiki was the leading plaintiff, and he was joined by other Traditional Owners of Mer as plaintiffs: Mr Sam Passi until his death, when Rev Dave Passi carried through the family's claim, Mr James Rice and, until she passed away, Mrs Celuia Mapo Salee.

Central to the case was the evidence, written and oral, that the people of Mer had their own laws that were given to them by their god, Malo. This god is often represented as an octopus. The plaintiffs challenged the idea that the entire continent and islands of Australia were given to the British upon 'discovery'. It was wrongly claimed that the Traditional Owners had no laws or system of governance, and that the land was not theirs.

This idea in British law is called terra nullius or 'land belonging to no one'; it was assumed that Aboriginal people had no laws or governance system

A meeting of Aboriginal representatives, ministers and Prime Minister Paul Keating, 27 April 1993. The group discussed ways of protecting Aboriginal rights in light of the High Court's *Mabo* decision. The painting is a work by Mr W. Rubuntja, who was also present at the meeting.

and therefore no one for the British to treat with. It was based on arguments by the British legal expert, judge and politician William Blackstone, who, in his *Commentaries* (1765–1770), argued that there were 'ceded' (given) and 'conquered' (taken by force) colonies. Australia was deemed to be a 'ceded' colony until the High Court overruled this legal nonsense in the case known as *Mabo v Queensland* (No. 2) in 1992.

For Koiki and the other plantiffs, the path was not easy. The Queensland government passed the *Queensland Coast Islands Declaratory Act 1985* to overrule any claims Torres Strait Islanders may have had to the land. The Act declared that when the Queensland government took over the Torres Strait Islands under the *Coast Islands Act* in 1879, title to the islands was transferred to the state of Queensland. This title could not be subject to other claims. In 1992, the plaintiffs from Mer appealed to the High Court, which found the *Queensland Coast Islands Declaratory Act 1985* contravened section 10 of the *Racial Discrimination Act 1975* (Cth) and was invalid. Barbara Hocking's thesis on native title provided the basis for Australian lawyers to pursue the rights that Koiki Mabo and others sought.

The High Court judges' decision said that if native title rights did exist, they should be viewed as part of the human right to own and inherit property. On those grounds, the Coast Islands Act unfairly compromised the property rights of people in the Torres Strait.

To understand why the myth of terra nullius was wrong and was finally dismissed as legal doctrine by the High Court, you can watch *Land Bilong Islanders*. This documentary was directed by Trevor Graham and released in 1989. It features historic film as audiovisual evidence that the Murray Island People's traditional practices have continued over the generations. For example, the dances filmed by A.C. Haddon in 1898 are still performed today. *Land Bilong Islanders* documents the four months of hearings in the Supreme Court of Queensland before the High Court case.

It looks at the evidence about the laws and customs that govern the Murray Island People's land boundaries and ownership of property. Graham and his crew travelled to Murray Island to film sites of significance to the case.

On 3 June 1992, ten years after Koiki, Passi, Rice and Mrs Mapo Salee lodged their case, the High Court of Australia handed down its decision. In a six to one majority, it agreed to the claim that the Meriam People of Mer Island should have their native title recognised by law. In this case, called *Mabo No. 2*, the High Court overturned more than 200 years of the legal fiction of terra nullius. It established that rights to land had existed before the arrival of the British and, under certain conditions, survived British sovereignty. Koiki Mabo did not live to see his victory in court. He died of

Eddie Koiki Mabo (with fishing spear) and Jack Wailu on the Island of Mer in the Torres Strait Islands, 1989

cancer not long before the judges gave their decision, but his memory has endured in the name given to this momentous decision.

This win in the High Court was a turning point in the long history of governments dispossessing with impunity from Aboriginal and Torres Strait Islander Peoples.

Following the High Court's judgement in 1992, there was a bitter national debate about the impact of the *Mabo* case on Australian land ownership. After more than a year of difficult negotiations involving Aboriginal leaders and representatives from the farming, grazing and mining industries, the *Native Title Act 1993* (Cth) was finally passed into Australian law when it received Royal Assent on 24 December 1993. In a speech in Parliament, then prime minister Paul Keating explained that the legislation '[would] make the Mabo decision an historic turning point: the basis of a new relationship between Indigenous and other Australians'.

To see why the High Court's *Mabo* decision was a key turning point in Australia's history, you need to understand how property law works. The most complete form of land ownership is called 'freehold title'. That means the owner has permanent possession of their land and can sell it when they want to. In Aboriginal or Torres Strait Islander Peoples' traditional laws and customs, there is a different relationship with land. Land estates are inherited as the joint property of descent-based groups, in some parts of Australia, called clans, but having great variability in their structure and rules of inheritance. For the most part, an individual cannot make unilateral decisions about the property of the collective and in any case, such decisions are themselves subject to a complex of laws, traditions and customs.

In law, the term 'property' describes rights in relation to things. In the 1999 case *Yanner v Eaton*, the High Court of Australia said:

> The word 'property' is often used to refer to something that belongs to another. But ... 'property' does not refer to a thing; it is a description of a legal relationship with a thing. It refers to a degree of power that is recognised in law as power permissibly exercised over the thing. The concept of 'property' may be elusive. Usually it is treated as a 'bundle of rights'.

The 'bundle of rights' that property involves acknowledges that rights over land can be divided. For example, the rights can be divided between an owner and a tenant. This means that many individuals may be able to claim various bundles of rights over one area of land.

Native title is also a 'bundle of rights'. What's in that bundle of rights will depend on the native title holders' traditional laws and customs, and Australian laws recognising the rights and interests they hold. For example, in *Yanner v Eaton*, the court found that the Gungaletta People had a native title right to hunt crocodiles on their traditional lands and waters. That is a limited right. In the 1992 *Mabo* case, the High Court agreed that the Mer People have native title to permanently own most of their traditional land.

In 1788, Governor Phillip claimed possession of the entire continent for a penal colony on behalf of the British government. All lands were taken in the name of the Crown, thus the name 'Crown lands', a colonial concept now overturned by the *Mabo (No. 2)* judgement. However, there were no valid treaties with Aboriginal and Torres Strait Islander Peoples. Of all the British settler states, Australia remains the one jurisdiction with no treaties with the Indigenous Peoples. No Indigenous Peoples ceded land to the British government – and so native title continues. Indigenous traditional laws and customs that form the basis of ownership over their lands *co-exist* with the claim of sovereignty by the British Crown.

Since colonisation, much of Australia has come under private ownership, Crown lease or some other private property arrangement. In most cases, the Traditional Owners were forcibly removed from their land. Australian law holds that such acts, which break the Traditional Owners' ongoing connection with their land, 'extinguish' or remove native title.

Yorta Yorta land rights appeal at the Federal court (image courtesy of AIATSIS, item ATSIC.006. CN-E00011_03)

Where the Traditional Owners' rights and interests in relation to their land under the traditional laws and customs are still observed, and they have a connection with their land by those traditional laws and customs, native title may be recognised by the common law of Australia.

The High Court of Australia established a form of recognition of native title that falls far short of the laws in Canada, the USA and New Zealand. While its terms are unjust, *Mabo* was a historic turning point for Australia for two reasons. First, because it gives Aboriginal and Torres Strait Islander Peoples the ability to have their land rights recognised and protected. Second, and most significantly, it recognised Indigenous laws and customs and brought them within the Australian legal system.

The terms of the *Native Title Act* regulate the circumstances in which native title can be recognised and survives. In many cases these terms have led to bitter disappointment for the Traditional Owners. Courts have dismissed claims when groups of people have been unable to prove their connection to land through an unbroken line of descent to a time before British colonisation. This is because of the lack of historical records – or, as in some cases, judicial preference for the accounts of white explorers and colonisers over the Aboriginal evidence. The *Yorta Yorta* case in northern Victoria was such a case.

On 12 December 2002, the High Court handed down its decision in the case of the *Members of the Yorta Yorta Aboriginal Community v State of Victoria and Others*. The Yorta Yorta People claimed their traditional rights in land and waters covering 2000 square kilometres along and around the Murray and Goulburn rivers. They sought to be recognised as the peoples belonging, by tradition, to that Country.

Justice Olney of the Federal Court found that before the end of the nineteenth century the Yorta Yorta People had ceased to occupy their traditional lands 'in accordance with their traditional laws and customs' and relied on a phrase in the *Mabo (No. 2)* judgement of the High Court: 'the tide of history'. Justice Olney wrote, 'the tide of history has indeed washed away any real acknowledgement of their traditional laws and any real observance of their traditional customs'. The Yorta Yorta plaintiffs appealed to the Full Court of the Federal Court, which upheld Justice Olney's findings. They then appealed to the High Court, which also confirmed Justice Olney's findings.

This case was widely debated because the courts' findings seemed unjust and discriminatory. Legal scholars turned to arguments about 'tradition', noting the findings of the Chief Justice of the Federal Court, Justice Michael Black, who was in the minority: 'far from being concerned with

Representatives of the Aboriginal Land Council attend rallies with sights set on the future (photo Wayne Quilliam)

what is static, the very notion of "tradition" as involving the transmission from generation to generation of statements, beliefs, legends and customs orally or by practice implies recognition of the possibility of change'.

Indigenous people have a long and brutal colonial history of land being taken from them and people being forcibly moved onto reserves. The Yorta Yorta People, understandably, felt that yet another great injustice had been done to them in their native title case. Not just courts, but governments also have extinguished native title. In the most egregious case, in May 1996, the newly elected Howard Government announced significant amendments to the *Native Title Act*. Industry and Indigenous groups took different views to the proposed reforms. Much like the situation in the lead up to the original legislation, the debate became polarised between groups who sought a watering down of the Act (the National Farmers Federation and the Australian Mining Industry Council) and the Aboriginal representatives who sought greater protection of native title interests. In November of that year, whilst debate was raging around the form any amendments might take, the High Court handed down its decision in *Wik*. The Howard Government immediately announced a new set of reforms, incorporating those already proposed, but arguing that the decision required a more substantial set of changes, incorporated into the so-called 'Ten Point Plan'. Indigenous parties vehemently opposed the amendments, arguing that the provisions delivered 'bucketloads of extinguishment', including all the areas that had been opened to potential native title claims by the *Wik* decision. As Tehan states, 'it was clear that the balance of interests had shifted'.

Only one reform area was welcomed by both sides of the debate: that relating to Point Ten of the 'Ten Point Plan', the introduction of a more comprehensive scheme for the negotiation of agreements. The 1998 amendments, despite the significant detrimental impact of the new extinguishment provisions and others relating to the recognition of native title, introduced provisions for a robust process for Indigenous Land Use Agreements (ILUA) and Section 31 Agreements (covering procedures for agreement over the doing of future acts), and in so doing paved the way for a more fruitful period of agreement-making, resulting in significant economic and social outcomes for native title parties.

Native title has had little impact on the lives of most Australians. After the High Court's findings in the *Mabo* case, opponents of Aboriginal land rights claimed that the outcome would cause enormous damage to the economy. However, this hasn't happened. It is a weak title compared with the usual freehold title that homeowners have, with its exclusive possession and far greater protection at law.

Aboriginal or Torres Strait Islander Traditional Owners usually make a native title application to the National Native Title Tribunal (the Tribunal). The Tribunal is an independent statutory body established under the *Native Title Act*. Its role is to administer and make decisions about matters arising under that Act. This includes matters relating to an Indigenous Land Use Agreement or other agreements made under the Act, or a Prescribed Body Corporate, which holds or manages native title.

When a Native Title Claim Group makes an application to the Tribunal, they make a declaration that they 'hold rights and interests in an area of land and/or water according to their traditional laws and customs'. The Claim Group must then mount a case and gather evidence to show that they have a continuing connection with their land by their traditional laws and customs. After making an application, the group can expect to wait decades before the court makes its decision.

If the group is successful, a court will recognise that their native title rights and interests exist. The court will do this at an occasion called a 'native title determination'. Successful native title determinations are usually held on the Claim Group's traditional lands. Many people attend and there are celebrations and ceremonies. Many claims have been successful, but most of those are in the remote areas of Australia.

The Act defines two kinds of acts that affect native title. The first are 'past acts', which were done *before* the *Native Title Act* commenced (on 1 January 1994) and that were invalid because of native title. An example of a past act is where native title existed on land leased by a state or territory. The lease becomes invalid because it extinguished, or superseded, the native title rights. Under certain limited circumstances, these native title holders have a right to compensation.

The second class of acts that affect native title are 'future acts'. These are acts done after the *Native Title Act*'s commencement that either affect native title or are invalid because of native title. For example, the Act provides that a valid lease, licence or permit prevails over any native title rights.

A future act is a proposal to deal with land in a way that will affect native title by extinguishing or suppressing it. Or it creates interests that are inconsistent with the continued existence, enjoyment or exercise of native title. Future acts may include the grant of a mining lease or the compulsory acquisition – for a development, for instance – of land over which native title rights exist. The Tribunal explains in 'About native title applications', July 2014, that:

> Future act processes are based on the principle that in general, acts affecting Native Title will only be valid if they can also be done on freehold land. These processes give effect to the principle that in appropriate cases, these acts should only be done after every reasonable effort has been made to secure the agreement of the Native Title holders. They also provide certainty by ensuring that future dealings with land are enforceable, notwithstanding the existence of Native Title.

The *Native Title Act* gives native title holders rights in relation to certain future acts. This may include the right to negotiate. For some future acts, native title holders have no rights. Native title holders or claimants don't often win under this system. There are many loopholes in the Act that developers can use to avoid having to negotiate with Traditional Owners. The *Native Title Act* does not allow Traditional Owners to stop any proposal.

Where they have a right to negotiate, it is often undermined

Where parties have negotiated but have not been able to reach an agreement, the Tribunal can host a mediation. Where this fails, the parties may apply to the Tribunal for a determination. The Tribunal will then decide whether the future act may be done; may be done subject to conditions; or must not be done.

The Traditional Owners' rights are often undermined where the government party thinks the future act can be progressed more quickly. This is known as the 'expedited procedure' – a fast-tracking process for future acts

Rallying for rights and traditional lands (photo Wayne Quilliam)

that would normally be subject to the right to negotiate but are considered to have minimal impact on native title. If this procedure is used, and no objection is lodged, the future act can be done by a government without following the right to negotiate.

Sometimes, the Act does work in favour of Traditional Owners. This happened in March 2018. It involved the Olkolo People, in Cape York Peninsula, who fought the Queensland Government and Gamboola Resources Pty Ltd. Gamboola is a goldmining company that sought an expedited exploration lease on land over which native title exists. Gamboola was trying to use this expedited procedure or fast-tracking process to bypass negotiations with the Traditional Owners.

The company claimed that the right to negotiate would not apply. The Tribunal found against the company because of the evidence that the project would 'interfere with sites of particular significance to the native title party', including a sacred 'mound spring area' and matchwood burial sites, and would cause a 'major disturbance' to the land and waters.

The interests of mining companies were at the forefront of the public debate after the *Native Title Act* was passed. The legislation acknowledged that mining companies and the resource extraction industry would seek access to, and the use of, native title land. Thus, the Act defines a range of future acts that, if done by a government, may be permitted to take place on native title land. These permissible future acts include:

- creation or variation of a right to mine, including explorations, prospecting and quarrying
- variation and extension of the period of a mining right
- compulsory acquisition by government of native title rights or interests to a party other than government.

The *Native Title Act* provides a right to negotiate the terms and conditions upon which land use and access could occur. For Traditional Owners, the right to negotiate is a beneficial provision of the Act, although it has limitations. For example, Traditional Owners have no right to stop dealings on land held under native title.

The right to negotiate has given Traditional Owners the opportunity to sit at the negotiating table with the government and mining companies, and – for the first time in Australian history – negotiate the use of their land and access to it. Its impact is significant because it shows the practical consequences of the rejection of the doctrine of terra nullius. Whereas terra nullius had denied Indigenous people access to the land market, the right to negotiate provides an opportunity for economic participation.

However, the procedures under the *Native Title Act* make it extremely difficult for Traditional Owners to gain legal recognition of their native title. Also, where a state or territory opposes a native title application, the Claim Group must face a long and expensive legal process (litigation). The High Court's findings in *Yorta Yorta* and more recent decisions have meant that litigation is often not an effective way to achieve good outcomes for Indigenous people. Only a small minority of successful native title determinations have resulted from court cases.

As well as court decisions that have found against the claims of Aboriginal people, the *Native Title Act* provides the means for native title to be 'extinguished' or declared unable to be recognised by Australian law. This aspect of the Act presents Indigenous people with a terrible dilemma: should they appeal to the courts for recognition of their native title and risk having it extinguished, or stopped, forever?

In view of these challenges, many Traditional Owners have tried to have their native title rights recognised through 'consent determinations'. The Agreements, Treaties and Negotiated Settlements Project in 2015 provided a useful explanation of what a consent determination is:

> *Consent determinations are an alternative to litigated determinations. [They] aim to provide an efficient and resourceful means of settling*

Native Title issues. The process has been described as: encouraging relationship building between Indigenous communities and others; less intrusive on Aboriginal culture than litigated determination ... In making a determination of Native Title, the court (or recognised body) must:

- *decide whether or not Native Title exists in respect of the determination area;*
- *identify the group that holds Native Title;*
- *state the nature and extent of the Native Title rights and interests; and*
- *set out other rights and interests in the determination area and the relationship between those rights and Native Title.*

The court or recognised body is allowed to make a determination without holding a hearing, where there is agreement (consent) between the parties, or where the orders sought by the applicants are unopposed.

Consent determinations are an opportunity for native title rights to be recognised through a negotiation process. The advantages of this process include saving time and resources, relationship building, and avoiding the stress and expense of lengthy hearings and cross-examination of witnesses. That is particularly important for Aboriginal people who are elderly and forced to reveal information about sacred sites and ceremonies to secure their native title.

The National Native Title Tribunal provides maps of determinations and Indigenous estates. Negotiation has been a more fruitful path for native title parties seeking a determination. However, with many hundreds of applications pending, the promise of a full recognition of native title through the determination process – either through a process of negotiation or through legal action – is still a long way off.

The content of these determinations varies enormously, with limited economic benefits for the native title holders coming from a determination alone. In the years immediately following the *Mabo (No 2)* High Court case, even consent determinations failed to produce the sorts of outcomes the native title applicants hoped for. The majority led to outcomes where native title was not recognised.

The amended *Native Title Act* now provides two main mechanisms for the negotiation of agreements for the use and access of land. They are section 31 and the 'right to negotiate' procedures. These provide that an agreement may be reached between the parties for any development on native title land. There is no provision for native title parties to stop a future act, only to negotiate its terms. In plain English, native title parties do not have a right of veto. Indigenous Land Use Agreements are legally binding on the parties and enforceable as a contract.

Traditional Owners are increasingly looking to other aspects of the native title system to secure more meaningful outcomes and to translate the recognition of their native title into economic and social benefits for their communities. Economic participation and wealth creation at far higher levels than in the 1990s are the two outstanding outcomes of the right to negotiate.

In 2019, the High Court of Australia ruled that the Ngaliwurru and Nungali Peoples, the Claim Group, from the Northern Territory town of Timber Creek be paid for 'the compensation for loss or diminution of traditional attachment to the land or connection to Country and for loss of rights to gain spiritual sustenance from the land'.

This test case was almost as important as the *Mabo* case because it was the first High Court ruling on native title compensation. It recognised the cultural loss the Traditional Owners experienced.

The High Court ruled that the Northern Territory government would pay $2.5 million in compensation to the native title holders for an area of 126 hectares. The trial judge recorded that 'The Ngaliwurru and Nungali Peoples' connection to Country is unique, deep and broad'.

Until this case, the official view was that native title was worthless, and that compensation, if found to be payable at law, would be a pittance or nothing. That view is wrong, not just because of the monetary value of native title that is now clarified, but because of the cultural loss that is an integral part of this decision.

To date, governments have settled out of court, but the negotiations and payments have been completely confidential. Clearly, the High Court judgement took into consideration the number of native title holders in the Claim Group. It also took into account the acts causing cultural loss that could not be separated from the content of the traditional laws and customs they observed, specifically the 'loss of connection to country suffered by the Claim Group'.

The spiritual loss was captured in the High Court's citation of this passage, observing that despite the evidence, Justice Blackburn maintained the fiction of terra nullius in his judgement in 1971, a state of affairs that did not end until 1992:

> *the connection which Aboriginal peoples have with 'country' is essentially spiritual. In* Milirrpum v Nabalco Pty Ltd *[(1971) 17 FLR 141 at 167]*, *Blackburn J said that: 'the fundamental truth about the aboriginals'*

> *relationship to the land is that whatever else it is, it is a religious relationship ... There is an unquestioned scheme of things in which the spirit ancestors, the people of the clan, particular land and everything that exists on and in it, are organic parts of one indissoluble whole'. It is a relationship which sometimes is spoken of as having to care for, and being able to 'speak for', country. 'Speaking for' country is bound up with the idea that, at least in some circumstances, others should ask for permission to enter upon country or use it or enjoy its resources, but to focus only on the requirement that others seek permission for some activities would oversimplify the nature of the connection that the phrase seeks to capture. The difficulty of expressing a relationship between a community or group of Aboriginal people and the land in terms of rights and interests is evident. Yet that is required by the [Native Title Act]. The spiritual or religious is translated into the legal.*[89]

This case has implications for governments that have extinguished or impaired native title since the *Racial Discrimination Act* came into effect on 31 October 1975. There will be litigation to determine whether – and if so, how much – compensation is payable to the native title groups affected. At the time of the High Court decision, there were 377 native title determinations to land over a total area of 2,836,842 square kilometres.

They would all be implicated if the states or territories had extinguished or impaired their native title.

In the future, governments will be careful to conduct negotiations over 'future uses' or proposals to impose projects or developments on land with determinations of native title, and they will be careful to do so within the confines of the law. Each claim in the future will need to be dealt with on a case-by-case basis. This may lead the Commonwealth to amend the Act so that governments don't have to pay compensation.

Unless the Commonwealth Government amends the *Native Title Act*, the judgement gives force to the present terms of the Act: compensation is payable for acts that impair or extinguish the Traditional Owners' native title rights. The compensation must be paid in money on 'just terms' and, subject to the 'just terms', be a maximum of the freehold value of the land.

13
The Stolen Generations

The term 'Stolen Generations' refers to the Aboriginal children who were forcibly removed from their families by the state, territory and federal governments of Australia from 1788 onwards. The children were placed in controlled institutions, or from a young age were made to work without pay in the homes of white people or adopted or fostered into white families. Most were never able to find their birth families again. This had terrible consequences for the mental and physical health of the children and their parents throughout their lives, and for Indigenous people down through the generations. It also resulted in cultural loss on a nationwide scale for the affected families.

The intention of the policies and laws that led to children being taken from their parents was to 'assimilate' part-Aboriginal people into the general Australian population, leaving the 'full bloods', as these people were called, separated and incarcerated on Aboriginal reserves. Governments regarded 'miscegenation', as mixed racial descent was known, to be a danger to the 'racial hygiene' and health of white Australian society.

For much of the twentieth century, most Australians had no qualms about this cruel practice or were unaware of it. In the 1980s, victims began to challenge the status quo by telling their stories and looking for their birth families. Their efforts led to the revelation that perhaps tens of thousands of children had been removed from their families. Growing evidence from the survivors, who numbered about 13,000, told of the sometimes extreme physical and sexual abuse they suffered at the hands of adoptive and foster families and employers (to whom some were indentured or enslaved). Aboriginal organisations called for a national inquiry.

Eventually, in 1995, the federal attorney-general established the National Inquiry into the Separation of Aboriginal and Torres Strait Island Children from their Families.

Two special commissioners were appointed, Sir Ronald Wilson QC, President of the Human Rights and Equal Opportunity Commission, and

May 26 is National Sorry Day, remembering The Stolen Generations and acknowledging the mistreatment of Aboriginal and Torres Strait Islander Peoples (photo Wayne Quilliam)

Professor Mick Dodson, the Aboriginal and Torres Strait Islander Social Justice Commissioner.

After taking evidence from across the entire country, the commissioners presented Bringing Them Home: The 'Stolen Children' Report to the Australian Parliament in 1997. Professor Dodson and Sir Ronald Wilson found that the race-based child-removal policies were a special instance of genocide under the definition in the United Nations Convention on the Prevention and Punishment of the Crime of Genocide.

The commissioners wrote:

> When a child was forcibly removed that child's entire community lost, often permanently, its chance to perpetuate itself in that child. The Inquiry has concluded that this was a primary objective of forcible removals and is the reason they amount to genocide. [Children are] core elements of the present and future of the community. The removal of these children creates a sense of death and loss in the community, and the community dies too ... there's a sense of hopelessness that becomes part of the experience for that family, that community ... (Lynne Datnow, Victorian Koori Kids Mental Health Network, evidence 135).

There have been similar conclusions in the comparable context of forcible removal to educational institutions of Native American children.

Because the family is the most fundamental economic, education, health-care unit in society and the centre of an individual's emotional life, assaults on Indian families help cause the conditions that characterise those cultures of poverty where large numbers of people feel hopeless, powerless and unworthy (Byler 1977 page 8).

A Congressional Inquiry in 1978 found that the removal of Indian children had a severe effect on Indian tribes, threatening their existence as identifiable cultural entities (US Congress 1978).[90]

This was clearly the case in Western Australia, for example, where the instructions and justification were aimed at eliminating the entire 'race'. This incited a national debate among many Australians and in May 1998 the first National Sorry Day was held, one year after the tabling of the report. On Sorry Day, 28 May 2000, around 300,000 people walked across the Sydney Harbour Bridge in the Walk for Reconciliation, and all around the country Australians were demanding a national apology to the Stolen Generations.

From 1996 until it lost the election in 2007, the federal government, led by then Prime Minister John Howard, refused to acknowledge the facts, and proposed an alternative explanation arguing that the stolen children were 'rescued'. On these – as has been repeatedly proven – grossly false grounds, John Howard refused to apologise.

Moments before Prime Minister Kevin Rudd delivered the Apology (photo Wayne Quilliam)

It was also claimed that an apology would establish the grounds for financial compensation; and of course, this would be the case for any other Australian, and is one part of the remedy for genocide set out in international law. In the Northern Territory and South Australia, survivors went to court to seek justice. The *Cubillo* and *Gunner* cases were unsuccessful, but a case in 2007 brought by Bruce Trevorrow in South Australia resulted in him being awarded $500,000 compensation. Mr Trevorrow died before the compensation was paid. In a further twist of the knife, the South Australian government ruled that his heirs were not entitled to the compensation payment.

At that time the nationwide campaign for an apology was growing. Tens of thousands of people signed 'Sorry' books to register their own apology and to demand an apology from the Australian government.

On 13 February 2008, then Prime Minister Kevin Rudd gave an apology in federal Parliament to the Stolen Generations. Here is the parliamentary transcript of his speech:

> *Mr Speaker, I move: That today we honour the Indigenous peoples of this land, the oldest continuing cultures in human history. We reflect on their past mistreatment. We reflect in particular on the mistreatment of those who were Stolen Generations – this blemished chapter in our nation's history.*
>
> *The time has now come for the nation to turn a new page in Australia's history by righting the wrongs of the past and so moving forward with confidence to the future.*
>
> *We apologise for the laws and policies of successive Parliaments and governments that have inflicted profound grief, suffering and loss on these our fellow Australians.*
>
> *We apologise especially for the removal of Aboriginal and Torres Strait Islander children from their families, their communities and their country.*
>
> *For the pain, suffering and hurt of these Stolen Generations, their descendants and for their families left behind, we say sorry.*
>
> *To the mothers and the fathers, the brothers and the sisters, for the breaking up of families and communities, we say sorry. And for the indignity and degradation thus inflicted on a proud people and a proud culture, we say sorry.*
>
> *We the Parliament of Australia respectfully request that this apology be received in the spirit in which it is offered as part of the healing of the nation. For the future we take heart; resolving that this new page in the history of our great continent can now be written.*

> *We today take this first step by acknowledging the past and laying claim to a future that embraces all Australians. A future where this Parliament resolves that the injustices of the past must never, never happen again. A future where we harness the determination of all Australians, Indigenous and non-Indigenous, to close the gap that lies between us in life expectancy, educational achievement and economic opportunity. A future where we embrace the possibility of new solutions to enduring problems where old approaches have failed. A future based on mutual respect, mutual resolve and mutual responsibility. A future where all Australians, whatever their origins, are truly equal partners, with equal opportunities and with an equal stake in shaping the next chapter in the history of this great country, Australia.*[91]

The cruel legacy of the policies of removing Aboriginal children from their families has been felt for generations. Even now, there would not be an Aboriginal person alive who has not been tragically touched in some way, directly or indirectly, by the impact of these policies.

Apologising to the victims of the historical policies of Aboriginal child removal achieved at least two important goals. First, it helped to restore the sense of dignity and legitimacy that the victims ought to feel but were denied. Secondly, it was a national acknowledgement of the wrong and harm done by previous governments to generations of people on the grounds of race-hate, an acknowledgement that should state explicitly that this should never occur again. The victims' inheritance has been denied by their removal. The denial of that inheritance is the key to their suffering and the correct grounds for compensating them: they were denied their family lines and their links to a family past and legacy, their material inheritance, their culture, and history, and most importantly, a sense of self shaped by the people who brought them into the world.

The primary significance of an apology must be for the victims of the policies of removing Aboriginal children from their families. But almost as significant is the effect of a formal apology on the citizens on whose behalf the apology was made.

In 2010, the Healing Foundation was established in Ngambri/Ngunnawal/Canberra to provide trauma support for the victims, assistance with commemorative events and to undertake research. Also, several monuments have been erected around the country to remind us of this tragedy, and families visit them on National Sorry Day every year. As there are so many, it is not possible to mention them all here, nor all the commemorative plaques. For example, the six plaques placed in culturally significant sites around Meanjin/Brisbane: King George Square, Teralba Park in Everton Park, Kalinga Park in

Nundah, Orleigh Park in West End, Sherwood Arboretum and the Wynnum foreshore. Instead, I will focus on three of the monuments.

STOLEN GENERATIONS MEMORIAL
Reilly Lane, Sydenham Green, Sydney, New South Wales

The Stolen Generations Memorial at Reilly Lane, Sydenham Green, is a sandstone sculpture by Aboriginal artist Joe Hirst.

Its inscription is taken from Link-Up, the organisation established by victims to find their families.

> *We may go home, but we cannot relive our childhoods. We may reunite with our mothers, fathers, sisters, brothers, aunties, uncles, communities, but we cannot re-live the 20, 30, 40 years that we spent without their love and care, and they cannot undo the grief and mourning they felt when we separated from them. We can go home to ourselves as Aboriginals, but this does not erase the attacks inflicted on our hearts, minds, and bodies by caretakers who thought their mission was to eliminate us as Aboriginals. Link-Up (New South Wales)*[92]

STOLEN GENERATIONS MEMORIAL
Phillip Creek Native Settlement, Manga Marda Waterhole, Tennant Creek, Northern Territory

In 1946, sixteen 'part Aboriginal' children were moved from the Phillip Creek Native Settlement at the Manga Manda waterhole to the notorious Retta Dixon Home in Darwin. This kidnapping was authorised by the Native Affairs Department of the Northern Territory government. In 2004, eleven survivors of the group taken from the Phillip Creek mission returned to the place where they were abducted to dedicate a memorial at the long-abandoned settlement. They used the dedication ceremony as a time to distance themselves from their shocking experiences at the Retta Dixon Home and rebuild their ties with their own families. The Phillip Creek mission was opened in 1945 as an interim ration depot for Aboriginal people. They had been displaced from their land after gold was discovered in the Tennant Creek region in the 1930s. By 1956, the mission was abandoned, and a permanent site was established at Warrabri.[93]

STOLEN GENERATIONS MEMORIAL GARDEN
Beinda Street, Bomaderry, New South Wales

This garden, created on the site of the Bomaderry United Aboriginal Mission (UAM), was dedicated on 21 October 2001. The mission was established in

1908, a year before the enactment of the *Aboriginal Protection Act* of 1909 and became the destination for many of the children in New South Wales who were taken from their families.

The inscription on the plaque at the garden reads:

> This plaque and memorial garden is dedicated to 'all' the Aboriginal children of the 'Stolen Generation' who were residents here at Bomaderry, the former 'United Aborigines Mission' (U.A.M.). Also to honour and respect the children who are now deceased. This site is the birthplace of the 'Stolen Generation' here in New South Wales.[94]

Remember the Dead

Advisory note: This section may distress some readers.

During the colonial and post-colonial times of massacres,[95] 'dispersion' and forced removals of Aboriginal populations, men and women obtained Aboriginal body parts – skeletal remains (skulls were particularly popular) to serve the eugenicist practice of scientific experimentation on our people, then cast as an 'inferior race' and 'scientific curios'. These ancestral remains were also traded among institutions and private collectors and exhibited to the public. In Australia, ancestral remains were acquired by museums until the 1980s, and there are still thousands of remains in museums worldwide as the international trade in body parts, ethnographic photographs and cultural objects continues.[96]

Truganini, a Nuenonne woman, the most famous of the palawa People of the island now known as Tasmania, witnessed the genocide of her people. She was one of the few survivors. Aware of the terrible practices of the colonists who used Aboriginal bodies for scientific experiments – even stealing them from graves and murdering people for this purpose – she begged that her body not be used in this way. She wanted her ashes scattered in the D'Entrecasteaux Channel.

When she died in 1876, her remains were exhumed and displayed in the Hobart Museum. After many years of demanding that her remains be returned for a proper interment, the museum agreed in 1976, one hundred years after she had passed. A closed service was held at the Cornelian Bay Crematorium on 30 April, attended by then premier of Tasmania, Mr Doug Lowe, Dr Allen Wallace, Roy Nichols, the state secretary of the Aboriginal Information Service, and other members of the palawa community. On the fortieth anniversary of this event in 2016, Dr Stan Florek gathered the memories of that day.[97] The late Aunty Ida West recounted that it was 'a lovely sunny morning':

The coffin was carried by Mr Roy Nichols and Mr Lowe to the furnace – placed in and Mr Nichols and Mr Lowe waited until cremation had taken place. Under police guard the ashes were taken for safe keeping till the morning of the 1st of May 1976.

The ashes were contained in a Huon Pine casket which was placed in the Egeria's *cabin and carried to a point south-east of the pilot station in the D'Entrecasteaux Channel. Mr Lowe formally handed the ashes to Mr Nichols and the following words were said, 'Truganini, may you now rest in peace'. On the* Egeria *were Mr Lowe, Roy Nichols, Members of the Aboriginal community and a police guard. A flotilla of craft accompanied us down the river ... It was a solemn affair – giving the important person a decent and dignified burial.*

Truganini's ashes were scattered on a lovely sunny morning ... a porpoise was swimming around us when the ashes went down. Truganini had asked for this to be done, but it took a hundred years to come about. My daughter Lennah and another lady were with the casket of Truganini before the cremation. Rosalind Langford made a speech at the cremation and it was very good.

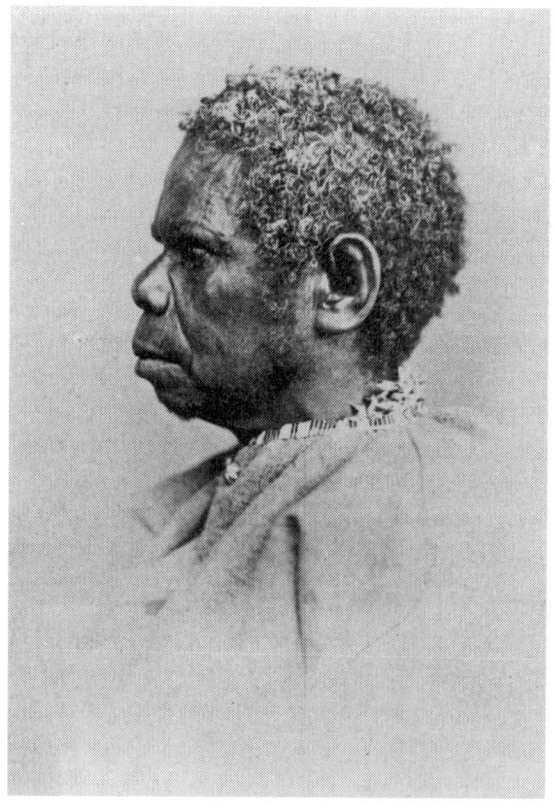

Side profile sketch of Truganini (image courtesy of AIATSIS, item RCS.001. BW-N00701_07)

> *On the 9th of May people from the Aboriginal community and myself all went up to open a park which was dedicated to Truganini. Mr Stephen Walker, a sculptor, made the commemorative plaque for the area which he set into a large stone and it looks lovely. Guest speakers were Mr Doug Lowe, Roy Nichols and Mr Bingham. We had some little children sitting on top of some rocks watching what was going on. My grand-nieces and nephews were sitting there too with a few white children. They had their arms around each other. We were all standing around while they gave their speeches, a big black dog was standing with us too.*

This event was one of the first repatriations of Aboriginal ancestral remains, inspiring Aboriginal people across the country to find their ancestors who had suffered the fate of Truganini and have them returned for a dignified burial or interment according to their traditions. Over many decades, Indigenous people have demanded that museums and other collecting institutions return ancestral remains and sacred objects, but around the world and here in Australia most of these institutions remained intransigent, insisting on their ownership and their 'right' to keep them for 'scientific purposes.'[98]

In the twenty-first century, when almost the entire human genome has been mapped, revealing that there is no sound scientific basis for the idea of 'race' and 'racial science', it is difficult to understand why institutions and collectors keep Aboriginal ancestral remains. A group of researchers at the Australian National University have attempted to explain the practice of keeping Aboriginal bodies and body parts. The *Return, Reconcile, Renew* project is a timely response to these practices, with the aim of assisting Aboriginal and Torres Strait Islander Peoples to repatriate their Old People. The project's website informs us that:

> *Ancestral Remains were taken from wherever the deceased can be found. The majority of remains were taken from funerary sites. Indigenous burial grounds were dug up, and remains were taken from caves, burial platforms and other areas of funerary ritual. Indigenous remains were also disinterred from European churchyards and cemeteries. Those seeking to obtain remains also targeted areas where Ancestral Remains had been revealed through erosion, whether through the actions of burrowing rabbits, wind or water. Ancestral Remains were also revealed through construction work when houses and new roads were built.*
>
> *Some Ancestral Remains were taken from massacre sites or places where people were known to have died a violent death.*

> In some instances, bodies were taken from hospital morgues and university anatomy departments, after executions or from people who had died in jail. Sometimes, as in the cases of Yagan, Kanabygal, Jandamarra, and Pemulwoy, eminent leaders were killed for their part in resistance to colonial expansion and their heads subsequently removed and sent to overseas institutions.[99]

As well, police departments handed over to universities and museums bodies disinterred in excavations and obtained by other means.

Even though those who came from the disciplines of 'comparative anatomy', 'craniology', eugenics and physical anthropology insisted that they took Aboriginal bodies from graves for 'scientific purposes', when Indigenous people have found ancestral remains in institutions, there are no records of who they were, where they came from, and how they got there. So much for their 'science'. Reputable scientists document their work according to the proper standards of science. Because of this gross negligence, there are thousands of unprovenanced ancestral Aboriginal remains that have been returned by overseas institutions to Ngambri/Ngunnawal/Canberra. Without any records, no one can know who they were nor where to return them. A national Keeping Place is envisaged for these Old People to dignify and memorialise them, although anonymous, and to acknowledge this history of stealing them from their graves and trading them among institutions for the 'racial' entertainment of the audiences of museums and to teach 'racial science' in universities. The University of Melbourne collected thousands of ancestral remains and is a major centre of the study of the now discredited field of eugenics.

In Victoria, the long saga of litigation and campaigning by Aboriginal people to have their Old People returned resulted in a major breakthrough when Gunditjmara Elder Uncle Jim Berg won a significant victory in the courts in 1984. His court injunction against the University of Melbourne and the Museum of Victoria was successful in preventing a collection of Australian Indigenous remains from Kow Swamp and Keilor being sent to America for an exhibition entitled 'Ancestors'. Changes in museum practices followed.

In 2016, the Victorian Aboriginal Heritage Council became the guardian for all unprovenanced Aboriginal ancestral remains and sacred objects in Victoria, but in the 1980s, Jim Berg's injunction, followed by moral persuasion and negotiation, turned the page on this horrible history, as explained by the council's website:

> On 22 November 1985, 38 Ancestors were reburied in Kings Domain, Melbourne. The site was chosen in the absence of being able to determine

their origins. This monumental event paved the way for collaborative repatriation efforts between Traditional Owners, state government agencies and academic institutions in Victoria. Since then, thousands of Ancestral Remains have been repatriated to their intended resting places. However, the repatriation process is often slow, frustrating, and difficult for Aboriginal communities for a variety of reasons.[100]

The eventual repatriation of the Kow Swamp ancestral remains ignited a worldwide debate about the merit of scientific experimentation versus the desires of the communities of origin to have their Old People's remains treated with dignity.

This debate continues because collecting the ancestral remains of Indigenous people and non-western cultures is a global practice and there are many testimonies about how deeply distressing the practice is to descendants. In some cases, the display of the remains of deceased people is permitted in highly restricted circumstances, such as in Cambodia at Choeung Ek (known globally as the Killing Fields).[101]

However, the work of Uncle Jim Berg led to an important change in Victorian legislation: the amendment in 2016 to the *Victorian Aboriginal Cultural Heritage Act*, which places all Aboriginal ancestral remains and sacred objects in the ownership of the Victorian Aboriginal Heritage Council, which has the responsibility to repatriate them to their communities of origin.[102] Uncle Jim Berg took a stand against these practices and he tells his story with Aboriginal curator, Shannon Faulkhead, in *Power and the Passion: Our Ancestors Return Home* (2010).

Then in 1984, when Uncle Jim Berg became aware of the George Murray Black Collection in the Anatomy Department of the University of Melbourne, he worked with Ron Merkel of the Victorian Aboriginal Legal Service to prepare 'a number of injunctions which were served against the University for breaches of the *Archaeological & Aboriginal Relics Preservation Act* (1972) for being in possession of Aboriginal skeletal remains. Discussions and court proceedings followed, with Berg winning the case and the Murray Black Collection was transferred to the museum.'[103]

The events that followed – particularly audits of the university's collections – resulted in the return of hundreds of ancestral remains for proper burial as instructed by Elders and communities of origin.

The Australian government has worked with Aboriginal and Torres Strait Islander Peoples and institutions such as the Australian Institute of Aboriginal and Torres Strait Islander Studies (AIATSIS) to assist in repatriating ancestral remains from overseas museums, universities and collecting institutions, in compliance with international laws. Some Australian domestic laws, although not entirely adequate, have been useful in bringing them home. As I have pointed out with my colleagues, Brook Andrew and Jessica Neath, in our contribution to the *Handbook on Genocide*:

> Despite the widespread acknowledgement of the inhumanity of the practice, still today, some museums like the Natural History Museum, London, and Cambridge University's Duckworth collection refuse to allow the repatriation of Aboriginal and Torres Strait Islander human remains in their collections.[104]

A National Resting Place for unprovenanced Aboriginal and Torres Strait Islander ancestral remains in Ngambri/Ngunnawal/Canberra was proposed in a 2014 report by the Advisory Committee on Indigenous Repatriation to the federal government and was the subject of a scoping study by AIATSIS, following Recommendation 4 of the Joint Select Committee on Constitutional Recognition relating to Aboriginal and Torres Strait Islander Peoples:

> The Committee also recommends that the Australian Government consider the establishment, in Canberra, of a National Resting Place, for Aboriginal and Torres Strait Islander remains which could be a place of commemoration, healing and reflection.[105]

I have worked with Wiradjuri/Celtic artist Brook Andrew on addressing the need for the memorialisation of massacres and other events in which Aboriginal and Torres Strait Islander people lost their lives in the colonial project, acknowledging that many took place in the twentieth century. Andrew established a visual arts research project with funding from the Australian Research Council, *Representation, Remembrance and the Memorial (RRM)*, to address this outstanding moral challenge for all Australians: how to represent the magnitude of Indigenous loss and survival in a national memorial. Andrew has involved a group of local and international peoples[106] to focus on case studies, including investigating international examples of monuments to genocide and community approaches to remembering frontier violence.[107] The challenge remains, and Aboriginal and Torres Strait Islander Peoples wait for a decision from the Australian government on a formal memorialisation of the Old People who suffered the indignity of being collected as 'scientific curios'. While debates continue as to whether what happened to Aboriginal people after 1788 can be classified as genocide,[108] it is nevertheless important to formally acknowledge the genocidal practices and politics that deem the remains of our ancestors as unworthy of ceremonial funeral services and return to their communities of origin.

14
Business and Tourism

If you are visiting Australia, you need to know about our history. I have explained that Aboriginal Peoples were the first humans to colonise the southernmost parts of the planet. Aboriginal people came from what is now Asia and moved across the whole continent before the last Ice Age.

The story that science tells is not so different from the traditional Aboriginal beliefs about our origins. Do the Wandjina tell of ancestral arrivals from the north-west on the monsoonal winds, among the lightning and giant cumulus clouds of the wet season? Rasmus Nielsen and his colleagues, writing in *Nature,* presented their findings in 2017 on likely human migration patterns in the last 60,000 years, confirming the 'out-of-Africa' thesis – modern humans evolved in Africa and expanded out across the world via a series of routes.[109] Genomic, archaeological and palaeontological methods enabled the direct determination of the genealogical relationships between humans as well as the elucidation of migration routes, diversification events and genetic admixture among various groups. DNA sequencing and methods for the enrichment and extraction of ancient DNA from the remains of ancient humans and our ancient hominid cousins has advanced rapidly and by 'including samples from a wide range of historical times and locations', new understandings of insights into human history have emerged. While there remain unanswered questions, a global picture of paths of migration has been determined from the evidence. Further population movements after the initial migrations may muddy some of the pathways, and several routes are 'controversial'.[110] It seems that our ancestors – who we now know arrived on the continent more than 65,000 years ago – came across the Eurasian continent from what is now the region of Iraq and Iran, and many thousands of years before that from southern Africa, according to this body of evidence.

Travellers coming to Australia fifty years ago would have found it almost impossible to visit Aboriginal and Torres Strait Islander communities and lands. Only the most determined adventurers succeeded in obtaining access at that time when government policies of racial segregation and exclusion kept most Indigenous people apart from the rest of Australia. Over the past thirty years, the Indigenous tourism industry has grown from a tiny number to hundreds of businesses today. Since the publication of the first edition of this book, there are many more Aboriginal and Torres Strait Islander businesses and a new online platform to assist travellers who want to find authentic Indigenous experiences. This new platform is also called Welcome to Country and can be accessed at: welcometocountry.com. It was created by the first not-for-profit online marketplace for Australia's First Peoples tourism experiences and products, and was launched on 2 December 2020 with a free virtual event directed by Aboriginal arts leader and festival director Rhoda Roberts AO. The goal of this online guide is 'to empower Aboriginal and Torres Strait Islander Tourism operators and communities by creating sustainable economic and wellbeing outcomes through tourism and products.' With an extensive list of immersive experiences listed, Welcome to Country online provides an easy-to-use single booking platform.

Tourists are now able to visit Country easily. But the opportunities for Indigenous people to build tourist facilities on their lands and in their communities did not come about so easily. The key industries in rural and remote Australia are mining, pastoralism and tourism – all land-based. As peoples with profound attachments to their land, a large part of the Indigenous population has sought to become involved in these industries. About a quarter of Australia's land mass is Aboriginal-owned and this preference for investment in their own assets and regions is a rational choice.

However, to make this happen successfully it was necessary to change the models of economic development that were available to Indigenous communities. A radical overhaul was designed to address the legacy of underdevelopment and exclusion of the previous two centuries.

Business

Changes in attitudes towards Indigenous business came slowly. First the iron-ore miners, then many of the top 200 Australian corporations, and now the Commonwealth Government has created an Indigenous supply chain by procuring goods and services from Indigenous businesses. The growth in the number of these businesses is a core achievement of a new approach to engaging with Indigenous Australians, and all Australians benefit from the outcomes. In 2007, the ANZ Banking Group collaborated with Reconciliation Australia and was the first major private sector company to develop a Reconciliation Action Plan (RAP).

Luke Carroll and Brooke Boney present the Indigenous Businesswoman of the Year award to Petina Tieman (Complete Business Solutions, Queensland) at the Supplier Diversity Awards, 2018 (photo Wayne Quilliam)

Reconciliation Australia is a non-government body that inspires and enables Australians by advising on ways to improve relationships with Aboriginal and Torres Strait Islander Peoples and create opportunities for them. Launched in 2006, Reconciliation Australia's RAP strategy has been enormously successful and has resulted in more than 1100 organisations with Reconciliation Action Plans with many more in development. Reconciliation Australia assists companies, government and non-government entities, educational institutions and other bodies to develop RAPs as frameworks to realise their vision for reconciliation. They are practical plans: 'RAPs create social change and economic opportunities for Aboriginal and Torres Strait Islander Australians'. In an evaluation report of their effectiveness by AusPoll in 2012, the RAPs are described as 'plans that organisations can make to identify clear actions with realistic targets that they can take to improve the relationship between Indigenous people and other Australians both within the organisation and more widely'.

Many major Australian corporations have adopted RAPs and this action has accelerated opportunities for Indigenous businesses as well as encouraging the acceptance of Aboriginal and Torres Strait Islander people in workplaces and recruitment strategies. During the mining boom, companies moved quickly to develop Indigenous business opportunities to demonstrate their commitment to the local Traditional Owners of land where they operated.

The results were outstanding. In 2011, Fortescue Metals Group announced its Billion Opportunities program 'to generate business opportunities for Aboriginal people' and to recognise that 'economic opportunity and participation is the key benefit to flow from native title agreements'. Since then, the company has awarded 244 contracts and sub-contracts valued close to $2 billion to 105 Aboriginal-owned businesses and joint ventures. In the last decade, Australian governments have caught up with the private sector and developed Indigenous business policies and programs.

Indigenous entrepreneur Michael McLeod and his non-Indigenous business partner Dug Russell were inspired by the National Minority Supplier Development Council in the USA. They developed the idea of creating the Australian Indigenous Minority Supplier Council (AIMSC) to achieve parity in procuring Indigenous goods and services and made a submission to the inquiry by Australian Parliament's Standing Committee on Aboriginal and Torres Strait Islander Affairs in 2008. Their submission outlined the creation of the council and focused on the development of Indigenous enterprises in Australia. One year later, the government announced it would invest $3 million to pilot AIMSC over three years. It was launched on 15 September 2009 at Parliament House in Ngambri/Ngunnawal/Canberra. In 2013, after successfully completing the pilot phase, AIMSC rebranded to become Supply Nation and has developed the largest membership in Australia of corporate, government and non-profit organisations committed to supplier diversity and Indigenous business development. It certifies Indigenous suppliers and registered businesses in every state and territory. Then it partners these businesses with companies and governments seeking to buy Indigenous goods

Fortescue Metals Group wins Corporate Member of the Year at the Supplier Diversity Awards, 2018 (photo Wayne Quilliam)

Evolve FM wins Registered Business of the Year and Outstanding Impact Award at the Supplier Diversity Awards, 2018 (photo Wayne Quilliam)

and services. Through the work of Supply Nation, private sector expenditure on Indigenous business services has grown dramatically. However, Indigenous business ingenuity, market forces and new government policies on Indigenous procurement account for much of this growth.[111]

In 2015, the Australian government recognised that Indigenous businesses had been largely excluded from its enormous purchasing power and announced a revised and improved Indigenous procurement policy. This led to the increase in federal government spending on Indigenous goods and services from $6 million in 2013 to $594 million in 2017, with the awarding of 4880 contracts to 956 Indigenous-owned businesses over a two-year period from 2015, when the Indigenous procurement policy was introduced. There is great interest in these developments because Indigenous businesses employ Indigenous people at far higher rates than other companies, as much as 100 times more, according to the Forrest Review of Indigenous Employment and Training, undertaken by Andrew Forrest, former CEO of Fortescue Metals Group, for the Australian government. Estimates are that there are between 3000 and 5000 Indigenous businesses nationally.

In 2015, the Community Development Program or CDP, a work-for-the-dole scheme, supported 37,000 people across 1000 communities. More than 80 per cent of the participants were Indigenous. This program has had several name changes in just a few years and many rule changes, none of which have improved the situation. The government's work-for-the-dole scheme applied in Aboriginal Australia has only had a 2 per cent success rate for transitioning its participants to jobs. According to Andrew Forrest's report, 'an additional 188,000 Indigenous Australians will have to find work in the next five years if we are to achieve parity. This will require a doubling of the current number of working Indigenous Australians'.

Indigenous Business Month is held annually in October throughout Australia (follow the Twitter account @IndigBizMonth) and events are held nationally to raise awareness of the Indigenous business sector.

Indigenous tourism sector

The Indigenous tourism sector is small and faces great challenges. For the foreseeable future, it will remain small-scale and attract smaller numbers than the most popular mainstream attractions. The COVID-19 restrictions in 2020, the closing of our national, state and territory borders, and the closing of the borders around Aboriginal lands has radically changed our access to Aboriginal-owned places of interest, tours and experiences. These measures were necessary to protect our highly vulnerable populations. A majority of Aboriginal and Torres Strait Islander people have underlying health conditions that put them at risk of serious illness and death should they contract the COVID-19 virus. Our Indigenous health sector responded swiftly and effectively, implementing pandemic plans in conjunction with Australian governments to protect our most vulnerable from the virus. As the vaccination program was implemented, more and more tourism businesses were able to open again, and visitors could travel to them.

Pamagirri Dreamtime Walk at Rainforestation Nature Park, Kuranda, Queensland

Before the pandemic, the Indigenous tourism ventures appealed mainly to visitors seeking boutique experiences in art, adventure and environmental experiences. 'There is low awareness amongst the domestic market that Indigenous tourism experiences are available in Australia,' says a research report, *Demand and Supply Issues in Indigenous Tourism*, by Dr Lisa Ruhanen and colleagues from the University of Queensland and Griffith University, which was published in early 2013. The situation has not improved since then. Commissioned by the Indigenous Business Australia (IBA), the federal Department of Resources, Energy and Tourism and the Indigenous Tourism Working Group, the report was based on interviews with more than 1300 international and domestic tourists and more than thirty Indigenous tourism operators. It revealed significant opportunities and challenges for the sector.

Only 5 per cent of international tourists cited Indigenous experiences as an activity they want to take part in while in Australia. Most wanted to stay on the eastern seaboard, especially in Sydney. According to the researchers, 'less than 25 per cent for domestic respondents and less than 20 per cent for international respondents' are aware of Indigenous tourism experiences available to them. 'Preferences for Indigenous tourism experiences declined to 12 per cent and intention/visit to 2 per cent'. Also, the researchers found that domestic visitors have little interest in Indigenous tourism.

I hope that readers will see from this book that Indigenous tourism offers opportunities to learn about another side of Australia, away from the mainstream attractions, and to have great fun in the process.

It is important to consider what tourists are looking for. Some people want short, relatively inexpensive, urban activities. This applies particularly to mainstream tour groups. Other types of tourism, such as adventure, art, cultural and environmental tourism, attract far smaller numbers of visitors, but these are the types of tourist attractions run by most Indigenous operators.

The researchers found that businesses can tailor their tour to suit particular groups. For instance, if an Indigenous tourism business wants to be included in a Chinese tour company's itinerary, the operators should produce an 'Aboriginal cultural show; bush tucker/story telling; guided nature/environment tours with Indigenous guide'. The researchers also advised that the venues should be 'located in close proximity to major cities/ urban areas, have a brochure and interpretation provided in Chinese', and offer souvenir and shopping opportunities. Indeed, there are such offerings to tourists in or near cities and towns. Many Indigenous operators in rural and remote areas would find it impossible to achieve all of the points suggested in the report.

Indigenous Business Australia (IBA) is using the information contained in this important report to inform its engagement with Indigenous tourism operators and the advice it provides on product development, particularly to assist potential tourism operators to better understand the domestic and international tourism market. The full report is available from the IBA website at www.iba.gov.au.

The research by Dr Lisa Ruhanen and her colleagues has also had an impact on improving government support for the Indigenous tourism sector. IBA, a government statutory body set up with the purpose of investing in Indigenous businesses, improved its Indigenous Tourism Champions Program thanks, in part, to the report. In 2013, it linked more Indigenous tourism operators to tourism industry expert mentors – from fifteen businesses in 2011–2012 to thirty-seven in 2012–2013. It also provided matched funding so Indigenous tourism operators can participate in trade events and access marketing and other business development services. Although these steps are small, they are essential if Indigenous tourism ventures are to achieve greater success in the future.

WHAT IF YOUR GUIDE IS NOT INDIGENOUS?

Aboriginal and Torres Strait Islander guides are employed at many places, especially in national parks that have joint management schemes with the Traditional Owners, such as Kakadu National Park and the Uluru–Kata Tjuta National Park, and at experiences offered by Indigenous-owned companies. However, it is unlikely that you will have an Indigenous guide at most popular tourist attractions. Instead, your guide will usually be a young white Australian. Also, it is sometimes the case that the guides will not mention Aboriginal history and culture at all, or, if they do, they sometimes repeat degrading stereotypes.

In 1997, two Hawai'ian women visited Australia. One was Mahealani Kahau, an important Hawai'ian cultural leader, who came to attend the Australian Reconciliation Convention in Naarm/Melbourne, and the other was her sister. Mahealani told me that her sister had taken a bus to northern Australia because she wanted to meet Aboriginal people in communities there. She was deeply shocked by what she saw, Mahealani said, but even more so when the bus driver, who acted as a guide, repeatedly made extremely racist statements throughout the trip. When she objected, the driver threw her off the bus and she had to find other means to return to Melbourne.

When I worked in Central Australia in the 1980s, visitors told me that tour guides would tell 'jokes' about the 'inferior' status of Aboriginal people.

Here's one: 'How do you make a gin squash? You run her over with your road train.' For those initiated into Australian everyday racism, 'gin' is a racist term for an Aboriginal woman. A road train is a truck towing one or more trailers and is used in rural and remote areas of Australia to transport goods. Other jokes are too crude to retell here.

These stories are not common now, although I do receive emails regularly with extraordinarily racist diatribes. The Australian reconciliation movement has brought about changes in attitudes and many racist ideas and habits are being recognised as such and are no longer tolerated in more and more social settings. Whereas in the past, Aboriginal people were despised and discriminated against, and excluded from Australian society, reconciliation has enabled many Australians to accept Aboriginal people as a part of Australian life without the fear and anger that typified earlier attitudes – at least for many Australians. Indigenous events, art exhibitions, films and television programs, as well as the National Indigenous Television service, and tourism experiences have led to greater understanding and awareness of Aboriginal and Torres Strait Islander cultures.

In some parts of Australia, however, rather than the experience of Mahealani's sister, you may find that there is absolutely no information about Aboriginal and Torres Strait Islander cultures and history available for tourists.

In 2017, I received an email from an Australian woman who visited Tasmania. This island state across the Bass Strait is infamous for the vicious campaign by British troops from 1824 to 1831, called the Black Wars in some history books, aimed at eradicating Tasmania's entire Indigenous population.[112] They almost succeeded, but you will hear nothing of this genocide from a guide in Tasmania. Historians still debate whether the Black Wars should be defined as an act of genocide. Governor Arthur formed 'roving parties' of civilians to capture Tasmanian Aboriginal People, offering them a reward of five pounds for each adult and two pounds for each child. The resistance was awe-inspiring. In April 1828, Governor Arthur was forced to defend his colony against the silent guerrillas who attacked the settlers ruthlessly and without warning. He declared martial law and made it illegal for Aboriginal people to go into any British settlement. Seventy years after the arrival of the British, the bloody wars came to an end in 1873. By that time, the sealers and whalers from the northern hemisphere, many from Cornwall, had already wreaked murderous havoc, especially on the smaller islands.[113]

My correspondent wrote:

> *I am currently holidaying in Tasmania for the first time (I live in mainland Australia), and am visiting many iconic historical and wilderness areas,*

on occasions on guided tours. What has appalled me is the (almost all) negation in tourist booklets and from tour guides, of information regarding Aboriginal Australians during first contact and beyond.

Although I have questioned tour guides about specific areas relating to the first peoples and their experiences, I have been stonewalled and in one instance told ... you do not want to know. Actually, I did want to know and responded accordingly. In another instance on the former penal colony of Sara Island, I was informed that the experiences of Aboriginal peoples during that time could not be spoken about, however there were places on this island that were restricted due to significant cultural Aboriginal heritage (good, re the latter).

Whilst I have furthered my knowledge about the experiences of convicts and their colonial masters, I remain frustrated at the omissions, bordering on negation of the real history of contact, by the rhetoric of the tourist industry.

What has been alluded to in rhetoric, is that contact history stories, are not to be told by non-Aboriginal people. Is this the case? If so, why doesn't the government allocate funding to have Aboriginal Australian guides contest and enrich the rhetoric, with Aboriginal truths?

I feel very uncomfortable in Tasmania because of the complete suppression of this history by the settlers. My limited access to the responses of the palawa – or Tasmanian Aboriginal People – is via palawa academics and artists. Photographer Ricky Maynard, artists and academics Julie Gough and Greg Lehman, and medical leader Ian Anderson have educated me about lives lived in the shadow of their terrible history with dignity and intellectual rigour. There are many excellent books on the history of Tasmania, and many of them confront the genocide. Particularly impressive is Cassandra Pybus' *Truganini: Journey through the Apocalypse* (Allen & Unwin, 2020).

The pall of the genocide in Tasmania is a visceral burden and its impacts are felt in many ways.

In August 2022, the Hobart City Council resolved to remove a colonial monument of the highly contentious character William Crowther, a surgeon who stole an Aboriginal skull from the town morgue. Paul Daley tells the story:

Crowther was a surgeon and honorary medical officer in Hobart in 1869 when Lanne – a well-liked whaler (and husband of Truganini, the famous nuenonne leader) – died. Lanne and Truganini were understood at the time to be 'the last full-blooded Tasmanians', so his skeleton was of great value to scientists and naturalists. A veritable bidding war over the rights to his body erupted between Crowther (on behalf of the Royal College of Surgeons in London) and representatives of the Royal Society of Tasmania.

Crowther lost. Angered, he and his son snuck into the morgue in the middle of the night, decapitated Lanne's corpse, peeled back his skin to remove the skull and replaced it with that of another corpse in the morgue. He then sewed the face back on and walked out. Lanne's hands and feet were removed by another surgeon to prevent Crowther from returning and nabbing the whole skeleton. His remains were never reunited, and their whereabouts are unknown.

Despite being held responsible for meddling with the corpse, Crowther went on to rise through the political ranks and, in death, was memorialised in bronze and sandstone paid for by public subscription. There is, of course, no statue of Lanne in Hobart.[114]

Crowther was memorialised in 1889 a few years after his death for his 'political and professional service to the colony' of Van Diemen's Land. For decades, palawa People have objected to the offence caused by this monument, located in Franklin Square in the city. It has taken more than a century for Lanne's right to dignity to be observed.

This is too often the challenge of travelling through Indigenous Australia: deciphering the deceit and outright lies about the Aboriginal presence and absence and seeking out Indigenous people for the story. Occasionally, I have met locals from the settler population who will talk about the history of their area, but the norm is the triumphalist colonial history about 'brave white pioneers'. The fate of Aboriginal people is rarely mentioned, and if it is, the accounts are often brief and inaccurate.

It is best to read the histories on these matters. There is a growing body of rigorous and honest history about the fate of the palawa People and too little space to recommend them all. The best I have read include the list I recommend below. The historians who doggedly told the story of Aboriginal people have been persecuted and hounded for doing so. Henry Reynolds, Lyndall Ryan and a growing body of scholars persist, however. If you are not a reader, there are DVDs, and I highly recommend *First Australians*, an eight-episode series on the history of Aboriginal Peoples since British occupation, and *The Australian Wars*.

- Henry Reynolds, *Fate of a Free People* (Penguin Books Australia, 1995)
- Lyndall Ryan, *Tasmanian Aborigines. A History since 1803* (Allen & Unwin, 2012)
- Cassandra Pybus, *Truganini: Journey through the Apocalypse* (Allen & Unwin, 2020)

- Cassandra Pybus, *Community of Thieves* (Minerva Australia, 1992)
- Ronnie Summers and Helen Gee, *Ronnie: Tasmanian Songman* (Magabala Books, 2009)

Gourmet food and culinary tourism

The high quality of Australian produce makes gourmet tourism experiences very appealing. Mark Olive, aka The Black Olive, was one of the first people to make it easy for tourists to sample and enjoy Indigenous food. This Bundjalung man is Australia's most famous Indigenous chef, and his cooking is highly regarded nationally. His television programs and corporate catering experiences introduced Australians and visitors to the world of wild bush foods and the experience of bush foods in gourmet cooking. Mark's company, Black Olive Catering, based in Naarm/Melbourne, is sought out for major events all around the country and his series *The Outback Cafe* is watched around the world. In his role as the Outback Academy Ambassador – Hospitality Programs, Mark has helped many Indigenous people to train as chefs and he has attracted chefs from around the world to experience Australian wild, or bush, food. Chefs looking for exciting new ingredients were not disappointed. Even Heston Blumenthal has experienced Indigenous wild food.

Josh Whiteland, owner–operator of Koomal Dreaming, runs foodie tours and bush-food walks on Wadandi and Bibbulmun Country, Western Australia

Another Indigenous chef is Clayton Donovan, the only hatted Indigenous chef. He is the star of his *Wild Kitchen* television program. Clayton lives in the Nambucca Valley, northern New South Wales, and brings Indigenous ingredients, both foraged and farmed, to a wide audience at festivals and events.

Mark Olive worked with the Indigenous bush foods farm Roelands Village, in the south-west of Western Australia, to bring their produce to a wide market. Roelands Village is a working farm, producing native bush foods, and a nationally significant heritage site set in a majestic environment surrounded by the rolling Seven Hills. It has accommodation, conference and catering facilities, and is a great food and wine destination. Formerly known as Roelands Mission, it was an institution for the Stolen Generations. From the 1940s to the 1970s, around 500 Aboriginal children were taken to the mission. Now some of those people are transforming Roelands Village into a place of social business, education and healing. In 2004, the Indigenous Land Corporation bought the property on behalf of Woolkabunning Kiaka Incorporated, representing the former residents, and its purpose now is to promote the overall development of the community.

Josh 'Koomal' Whiteland, a Wadandi man, operates Koomal Dreaming at Yallingup, west of Dunsborough in the south-west of Western Australia. Josh offers cultural tours and gives visitors the opportunity to taste native foods, learn about bush medicine and explore the beautiful Margaret River region, three hours south-west of Perth. Sampling the fresh wild food from the sea and the land that Josh knows so much about, as well as swimming at the pristine beaches and walking through the natural environment makes Koomal Dreaming a special experience. Josh took part in the first Margaret River Gourmet Escape in November 2012, along with some internationally renowned Australian chefs. He introduced the chefs and other visitors to the Noongar People's calendar of six seasons and the abundant wild food of the area, including edible flora, kangaroo, emu, abalone and squid. This major annual food festival is a popular attraction for gourmands.

Immersive cultural experiences

The Garma Festival is one of the best cultural festivals in Australia. It has been held since 1999. The festival was cancelled in 2020 and 2021 because of concerns about the difficulty of coping with the potential for positive COVID-19 cases in a remote area with extremely limited medical facilities. The Garma Festival has offered a unique combination of traditional Yolŋu ceremonies, held every afternoon, and a forum that pre-

Dancers from Yolŋu clans throughout north-east Arnhem Land take turns to perform at the buŋgul, each adorned in their respective colours and clan designs

COVID-19 attracted a gathering of 2500 political and business leaders from across the globe to share Yolŋu knowledge and culture and to discuss the most pressing issues facing Indigenous Australians.

Coordinated and programmed by the Yothu Yindi Foundation (YYF), the proceeds are used to improve the lives of Yolŋu People in north-east Arnhem Land through education and community development programs. Garma incorporates visual art, ancient storytelling, dance – including the famous nightly buŋgul, or traditional dancing – and music. As well, important forums are held and education and training programs relevant to cultural tourism, craft, governance and youth leadership are run during the festival. Garma is presented by the YYF in early August each year. YYF is a not-for-profit Aboriginal corporation with tax deductibility gift recipient status.

Tourism in the outback: the landscapes of Indigenous Australia

The ancient landforms in the Gariwerd Grampians National Park date from the Gondwana period, and it shows. These mountains and valleys look and feel old. And they are: about 180 million years old. This is a unique place because of its geological history and because it is rich in Aboriginal history and culture. The Traditional Owners are the Jardwadjali and Djab Wurrung Peoples. Most of the rock-art sites in Victoria are in the Gariwerd, with some dating back 22,000 years. Their Traditional Owners are still involved in Gariwerd and maintain the culture and the stories of the land. Like other Aboriginal groups, the Jardwadjali and Djab Wurrung Peoples have six distinct seasons that have an impact on the times when plants flower and fruit, and on animal behavioural patterns.

15
Cultural Awareness for Visitors

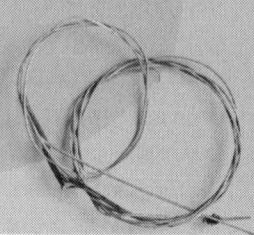

The Aboriginal way of welcoming visitors to their homelands is often a very simple affair, with just a few words of welcome, sometimes in the local language and in English. Some groups light a fire, wetting special leaves such as ti-tree or gum to make a fine smoke and ask visitors to walk through the smoke, while others splash water on their guests. Occasionally, more elaborate ceremonies are held, which involve singing traditional songs. Participating in these rituals is the best way of showing respect for Aboriginal and Torres Strait Islander hosts and guides. Showing respect for Aboriginal and Torres Strait Islander Peoples is often explained in unnecessarily complicated language in cross-cultural awareness programs. As travellers you will probably have met people from many different cultures and usually you will find that it is easy to talk to people in a normal tone of voice and say the usual greetings, such as, 'Good morning. How are you?' Or, 'Hello, my name is…' Also, you will learn a great deal by listening to and observing what your hosts and guides say and do.

In most of Indigenous Australia, English or a form of English is spoken. So there is no need to buy a phrase book that provides translations of everyday expressions such as 'hello' and 'where does the bus leave from?' – if, indeed, phrase books for travellers in Indigenous languages are available. I think it is more fun to get to know people and ask them questions such as, 'How do you say "hello" in your language?'

As I have explained, there are about 120 Indigenous languages still spoken in Australia. This astonishing diversity of languages is one reason why there aren't many, if any, language books for travellers or many other books and guides about Indigenous languages for the general reader.

Many Indigenous people were prevented from speaking their mother tongues during the assimilation period and were often punished for doing so. That history combined with residual racism has resulted in a great reticence on the part of Indigenous Australians to speak their languages except in their own social settings. Fortunately, there are many grammars

Many remote communities use English as a third, sometimes fourth, language (photo Wayne Quilliam)

and dictionaries published by linguists and language revival programs, but this does not make it any easier for the visitor to engage in basic conversations in local languages.

Showing respect for your host is as simple as trying to say some words in that person's language, if you meet an Indigenous person who is willing to share their language.

Speaking a few words of a First language is a great way to make friends, too. Your teacher will want to share more if you show a keen interest. Increasingly, many Indigenous tour guides are very proud and happy to share words about the flora and fauna and their traditional environmental knowledge, such as the names of seasons and weather patterns, and the behaviour of plants and animals during those times. The training provided by Indigenous ranger programs has enabled people to discuss their traditional knowledge openly and without fear.

Nura Gunyu provides experiences ranging from bush food walks to cooking demonstrations in the Budawang bush, New South Wales

Questions

You need to know that not all questions are welcome, even if you are sincerely interested in finding out more about a place or a cultural point. In some areas of Australia, Aboriginal people will not respond to questions. Either the question makes no sense culturally, or it breaches local customs. Often an Aboriginal person – whether a man or a woman – is not permitted to discuss local customs without the permission of their group or clan. Instead of saying, 'I am not authorised to answer that question,' an Aboriginal person will remain silent or answer another question. This is still the Aboriginal way in many areas today.

Asking too many questions can be seen as intrusive, even though meant with goodwill. Some trained guides and rangers are accustomed to the inquisitive visitor and deal with questions in a way that the visitor expects of a commercial guide. Aboriginal hosts are not always trained, and even if they are, will not bend their local rules.

A good way to get a conversation going is with an observation about what you are being shown.

For example, if you are walking by a forest at sunset and the trees are alive with flying foxes, or bats, you might say, 'That's a lot of bats. I have never seen so many.' This might start a discussion about the bats, the forest they live in, the season and local customs. Or not, but if you are in a different culture, such differences are to be expected.

When to use names of people and places and when not to

Visitors using Aboriginal and Torres Strait Islander names of people and places is not a problem when it is clear that this is allowed because your host has used the names, or they appear on signs. Some Aboriginal and Torres Strait Islander names are difficult to pronounce, but it is always worth trying. You may get it right, and no one will be offended if you tried and didn't say it correctly. There are rules about names that cannot be used, but this practice is usually confined to the members of an Aboriginal society. Visitors are not expected to follow these rules unless the hosts have explained that particular names may not be spoken.

In many areas, when a person dies, the name and images of that person cannot be used at all until the family of the deceased makes a public declaration that the taboo has been lifted. In the case of famous Aboriginal people, it may be some years before this happens. For famous Aboriginal musicians, an elliptical way of referring to the deceased will be used, such as 'that lead singer of the Yothu Yindi band'. Place names that are the same as, or similar to, a deceased person's name will not be used by Aboriginal people in the areas where these traditions are followed. For some years, Alice Springs was referred to as Kumunjayi by local people because of the death of a woman with the same first name as the town.

Television stations and websites in Australia that broadcast or publish photographs and videos of Aboriginal people provide warnings at the beginning of the content so that Aboriginal and Torres Strait Islander people will be aware that they are likely to see images of deceased people. These practices have been in place for the last two decades and are commonplace. They show respect for the cultural protocols of the First Australians and help other Australians to understand these cultural differences.

Language rules

In every language in the world there are rules about what is appropriate to say in public. Aboriginal groups may have words that only women are permitted to use, or that only men are permitted to use. There are words that are not allowed to be spoken in public but are confined to ceremonies. The esoteric languages of many Aboriginal societies are used only in ceremonial or ritual contexts. Visitors may have read in books by anthropologists about Aboriginal cultural practices such as rituals. In many cases, it is not polite or acceptable to speak about these matters in public.

When in doubt, don't ask questions about anything that you think might be sensitive, and do not share what you have read in an obscure anthropological text.

I was in Paris many years ago at an international conference on Indigenous cultures when it was the fashion in French universities for students to interpret the 'meanings' of Aboriginal rock art through the lens of European psychological theories about sexual deviation. On a table in the foyer of the conference centre were piles of various documents published by a local publisher. I flipped through a few and my skin crawled. The texts bore no resemblance whatsoever to the meanings of the rock art as explained by the Traditional Owners. One of these texts stated that the art referred to a particular sexual deviation, when in fact the rock art represented a Lightning Ancestor who rouses the world during the monsoon season with thunder and flashes of light. None of the students had been to Australia, and clearly there was a theoretical formula imposed by a Freudian anthropologist in a faraway Parisian classroom. My advice: Don't try out European theories on Aboriginal people.

Photographs and videos

You must ask permission before filming or taking photographs of people, especially children. Aboriginal and Torres Strait Islander people do not feel comfortable with visitors taking photographs or videos of them or their family members without explicit permission. Aboriginal hosts at public events and tourist events will make it clear if photography is permitted.

There have been a number of legal cases involving unauthorised photography, commercial use of photographs in publications without permission, and the distribution of photographs and videos. The use of unauthorised photography and video on social media platforms is also becoming a problem, and complaints from Aboriginal people have been acted on by police.

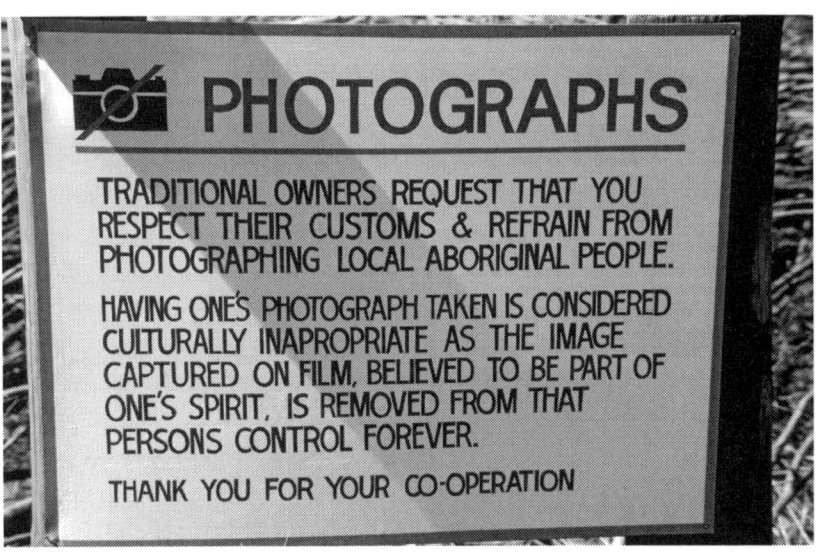

A sign near Uluru asking visitors to respect the traditions of the Anangu People

Signs and published cultural rules and protocols

Because of the great diversity, culturally and linguistically, in Indigenous Australia, many groups publish their own rules and protocols. A good example is the 'Protocols and Conduct' section published on the website of the Garma Festival hosted by the Yolŋu People of north-east Arnhem Land in the Northern Territory. It is a thorough and useful guide to the rules and protocols in the area. There are some differences from area to area, so keep in mind that something that is acceptable in one area or at one event might not be elsewhere.

You are guests on Yolŋu land and entering Yolŋu time.

Yolŋu perceptions, priorities and preoccupations are different from those of mainstream Australia.

Be patient and try to leave at home your expectations of how things are learnt and how events should run. Traditionally Yolŋu learn by observation, by looking and listening. Asking too many questions can be inappropriate. When you have questions, choose them carefully and thoughtfully.

Respect people's personal space, particularly in the camping areas and each guest's tent. Sticking to the walking paths provided is important.

We ask that guests respect the community and stay within the festival areas and camping zones. Guests should NOT leave the Gulkula site on their own and should only walk along specifically marked trails. This is also for your own safety and wellbeing as we have wild buffalo wander this country and organisers spend considerable effort in monitoring their trails before Garma each year. Please ensure someone knows where you are travelling around the site. Avoid strolling around and visiting Yolŋu campsites unless specifically invited and accompanied by Yolŋu.

Please exercise courtesy and sensitivity when taking photographs, and posting images to social media. Always seek the permission of your subjects if taking close-ups, or photographs of small groups. We kindly ask guests not to bring professional cameras with long lenses to Garma.

Example of warnings displayed in respect for Aboriginal and Torres Strait Islander Peoples

> *Treat the old people with the greatest of respect – they hold the knowledge and the power.*
>
> *Dress conservatively and be sun-wise. Too much skin on display draws inadvertent attention and is not appropriate for this event. Schools attending the festival should advise their students of this policy. Our dress standards also protect our participants from harsh weather conditions. Plan a sensible and modest wardrobe, knee length skirts/dresses/shorts, covered shoes and include a hat to protect you from the elements.*[115]

You might wonder how practical advice about wearing hats and covered shoes might be cultural protocols. This is a good question. Aboriginal people become very upset if their visitors are injured or become sick while visiting their homeland, because they feel a great sense of responsibility for visitors. They might think that they have not done their job well as responsible Traditional Landowners by reassuring the spirits of the land about their visitors. Other Traditional Owners may blame them for not paying attention if someone becomes sick or injured while visiting. The cultural belief in the power of the spirits in places is still very strong in many parts of Australia.

In November 2017, the Chairman of the Uluṟu–Kata Tjuṯa National Park Board of Management, Sammy Wilson, an Aṉangu Elder and Traditional Owner of the land, announced his intention to the board that the climbing of Uluṟu should cease. Sammy Wilson's full statement to the board can be read on the Parks Australia website.[116]

In 2019, the Traditional Owners of the Uluṟu–Kata Tjuṯa National Park were finally able to achieve their long-held desire to stop visitors climbing Uluṟu. Their representatives on the National Park Management Board worked with the board to announce well in advance their intention to close the climb. In 2019, the board announced that it would close the climb to the top of Uluṟu on 26 October 2019. The board's public statement said:

> *The date of 26 October 1985 is significant to the park's traditional owners, as it was the date the park was handed back to them.*
>
> *In 2010 the Board committed to giving the tourism industry at least 18 months' notice to adjust any itineraries or marketing strategies. With their decision to close on 26 October 2019, people can continue to climb if they choose and it is safe to do so, for the next two years if they wish.*[117]

Forty years before, they had expressed their desire to stop the climbing of this sacred place, but the opposition was extreme at that time, as was the opposition to the hand back of their land under the terms of the *Aboriginal Land Rights (Northern Territory) Act 1976*.

Once they had received title to their land, they leased it to the Commonwealth to create this national park to allow access to other Australians under the management of the Management Board. They had given up their rights to their land – any say about who could come onto their land and their right as owners as to its use – in order to have legal title. Even though the Federal Court judge who heard their case as the Aboriginal Land Rights Commissioner recommended the return of their land to them, the Commonwealth Government would only return it if they agreed to the complex leasing arrangements to created this Commonwealth controlled National Park.

They placed a sign at the commencement of the climbing track established many years before by non-Indigenous people. The sign stated:

> Please don't climb.
> We, the Anangu traditional owners, have this to say
> Uluru is sacred in our culture. It is a place of great knowledge.
> Under our traditional law climbing is not permitted.
> This is our home.
> As custodians, we are responsible for your safety and behaviour.
> Too many people do not listen to our message.
> Too many people have died or been hurt causing great sadness.
> We worry about you and we worry about your family.
> Please don't climb.
> We invite you to walk around the base and discover a deeper understanding of this place.

In late October 2019, hundreds of visitors lined up to climb Uluru for the last time, some behaving in disgusting ways to show their disrespect for the Traditional Owners. On 25 October, the last person 'permitted to ascend Uluru ... reached the base of the climb.' Rangers permanently closed the climb at 4:00 pm at Australian Central Standard Time and stopped the hundreds still waiting from proceeding. The Traditional Owners celebrated at the base of the rock as a new sign was set up notifying visitors the climb was permanently closed. Australian law had finally respected their wishes.[118]

Rarely can Aboriginal Traditional Owners set out their protocols as clearly as the Yolŋu in their Garma protocols or the Anangu in closing the climb to the top of Uluru. In some places the Traditional Owners assert their rights to state what should and should not happen on their land, which they own under Australian law. In other areas, even when the Traditional Owners

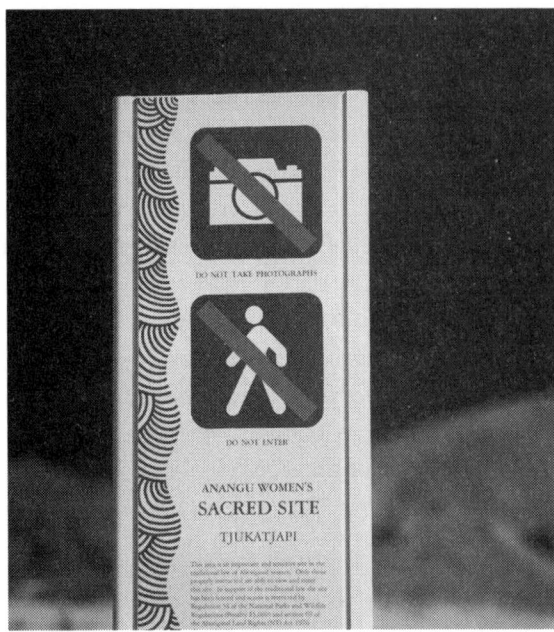

Sign erected at Tjukatjapi, Uluru, Northern Territory

legally own the land, they might not have the means to erect signage about their protocols.

In many places there are hidden dangers that Traditional Owners and custodians know about, but non-Indigenous guides are unaware of. When rules and protocols are explained in signs and publications, everyone should observe them for their own safety.

In most national parks and conservation areas, government authorities install signage for visitors' safety. In north Australia, for example, there are the ubiquitous signs warning about crocodiles and the dangers of swimming as sharks, stingray, stone fish, gropers, fresh and saltwater crocodiles, sea snakes, eels, poisonous jellyfish, 'stingers', and other dangerous creatures inhabit the seas, rivers and waterholes. In other parts of Australia, Aboriginal custodians and government authorities are particularly concerned about the dangers of drowning, people being washed out to sea and bites or injuries from the many dangerous creatures. In view of these and other hazards, signs warning against swimming are common in some areas and should always be taken seriously.

There are many protocols that are not mentioned in tourist guides. I have learnt about fishing protocols, for instance, from Traditional Owners. In northern Australia, when Traditional Owners have taken me on fishing trips, they would speak to the ancestral spirits or hold the fishing line over a smoky fire and tell me a few rules. It is forbidden to gut fish near water and leave the entrails near bodies of water or on beaches. Clearly this is a practical safety rule because of the constant presence of saltwater crocodiles and wild boar. The smell of fish entrails will attract them very quickly and present an immediate danger. I never sleep or camp near water for the same reason. There are religious rules about this practice as well: it is an offence to the ancestral spirits to leave the remains of fish or other animals near water bodies. There is the constant concern of Traditional Owners that fresh water should not be contaminated, and the traditional way to drink from scarce fresh water sources, especially in arid areas, is to kneel at the edge of the water and sip it, or carefully fill a container without contaminating the water. Most visitors will not encounter these situations, but if you are travelling in the outback, it is good to know the basic Aboriginal rules, for your own safety as well as out of respect for the Aboriginal custodians.

In all cases around Australia, my advice is: Do not ignore the safety signs.

16
Undoing Racist Australia

Trigger warning: This chapter looks at racism towards Indigenous people.

I often find myself talking to other Aboriginal people about their latest experiences of racism. We compare our experiences, and we sympathise. We talk too much about racism because there is too much racism. The harm that racism causes us and our families is indescribable. I struggle to find the words, but I must start with the permanent pain that is left in my psyche by the hateful words and deeds of people who believe that I am a member of an 'inferior race'. Not just any 'inferior race' but that one that white Australia has been at war with for nearly 250 years. It's not just a psychological war, although it is that too. Every day I fear that another Aboriginal person, maybe a woman, a man, or a child, has been killed. I know that there will never be justice for them.

What I have learnt is that there is no simple way to explain why some people are racist and why they commit acts of racism. We suffer these insults all too frequently. I know just how wearing and sickening the 'microaggressions' or 'casual' insulting statements made in conversation or in passing are. Their long-term impact lives with me. I remember vividly the insults from 50 years ago, 20 years ago, and yesterday.

Do racists remember their insults to us? What do they feel about their unjustified attacks on me, and people like me? How do people who throw bananas at Eddie Betts or compare Adam Goodes to an ape justify these blatant acts of racism? They don't. It is impossible to find out why they act like this because they do not and will not give an account of themselves, other than to make incomprehensible excuses: Eddie McGuire's response to his racist references to Adam Goodes do not make sense.

Most people deny that they are racist and claim that what they said was not meant to offend. Most say they 'don't see colour'. Yet, I know from many encounters like this that they have a very clear sense that I am Aboriginal and that their statement was directed at me and my Aboriginality. They cannot see that their lack of logic and denials are misconceived and that they form a larger pattern of contradictions and misconceptions. Most such people are repeat offenders.

There are others who try to overcome their racism, to think about the ways that racism is expressed, and work to prevent racism in our workplaces and public spaces.

Being Aboriginal in Australia involves the constant presence of racism and the quest to find ways to limit its impact. Racism is the norm for Aboriginal people and other people of colour in Australia. Because it is customary, racists fail to see it.

It is as though they harbour a deep fear of racial contamination by being in the presence of an Aboriginal person. When she grabs her handbag because she thinks I might steal it, I wonder if she has any understanding of history: white people stole our land and our children. When he asks who wrote this for me, I know that very little has changed. I remember my years as an undergraduate at the Australian National University in the 1970s and early 1980s, where I was regularly physically assaulted and abused for being Aboriginal, and my years at the Macquarie University in the 1990s writing my doctoral thesis under the glare of racist condescension. For still far too many white Australians, Aboriginal people remain the enemy, always cast as inferior and incompetent. With some notable exceptions, non-Anglo immigrants have acquired the same attitudes. It's as if they believe that to be the right kind of Australian one must hate Aboriginal people, even if they themselves are reviled.

Still, it is encouraging that there is a large and growing minority who recognise and understand the evil of racism and want to do something to stop it.

Race and racism

There are many definitions of 'race'. It is important to rely on reputable sources. *Britannica* defines it:

> race, the idea that the human species is divided into distinct groups on the basis of inherited physical and behavioural differences. Genetic studies in the late 20th century refuted the existence of biogenetically distinct races, and scholars now argue that 'races' are cultural interventions reflecting specific attitudes and beliefs that were imposed on different populations in the wake of western European conquests beginning in the 15th century.[119]

Some of the historical developments that led to the idea of 'race' as it was understood by its most vociferous proponents, including Adolf Hitler, will be discussed further, along with the distinctly Australian versions of this evil idea.

There are many definitions of racism, and again, it is important to rely on reputable sources. The legal definition in the *Racial Discrimination Act 1975* implements Australia's commitment to the United Nations Convention on the Elimination of All Forms of Racism and declares that racial discrimination is illegal in Australia. The Act promotes equality before the law for all people regardless of race, colour or national or ethnic origin. It is illegal to do anything that treats people differently or infringes their 'human rights or fundamental freedom in the political, economic, social, cultural or any other field of public life'.

All Australians should be familiar with these prohibitions on racism, and yet the frequent acts of racism tell us that there is either ignorance of them or a wilful flouting of these laws. The most important sections are 9–8 in the *Racial Discrimination Act*.

Racial hygiene

The notion of 'racial hygiene' is deeply rooted in Australian ideas about Aboriginal people. It was applied in the Australian colonies and continued into the twentieth century under the guise of policies of 'protection' and 'assimilation'.[120]

This concept adopted now disreputable ideas about human biology, heredity and 'race'. It is a politically extreme variation of eugenics that held sway from the nineteenth century and lasted long after the Holocaust when Nazism adopted this idea to exterminate the Jewish people.

The Nazis established legal and institutional measures to uphold 'racial hygiene' to exclude anyone deemed hereditarily 'less valuable' or 'racially foreign'.[121] Mass murder and sterilisation were the primary methods, but to implement their war crimes, the Nazi regime established a genealogical records office and labelled and segregated all Jews, and eventually sent millions to die in death camps.

The 'dying race'

The belief in the inevitable and 'natural' extinction of Aboriginal people is deeply rooted in the beliefs that make up the peculiar style of Australian racism. This was a convenient mythology to hide the widespread murder and other atrocities committed against Aboriginal people, and to provide an excuse for protectionism and segregation. Newspapers, politicians and professors peddled the ideas of Social Darwinism and the 'natural' survival of the fittest, while the frontiersmen murdered tens of thousands of Aboriginal people on their behalf.

Sometimes this was cloaked in euphemism: 'Smoothing the pillow of

Laura Dance Festival (photo Wayne Quilliam)

the dying race' was one that was regularly used. Jennie Carter, Coordinator Information and Cultural Resources, Aboriginal Affairs Department in Western Australia, wrote in a discussion among historians about the phrase: 'Smoothing the dying pillow is a fascinating example of the catchphrase that is often quoted without attribution'.[122] And yet, it is clear that this was a concept in common usage in the late nineteenth and the first half of the twentieth century.

She cites the anthropologist A.P. Elkin (who was a keen participant in the racial categorisation of Aboriginal People) in *The Australian Aborigines* (first published in 1938):

> we find as early as 1843 some sentimental regret was expressed for the tribal remnants. A writer in that year wrote in the New South Wales Magazine; 'I wish to see our means applied to rendering the current of events by which the grave is closing on our sable brethren, smooth and regular.' 'Smooth the Dying Pillow' became the comfortable rationalisation to justify the passing of a 'stone age people' confronted by civilisation ...[123]

Then there are the words of economic historian, C.D. Rowley, in *The Destruction of Aboriginal Society* (published in 1972):

> The way had been prepared for those who spoke of the passing of the Aboriginal and the need to smooth (as cheaply as possible) his dying pillow.[124]

And more recently, Anna Haebich in *For Their Own Good*, published in 1992, wrote '[Premier Sir John] Forrest played a major role in the formulation of the protectionist policy of "smoothing the dying pillow" adopted in Western Australia during the 1880s.'[125]

The *Cairns Post* on 5 May, 1925, under the headline, 'Our Aboriginals, Smoothing the Pillow of the Dying Race. Missionary's Efforts' reported:

> Rev. J. S. Needham, speaking at Holy Trinity Anglican Church, Balaclava, said it was twenty years since four white men were hanged at Maitland gaol for the massacre of thirty blacks. So far as he could ascertain not a single white man had since suffered death for killing blacks, though large numbers had been shot by whites. Some were poisoned through arsenic being mixed with their food.[126]

Possibly it was too late to save the blacks, but at least they could smooth the pillow of the dying race. 'Australia's treatment of the aboriginals continues to be a shameful blot on our fair name. I have taken a solemn oath,' added Mr Needham, 'before people who have a conscience, and I shall work to have that blot wiped out. I am going through the length and breadth of Australia to see if I can arouse a sense of shame amongst the people of Australia.

'There are about 72,000 blacks left in the Commonwealth and if they are to be saved, they must be segregated, for it has become an axiom that the black man of Australia cannot live among white men.'[127]

Dehumanising Aboriginal people and people of colour

People of colour have been and are continually labelled and treated like animals and regarded as subhuman. The most egregious example is the historical displays of Aboriginal people in zoos.[128] At least 20 Aboriginal people were kidnapped from Palm Island in Queensland and put on display in human zoos across Europe and North America until at least 1940. They were a few of the tens of thousands from the colonies in Africa and Australia who suffered this degrading fate.[129] These human zoos served to inculcate racism:

> The exhibition of men, with animals or alone, in locations usually reserved for animals, such as zoological gardens, is hardly an anodyne act. And their presentation as specimens of un-evolved and uneducable 'races' played a major part in laying down the solid foundations of a popular racism.[130]

'White privilege'

White privilege is the term used to describe how white people continue to derive advantages from racism. They need not be aware of this or not. Individuals may not be racist, but they can still benefit from systems that privilege white faces and voices.[131]

There are many major institutions that accumulated wealth from the enslavement of black people. Harvard University is an example. In 2019, Harvard President Lawrence Bacow formed a committee to investigate slavery in its history. The report uncovered its roots in slavery leading to proposals for reparations. It found that:

> Harvard faculty and staff enslaved 70 people from the school's founding in 1636 until the banning of slavery in Massachusetts in 1783 ... Enslaved men and women served Harvard presidents and professors and fed and cared for Harvard students ... throughout this period and well into the 19th century, the University and its donors benefited from extensive financial ties to slavery.[132]

This included wealth gained from slave trading, textile manufacturing using cotton harvested by slaves, investments including loans to Caribbean sugar planters, rum distillers, plantation suppliers and cotton manufacturing. The vital economic link between the industrial north and the slaveholding south was described as 'unhallowed alliance between the lords of the lash and the lords of the loom.' Harvard's donors in this period were vital to the University's growth.[133]

Many Australian institutions were established using the money given to slaveowners when slavery was abolished in Britain in 1834. Some early settlers created a slave trade in the colonies, bringing people from Pacific Islands to work under duress.

Even Australian plants have been made memorials to racism. The genus *Banksia* was named after Joseph Banks the naturalist and botanist who accompanied Cook on his voyage. He later advised King George III on colonising Australia and identified Botany Bay as the 'ideal' location for a penal settlement. He too was involved in slavery. He wanted to bring breadfruit plants from the Pacific to the Caribbean to feed slaves more cheaply. He took 30,000 plant specimens from the lands Cook visited back to Britain.

It is difficult to travel anywhere in Australia without finding a place, a memorial, a road, a creek, or a university that does not have a name associated with racists, savage acts of racism committed in the name of white supremacy.

If we think about how non-Indigenous Australians are privileged by racism, we need to remember that before colonisation, the entire country was owned by Aboriginal and Torres Strait Islander Peoples. Their societies had thrived for thousands of years, but they became the target of a continent-wide campaign of violence. Over almost 250 years, the descendants of the First Peoples have been marginalised and impoverished. This terrible history owes its logic to ideas about race and acts of racism. What once belonged to us now belongs to a citizenry that is defined by its history of racism.

Australia's dangerous fiction of race

The idea of Australia was based on a dangerous fiction of an empty land. The fiction of 'race' added to this and took several forms in the new nation in 1901. As a result, Aboriginal people were not recognised in the Constitution, were denied the right to vote, and the first parliament passed legislation to deport Pacific Islanders and ban 'non-whites' (White Australia Policy). This made racism normal; some people were considered lesser humans because of the colour of their skin or their cultural heritage. Scientists in the twentieth century proved that there is no genetic difference between people of different ethnic backgrounds, but racism has endured and remains tangible and measurable.

Racism has many forms and types; its impacts are huge and last for generations. Racism is life-threatening. It impacts on the health of those who are its target. It causes most of the poverty in the world, either directly or indirectly, because of centuries of slavery, indentured labour, colonial conquest, segregation and apartheid. Legal and administrative forms of racism persist in many countries, including Australia.

I will outline these dangerous fictions so that you have the tools to understand why Indigenous Peoples – the First Peoples – are wary of jingoistic descriptions of the nation that exclude us. We are not only deliberately absent from the founding of the nation, but also discriminated against on the grounds of this dangerous fiction of 'race'.

Are you Australian? If your answer is yes, you will need to explain, at least to yourself, what this means.[134] As you consider your understanding of the idea of 'Australia' and what it means to be an Australian citizen, and what this involves, you may educate yourself about the history of Australia.

Why do you need to know this? Let's begin with a summary of a few highly relevant historical events that shaped Australia as a nation and shaped your identity, whether you are aware of this or not. Of course, Australia begins, not in 1770 with Lt James Cook's declaration at 'Possession Island' of British annexation of the eastern half of the continent, nor in 1788 with the First Fleet's arrival in Port Jackson to establish the British penal colony to dispose of criminals and undesirables – but in 1901.

The Australian Constitution drafted during the Australian Wars

On 1 January 1901 the *Australian Constitution Act* came into force on this continent. It was an Act passed by the British House of Commons and signed by Queen Victoria in Britain – the *Commonwealth of Australia Constitution Act 1900*. It has subsequently been amended and since 1988 the British courts are no longer the final court of appeal.[135]

The *Commonwealth of Australia Constitution Act* begins with the handing of a new national identity to the people of the colonies. The Constitution was drafted at a series of conventions in the late 1800s attended by white colonists, all men. They were aware of the violent frontier that moved across the country as the British moved further inland from Sydney, Victoria and Adelaide, and eventually, Brisbane and Perth.

Indigenous filmmaker Rachel Perkins called these conflicts *The Australian Wars* in a three-part documentary series. The most prolific historian of the wars, Henry Reynolds, who fought against Aboriginal people on their own land explained they 'determined the ownership and sovereign control of a

Preparing to march in Sydney on 26 January at the front of Parliament House (photo Wayne Quilliam)

234　Welcome To Country Handbook

whole continent.' In the series, he asked, rhetorically, 'what can be more important than that to us?'[136]

These wars were never declared, and contravened British laws, but had to be won for the settlers to claim Australia. The wars were waged by the British against the First Peoples for 'more than 100 years, from the landing of the First Fleet in 1788 until the 1920s.'[137] Rachel Perkins interviewed expert historians and descendants of the protagonists, and presents evidence of the tactics and strategies used by Aboriginal Peoples in 'defending their land and survival'. Historians Heidi Norman and Anne Maree Payne emphasise that the 'violence was often very well documented', and yet, 'overwhelmingly unmarked, unobserved, save for colonial names: "Blackfellows Bones", "Victory Hill". The silence continues.'[138]

Most Australians remain unaware, or perhaps even wilfully ignorant, of what happened to the First Peoples after 1788 in the British colonies and continued after 1901 in the new nation. It is now estimated that at the time the First Fleet arrived there were about a million people living on this continent; by the time of Federation the Aboriginal population was about a hundred thousand. This demonstrates the enormous death toll of Aboriginal people because of war, murder and disease. In Tasmania and parts of Queensland, this was a campaign of genocide, as Rachel Perkins found in researching the documentary series. Yet the First Peoples survived, the myth of a 'dying race' was a convenient fiction.

This book has canvassed some of that history. This chapter is concerned with the legacy of racism that grew from it. The simple and fantastical idea of an 'inferior race' took hold in accordance with pseudoscientific beliefs about 'race'. The idea of 'aborigines' as a 'race' was written into the Australian Constitution to exclude our peoples from the nation.

What is the meaning of 'race'?

The question must be asked: what is the meaning of 'race'? The answer is simple: there is no evidence of a physical reality which conforms with the concept of 'race'. This understanding is set out in detail in a statement of the American Anthropological Association, which I cite at length below, because of its importance:

> *Historical research has shown that the idea of 'race' has always carried more meanings than mere physical differences; indeed, physical variations in the human species have no meaning except the social ones that humans put on them ... From its inception, this modern concept of 'race' was modelled after an ancient theorem of the Great Chain*

of Being, which posited natural categories on a hierarchy established by God or nature. Thus 'race' was a mode of classification linked specifically to peoples in the colonial situation. It subsumed a growing ideology of inequality devised to rationalise European attitudes and treatment of the conquered and enslaved peoples.

Proponents of slavery in particular during the nineteenth century used 'race' to justify the retention of slavery. The ideology magnified the differences among Europeans, Africans, and Indians, established a rigid hierarchy of socially exclusive categories underscored and bolstered unequal rank and status differences, and provided the rationalization that the inequality was natural or God-given. The different physical traits of African-Americans and Indians became markers or symbols of their status differences.

Early in the 19th century the growing fields of science began to reflect the public consciousness about human differences. Differences among the 'racial' categories were projected to their greatest extreme when the argument was posed that Africans, Indians, and Europeans were separate species, with Africans the least human and closer taxonomically to apes ...

Ultimately 'race' as an ideology about human differences was subsequently spread to other areas of the world. It became a strategy for dividing, ranking, and controlling colonized people used by colonial powers everywhere ... But it was not limited to the colonial situation. In the latter part of the nineteenth century it was employed by Europeans to rank one another and to justify social, economic, and political inequalities among their peoples.

Given what we know about the capacity of normal humans to achieve and function within any culture, we conclude that present-day inequalities between so-called 'racial' groups are not consequences of their biological inheritance but products of historical and contemporary social, economic, educational, and political circumstances.[139]

Despite modern scientific understandings of human genetic and biological variability, in Australia, Aboriginal People have been – and still are – defined tautologically in at least 70 and perhaps up to 100 legislative acts as 'members of the Aboriginal race'. It needs to be said, again, that the 'Aboriginal race' does not exist, except in the racist imagination, our common law, legislation, racist literature and media, in one clause in our constitution (S. 25) and, arguably by the decision of the High Court of Australia with respect to S. 51 (26).

Another important question demands answering: why is the concept of 'race' so fundamental and pervasive in our national polity and politics?

The answer to this question is far more difficult. The notion of 'race' is an invention of the late seventeenth century, arising from the pre-idea based on the Latin *gens* or clan. The notion had its greatest influence in the twentieth century; it was the key idea in world affairs in that twentieth century, along with the conflict between fascism and communism. This idea accounts for the genocides and conflagrations of that century. An estimated six million Jews were exterminated by the administrative and military machinery of a state based on the idea of race, simply because they were defined racially as Jews and undesirable. The process of the balkanisation of the world into 'ethnic groups' in this century is driven by concepts of 'race'. The Holocaust, the Armenian and Rwandan genocides, the Bosnian wars and other horrors of the twentieth and twenty-first century are based on concepts of 'race'. But why?

The concept of race was exploded by the biological sciences in the twentieth century. In the 1950s Francis Crick, J.D. Watson, Maurice Wilkins and Rosalind Franklin added to earlier discoveries about DNA and the human genome, and this new science contributed to the critique of racism. This called into question the assumptions that had informed two centuries of thought.

Following the Second World War, world leaders met to adopt policies to prevent the excesses of race theory. The United Nations was established to further justice, the rule of law, and human rights and freedoms without distinction of race, sex, language or religion.

At the sixth session of the United Nations Economic and Social Council, it was agreed that a program should be adopted to disseminate scientific facts to remove race prejudice. The director-general was instructed to collect and study scientific data and to mount a widespread educational campaign based on these studies. 'The Race Question' (also referred to as the UN Statement of Race of 1950) was the first of four statements UNESCO. The Statement referred to this project as 'one of the most important contributions in the last century to an understanding of race and racialism'. The practical program of action accepted the psychological propositions of the American race relations schools and adopted them to try to remove racial prejudice in the world. The two most influential American intellectuals from this school of thought, Franklin Frazier and Ashley Montagu, explicitly assumed that people would change their minds based on reason and critical thought that:

- an intellectual appreciation of the harm done by race prejudice would educate them into better ways
- stereotypes could be broken by accurate information about 'causes'
- an intellectual attack should be made whenever biological explanations were applied to social phenomena

- penal legislation would ensure successful removal of race prejudice
- success depended upon the transmission of healthy attitudes through children.

The UN education program has had some success, but it has not eliminated racism. We now know that emotion often guides responses more than reason. While some member states have ratified and implemented the Convention on the Elimination of All Forms of Racial Discrimination, many ideas about race continue to flourish. The Ku Klux Klan has spawned hundreds of far-right groups, some of them with armed militias who have carried out acts of terrorism and violence against the United States federal government. Their adherents in the academy perpetuate these ideas as if they were natural.

The racialisation of Aboriginal people by white Australians and the associated set of assumptions about our intellectual and social capacities, contrary to all reliable scientific evidence, clearly has deep psychological roots in Australian society.

Many Australians, including some influential academics, are not aware that the concept of 'race' has been rejected by most reputable scientists and social scientists as a valid marker of human physiological and other social differences. Since the ground-breaking work on human genetics, the evidence concerning the genetic variation in and between human populations has grown. This has led to recognition that there are more similarities between people of different groups, traditionally called 'races', than between the members of these 'races'. The evidence from those working in genetic research has exposed the criteria for the division of the world's population into 'races' – skin, hair and eye colour, and a few other physiological characteristics – as a miniscule range of the thousands of characteristics encoded in humanity's gene files. The 'racial' characteristics are so limited in comparison to the identified genetically inherited features and their actual distribution is an adaptive response to the environment. The distribution of human blood types, for instance, bears no similarity to, or coincidence with, the perceived distribution of 'races'.

In the 1950s and 1960s, law makers repelled by the Holocaust re-examined 'race theories' to rid the world of evil ideologies based on eugenics, and to take steps to ensure that genocide could not recur. UNESCO coordinated the multinational and multidisciplinary effort to depose racism as the preeminent organising idea in world affairs. Australians were not affected by this profound and influential intellectual effort.

Stephen Jay Gould later surveyed the false scientism of 'race' theory, eugenics, and its related schools of thought in 1981 in *The Mismeasure* of Man.¹⁴⁰ He showed that phrenology – the measuring of heads and other physiological characteristics as 'proof' of perceived 'racial' and class characteristics – was based on unscientific data and argument. Meanwhile physical anthropologists in Australia surreptitiously guarded their storerooms of Aboriginal body parts, particularly skulls, in the belief that they would one day announce a great scientific discovery concerning the place of 'primitive' Aboriginal people in human evolution.

The idea of Indigenous people as 'the missing link' in human evolution was firmly embedded in popular Australian thinking. It was not quarantined from the scientific world. Of course, there were discoveries to be announced concerning Aboriginal people and human evolution based on examinations of skeletal material, but there was no suggestion that Aboriginal people were not fully part of the modern human species, *homo sapiens sapiens*. No reputable scientist would make such a suggestion.

The belief that Indigenous people are a pre-human type is a mythology of imperial white supremacism, one which lingers. Australia remained a backwater of eugenicist thought well into the twentieth century. Some professors of anatomy and anthropology kept ancestral remains in their offices and homes until the 1980s, even though this practice was illegal. In Victoria, the failure to return them to their families and communities – when there is sufficient information – remains an outstanding challenge. This problem is being addressed by the Victorian Aboriginal Heritage Council and the Australian Institute of Aboriginal and Torres Strait Islander Studies to ensure their repatriation.

Interpersonal racism

In many cases, people are not aware that they are being racist. Yet, in so many instances, the intention of people to be racist is very evident. One very public example of interpersonal racism shows how it is expressed, how it is denied, but also how divided Australians are about racism.

Adam Goodes, the AFL player and 2014 Australian of the Year, was the victim of booing, jeering and racist hysteria from AFL fans and media personalities throughout the 2015 season. He was the code's most prominent Indigenous player and a two-time Brownlow medallist, the game's highest honour. He had been an outstanding advocate for Indigenous issues, such as the Recognise campaign, seeking constitutional recognition for Indigenous Australians, and supported youth. To this day, his Go Foundation established with other Indigenous AFL stars supports young Indigenous Australians in education to overcome the obstacles they face.¹⁴¹

In the documentary *The Final Quarter* (2019), directed by Ian Darling, the persecution of Adam Goodes is depicted blow by blow. It exposed the relentless racism, lies and character assassination that he endured from shock jock personalities, such as Andrew Bolt and Alan Jones, during those terrible months, much of it passing without notice from other media. Goodes was accused of staging for free kicks, castigated for performing an on-field war dance celebration and wrongly accused of targeting the girl who shouted abuse. Another documentary *The Australian Dream*, written by Stan Grant, detailed the toll the experience took on the footballer and showed how after years of abuse fans and clubs rallied to support him. At the end of the 2015 season, he retired from the game, refusing to do the honour lap at his own club, the Sydney Swans. It took years before the AFL formally apologised to Goodes.

This saga of persecution of a star Indigenous sportsman is so prominent in Australia's history of racism that it is featured on the website of the National Museum of Australia. It points out that five years after the campaign of racist abuse, on 7 June 2019, the day *The Final Quarter* was to premiere at the Sydney Film Festival, the AFL and its 18 clubs made a formal apology to Goodes for the game's failure to stand up for him and 'call out' the treatment he was receiving. The apology stated, 'We never want to see the mistakes of the past repeated.' Goodes acknowledged the apology but did not return to Australian football.

Eliminating racism from Australia's sporting culture is a high priority for the safety of sportsmen and women, and the fans whose loyalty is the backbone of clubs. It is also a high priority for the wider society because if it is allowed to fester – and this is precisely what has happened while McGuire was at the helm of the Collingwood Football Club – the dangerous impacts of racism on the players and on the reputation of the codes and their clubs worsened. After an inquiry that found that systemic racism was still alive in the club, Eddie McGuire resigned as chairman in 2021.

As my friend and colleague, Melinda Sawers, pointed out in her teachers' notes for classes on the relentless booing of Adam Goodes, prepared for *Welcome to Country* for young Australians:

> *People who wouldn't normally think about racism towards Indigenous Australians became aware of it through the publicity this incident received and realised that more has to be done to reduce racism in Australia in general.*

There are Australians who want leadership on the problem of racism, and it is also the case that our national leaders are too slow to act, and ineffective

Kundat Djaru, a small community in Western Australia in the 80s (photo Wayne Quilliam)

when they do. This is why resources for understanding and overcoming racism are necessary in our nation's classrooms and workplaces, not least the Australian Football League Commission and clubs.

Just as important is the need to provide tools for living with racism, especially so that those who are the victims or potential victims of racism can maintain their health and wellbeing in the face of the relentless 'casual' racism that poisons Australian society.

Racism in everyday life. Tools for living.

Like myself, every person who is visibly Aboriginal and Torres Strait Islander – that is, typically, has a darker skin colour than about 60 per cent of Australians whose ancestry is British, colonial British (such as white South African), or northern European – encounters racism in everyday life. It may be a denial of service in a shop, or verbal or physical abuse, or exclusion from workplace or neighbourhood events. These everyday acts, or microaggressions, are classified as interpersonal racism.

Like myself, many Aboriginal people and other people of colour find themselves assessing each encounter with a white person to determine whether there will be an incident of racism and to prepare for the emotional impact. This constant vigilance is a source of trauma. Whether or not an incident of racism occurs, the well-known pain of racist insult is relived in the moment as one contemplates how to respond to avoid this pain.

Whether racist occurrences are 'unconscious' or intended, the impact is painful, destabilising one's sense of self. Assessments are made from the beginning and decisions are rehearsed. Should I leave? Should I speak about the racism? Will I be penalised if I speak about the racism? All these calculations made in moments create a sense of hyper-vigilance that causes constant stress.

Avoiding this stress by changing the response from one of fearful anticipation to a more empowering stance is learnt from others who have overcome the trauma of racism caused by interpersonal aggressions. Role models are often critical thinkers and people who practise positive thinking. They don't allow the pain of past racism to infect every moment of their lives. They change the narrative by understanding the nature of racism.

A simple but effective principle for disempowering racism is to understand that racists are wrong in their understanding of humanity. Racists invoke destructive emotions of hate, fear and animosity, which lead to behaviour that is antisocial. This includes insults, efforts to humiliate others, and often violence. This is the reason racism is illegal in Australia. The victims of racism have usually done nothing wrong. They are the targets of these destructive emotions and behaviours.

Overcoming the pain of being targeted by the microaggressions requires believing in one's own self-worth and seeing the racist's behaviour as not just loathsome but also the rage of people with no sense of common humanity, no compassion, or self-respect. A self-respecting person would not cause harm to others because such behaviour diminishes one's own humanity. The racists are the ones who suffer from a diminished sense of humanity. They are weak and, like startled animals, strike out when their fragile sense of self is threatened.

They are afraid of a phantasm; the Aboriginal person they insult is not perceived as fully human but subhuman. The idea of Aboriginal people as a fearful enemy, ogres, subhuman, or animal-like is learnt from socialisation in racist white Australia. Their distorted sense of humanity displayed towards Aboriginal people is, in large part, of their own making. While these ideas are inculcated in imperceptible ways, an intelligent person should be able to see that they are nonsense. That there are people who do not have the critical thinking to overcome these fears tells us that they are ignorant.

Systemic or institutional racism

The problem is much bigger than these incidents of interpersonal racism. Institutions have been shaped by, and are dependent in many ways, on practices of racism.

As Mary Frances O'Dowd explains, 'interpersonal racism cannot be disentangled from systemic racism'. It needs to be considered at 'a systems level: taking in the big picture of how society operates, rather than looking at one-on-one interactions.'[142]

Institutional or systemic racism originates in the beliefs and ideas that the dominant group has been acculturated into through language and social systems. The language and actions we use are the vehicles for both systemic and interpersonal racism. This includes laws and regulations, questioned social systems, education, hiring practices and access.

These systems of racism are almost invisible, O'Dowd explains:

> Systemic racism assumes white superiority individually, ideologically, and institutionally. The assumption of superiority can pervade thinking consciously and unconsciously. One most obvious example is apartheid, but even with anti-discrimination laws, systemic racism continues. Individuals may not see themselves as racist, but they can still benefit from systems that privilege white faces and voices.[143]

Describing cultures of discrimination, she observes that 'under systemic racism, systems of education, government and the media celebrate and reward some cultures over others'.[144]

Systemic racism shows itself in who is disproportionately impacted by our justice system. In Australia, Indigenous people make up 2 per cent of the Australian population, but 28 per cent of the adult prison population.[145]

Yin Paradies, an Indigenous Australian expert on the impacts of racism, published a systematic review of empirical research on self-reported racism and health, and writes about the invisibility of racism:

> The manifestations of racism vary considerably across time and place but in general ensue from societal systems that produce an unequal distribution of power (and hence resources) in societies based on the notion of 'race', where race is a social rather than a biological construct ... Owing to its pervasive nature in contemporary societies racism is frequently not perceptible to individuals or, perceive if perceived, may not always be reported.[146]

Can Australians overcome racism?

Most of us want our answer to this question to be 'yes'. But the next question is 'how?'

In his 2022 Boyer Lectures, Noel Pearson argued that successful passage of the referendum to create an Indigenous Voice to Parliament in the Constitution so that Aboriginal and Torres Strait Islander people can advise the Parliament on legislation affecting them, will create the conditions for racism to end. He said:

> My realisation after Goodes and his travails was that without sorting out that complex matters under the rubric of 'recognition' we will forever think that what we call racism is at the heart of our problem as a nation, rather than knowing who we are. Of all the claims I make in these lectures, this is the boldest and the one of which I am most convinced: racism will diminish in this country when we succeed with recognition. It will not have the same purchase on us: neither on the majority that has resorted to it over the past two centuries, nor the minority that lives with it, fears it and who too often succumb to the fear itself.

In this book I have given my own view of Indigenous Australians, our achievements, our history, our cultures and our successes. My views are based on evidence and on my life experience, not colonial myths that still linger. I have written this in the hope that when Australians have the knowledge to recognise both the strengths of our cultures and the invisible racism that surrounds them, they will change. That more Australians will begin to treat Aboriginal and Torres Strait Islander people with respect. That they will recognise that we are the descendants of the First Peoples of this land, not the enemy. That they will regard us as fellow citizens whose acceptance and recognition would be the basis for an honourable nation, free of its racist past.

17
Looking to the Future for Indigenous Australia

In his remarkable essay 'Moment of Truth', historian Mark McKenna observes:

> It is not only the absence of any acknowledgment of the country's violent foundation that makes the silence palpable, but also 65,000 years of Indigenous occupation. If it were not for the Tent Embassy and the easily missed Reconciliation Place, Indigenous Australia would have no obvious presence within the Parliamentary Triangle.[147]

This absence of Aboriginal and Torres Strait Islander people, their histories and cultures from the story of the Australian nation cannot be understated. I watched with interest on 26 January 1988 as Australians – not all, but most – celebrated 200 years of the Australian settlement. Without any irony, but with some slight and insincere acknowledgement of the existence of the First Australians, the official bodies organised re-enactments of the arrival of the British. Tall ships sailed into Sydney Harbour, and proud white Australians dressed up as convicts and colonists.

There was an Aboriginal protest and a march in Sydney – with several thousand people walking down the main thoroughfare behind a banner that read, 'We have survived'. The slogan was borrowed from the title of Bart Willoughby's song, performed by No Fixed Address, and released in 1981. It quickly became an anthem throughout Indigenous Australia as the nation prepared for its 1988 bicentennial celebrations of the arrival of the British on our shores. The song was first heard on the award-winning film *Wrong Side of the Road*, in 1981, and on the soundtrack album. This film was a tribute to Us Mob, Coloured Stone and No Fixed Address, which were among the first Aboriginal bands to play rock or reggae with a strong political message, while most Aboriginal musicians were playing country music.

The march moved on to La Perouse, where the 'We Have Survived' Festival was held on 26 January each year to counter the propaganda of the Australia Day celebrations. The festival eventually became the Yabun Festival in 2001. Yabun means 'music to a beat' in Gadigal language. It is a

Whether in a city or a remote community, Aboriginal people have kept many of their traditional customs (photo Wayne Quilliam)

free event that features traditional Indigenous cultural performances, music and activities for the Aboriginal and Torres Strait Islander community in Sydney. Similar festivals are curated in other cities and towns.

More than thirty years later, little has changed. The Indigenous protests against the idea of Australia's national day being a celebration of British colonisation grow larger. Indigenous festivals on the day remain distinctly separate and unrelated to the celebrations of many non-Indigenous people for their idea of our nation. The pall of 1950s-style racialist segregation hangs over the day.

Holding the national day on the date that the British established a penal colony at Port Jackson, rather than on 1 January, which was the date in 1901 when the Constitution of Australia was implemented, presents Australia's citizens with a convenient but troubling myth about the foundations of the nation. In the past, only a few stopped to consider the implications of this for their sense of what it means to be Australian; now, the number is growing.

Television presenter and political journalist Stan Grant, in the following edited extract from his book *Australia Day*, asked all the questions that Australians should ask on the national day, 26 January.

> We all seek identity: which communities we belong to; which football club we follow; what music we like; how we dress; where we live; religion;

race; culture. All of this gives us a sense of who we are, somewhere to belong. But there is a darker side to identity, a stifling conformity; an us and them; identity that pits us against each other. It keeps returning me to that question: am I Australian? Am I Aboriginal? Can those things be the same?

As a Wiradjuri man himself, Grant turned to Thomas Keneally's famous novel *The Chant of Jimmie Blacksmith*, about a historical Wiradjuri character, Jimmy Governor, to draw out the 'puzzle not easily explained, nor simple to comprehend' that these questions leave us with:

> *As modern Australia celebrated its birth at Federation in 1901, the historical inspiration for Jimmie Blacksmith, the real Jimmy Governor, sat in a Darlinghurst jail cell, alternating between singing songs in his traditional Wiradjuri language and reading the Bible – the synthesis of the old and new worlds that collided here so violently, given form in a man soon for the gallows. It is a synthesis Thomas Keneally saw as contradiction; and yet it is the essence of being Australian.*[148]

It would be superficial to say that Australians have got the date wrong. It should be obvious that it is wrong. Australia did not come into existence as a nation for another 112 years after Arthur Phillip unloaded his convicts at what is now Darling Harbour. How could the choice of this date, which

Rallies and marches bring Indigenous and non-Indigenous Australians together to celebrate and work towards a future for Indigenous Australia (photos Wayne Quilliam)

commemorates the founding of a penal colony, be seriously considered as providing the foundational myth of this robust, multicultural nation with a history of human society that commenced here at least six millennia ago?

Writers have referred to the British-born or British loyalists who are afraid to cut the 'apron strings' with their motherland. Nicholas Reece, writing in *The Guardian* on 7 June 2015, pondered on the significance of the Queen's Birthday holiday to Australians. It is celebrated each year on different dates across the Commonwealth, few of which are the Queen's actual birthday: 'In truth, the Queen's Birthday holiday is a meaningless excuse for millions of Australians to have a day off work. It is a sorry hangover from a bygone era when Australians clung to the apron strings of the Mother Country.'

Such sentiments usually come from republicans, such as Greg Barns, who chaired the Australian Republican Movement from 2000 to 2002. He wrote, on 9 April 2018 in *The Mercury*, on the occasion of a visit of Prince Edward to Tasmania, that the survival of the British monarchy in the Australian constitutional structure 'is inconsistent with the notion of equality. It does not befit a nation that purports to assure its citizens the impediments of birth or title do not prevent a citizen rising to high office'. Further, he wrote:

> There is also the projection of Australia in the 21st century. We live in the Asia-Pacific region and one of the major roadblocks to being embraced by other nations is Australia maintains anachronistic links to its former colonial master.

We may hold republican views or remain loyal to the British monarchy. Either way it makes no sense that our national day should not be on the day that Australia came into existence, even if it was a political artefact of the British Parliament, on 1 January.

The First Australians have been excluded from Australian constitutional, political, social and economic life for most of its history. Most likely, this comes from a sense of loyalty to the British motherland as the foundation of the colonies, if not the nation. The Indigenous people are relegated to the status of permanent enemy – if not declared as such, then certainly treated that way. There has been no formal end to this, except perhaps for the creation of the Council for Aboriginal Reconciliation that was formed in 1991 following the recommendation of the Royal Commission into Aboriginal Deaths in Custody. The council was established as a statutory body under the *Council for Aboriginal Reconciliation Act 1991*, passed by the Commonwealth Parliament, with unanimous cross-party support. It ceased to exist on 1 January 2001 in accordance with the Act. As stated in section 5 of the Act:

> *The object of the establishment of the Council is to promote a process of reconciliation between Aborigines and Torres Strait Islanders and the wider Australian community, based on an appreciation by the Australian community as a whole of Aboriginal and Torres Strait Islander cultures and achievements and of the unique position of Aborigines and Torres Strait Islanders as the indigenous peoples of Australia, and by means that include the fostering of an ongoing national commitment to co-operate to address Aboriginal and Torres Strait Islander disadvantage.*

In 2001, after the council was closed, concerned citizens created Reconciliation Australia. As explained in its vision statement, it was to be an independent, not-for-profit organisation to lead the reconciliation project and build 'relationships, respect and trust between the wider Australian community and Aboriginal and Torres Strait Islander peoples'. The founders envisioned national reconciliation as based on 'five critical dimensions: race relations, equality and equity, institutional integrity, unity and historical acceptance'.

The work of Reconciliation Australia has made a profound difference to Australian life. It has helped to build relationships of respect between Indigenous and non-Indigenous people. Narragunnawali, a program of Reconciliation Australia, as noted on its website narragunnawali.org.au, 'supports all schools and early learning services in Australia to foster a higher level of knowledge and pride in Aboriginal and Torres Strait Islander histories, cultures and contributions'.

As I have discussed earlier, among Reconciliation Australia's many other programs, the Reconciliation Action Plans (RAP) have been extraordinarily successful. A RAP is 'a strategic document that supports an organisation's business plan. It includes practical actions that will drive an organisation's contribution to reconciliation both internally and in the communities in which it operates'. Hundreds of institutions and companies, including most major Australian companies, have Reconciliation Action Plans with targets for engagement with Indigenous people, employment and supply-chain goals, and other goals that are relevant to their operations.

I have written about the proposals advanced by Indigenous Australians, such as the Uluru Statement from the Heart, which calls for Voice, Treaty, Truth. The grounds for this proposal, like many others, are the historical injustices that plague our politics, governance, and relationships.

Australia, unlike other former British colonies, has no treaty with its Indigenous people. Customary systems of law pre-date the arrival of the British by many thousands of years and survive, often in highly adapted forms, in many parts of post-colonial Australia. Native title was recognised in Australia only in 1992. This is in contrast to other common law jurisdictions, such as New Zealand and Canada, where native title has been recognised for at least 150 years. These countries have superior legal and political regimes for recognising and dealing with Indigenous systems of law and governance. In part, this is because of the treaty rights that were negotiated in their colonial period.

For more than a decade, Indigenous leaders have sought the agreement of successive governments to hold a referendum to change the Australian Constitution to recognise Aboriginal and Torres Strait Islander Peoples and their cultures.

It was the late Yunupiŋu who gave form to this existential crisis facing all the First Peoples in Australia. In 2008, as leader of the Gumatj clan in north-east Arnhem Land, he presented the then Prime Minister, Kevin Rudd, with a petition. It asked that Australia recognise the right of the Yolŋu clans to exist, and to be acknowledged in the Constitution.

> We, the united clans of East Arnhem land, through our most senior dilak, do humbly petition you, the ... Prime Minister of Australia, in your capacity as the first amongst equals in the Australian Parliament, and as the chief adviser to Her Majesty ... to secure within the Australian Constitution the recognition and protection of our full and complete right to:
> Our way of life in all its diversity;
> Our property, being the lands and waters of East Arnhem land;
> Economic independence, through the proper use of the riches of our land and waters in all their abundance and wealth;
> Control of our lives and responsibility for our children's future.[149]

It is important to acknowledge that 250 Indigenous leaders taking part in the National Indigenous Constitutional Convention held in May 2017 at Uluṟu, one of the most sacred and iconic places in Aboriginal Australia, unanimously supported the Uluṟu Statement from the Heart. The Australian government did not agree to the approach outlined in this elegant statement, which calls for the establishment of a First Nations Voice in the Australian Constitution and a Makarrata Commission to supervise a process of agreement-making and truth-telling between governments and Aboriginal and Torres Strait Islander Peoples. In response, the government issued a cursory statement in November 2017. But the Indigenous leaders are committed to pursuing their goal, just as their forebears did. And, in 2019, Indigenous Australians minister Ken Wyatt made his pledge to find a 'consensus' that would lead to a referendum to recognise Indigenous Australians in the Constitution within three years. With the election of the Albanese Labor Government in May 2022 the referendum was back on the political agenda, with a commitment that it would be held within the first term of the new government.

This is one of the reasons for learning about Aboriginal and Torres Strait Islander histories and cultures in schools. Better understanding of the issues that are bound up in the referendum. Better understanding of the cultural riches of the First Australians will contribute to the intergenerational change of which people such as Megan Davis, Noel Pearson, Stan Grant, Mark McKenna, Bruce Pascoe, Bill Gammage and so many other Australians are a part. Their intellectual contributions explain the growing impatience with the resistance by governments to righting the fundamental injustice of excluding First Australians and our ancient legacy from the idea of the nation.

Noel Pearson, in his essay 'A Rightful Place', written in 2014, refers to this predicament as 'fragmentation': it is the legacy of settler colonialism that created similar grievances around the world, capturing Indigenous peoples in the imperial grasp and denying their right to exist. Pearson states that there are 'four focuses of grievance: identity as a people; the territorial lands of a people; language; and culture. Peoples hold hard to these four things'. He asks the crucial question: 'So the problem of the world is: how do 10,000 distinct peoples live well and prosper – and get along with each other – within 200 nation-states?'[150]

Two events in 2020 made us aware of the fragility of our existence, the Black Lives Matter movement and the COVID-19 pandemic. The implications of these events will be long-lasting and the changes to our ways of life – and what we have taken to be 'normality' – will be profound.

Black Lives Matter

Throughout the first half of 2020, as people chanted 'Black Lives Matter' across the world in protest at the killing of George Floyd and too many others, *Guardian Australia* conducted a study of Aboriginal deaths in custody in Australia. After reading 589 coronial reports, the team at *Guardian Australia* found a record of systemic failure and neglect and reported on key issues that are too often ignored by police and the criminal justice system. There are too many myths about trends in death and incarceration rates and how Aboriginal people in custody are treated both by the police who charge them and when they are in custody, whether in police custody or in a correctional facility:

> The key finding of the royal commission was that Aboriginal people are more likely to die in custody because they are arrested and jailed at disproportionate rates. That remains as true in 2020 as it was in 1991.
>
> In 1991, 14.3% of the male prison population in Australia was Indigenous. In March 2020 it was 28.6%. And, according to data released by the Australian Bureau of Statistics this month, 4.7% of all Indigenous men are in jail compared with just 0.3% of all non-Indigenous men.[151]

After the primary recommendation of the Royal Commission into Aboriginal Deaths in Custody that investigated ninety-nine cases from 1989–1990 – that incarceration (or arrest and imprisonment) of Aboriginal and Torres Strait Islander people should be a last resort – the key recommendation pertained to the principle and implementation of duty of care by all involved in the criminal justice system, from police to correctional service officers. The evidence unearthed by the *Guardian Australia* team shows that the failure of police and correctional service officers to exercise duty of care remains the primary contributing factor to Aboriginal deaths in custody. No police officer or correctional services officer involved in these Aboriginal

The symbolism of the Aboriginal flag unifies our people (photo Wayne Quilliam)

deaths in custody has been convicted of a crime and none has been held responsible. The situation gets worse because of an intransigent culture of blaming Aboriginal people when every Australian should be entitled to be released from custody or prison alive. Non-Indigenous people die in custody too, but the disproportionate rates of arrest and imprisonment – the result of racism and discrimination – make Aboriginal people particularly at risk, especially given their underlying health conditions. There has been no justice, no prosecutions, just a cold silence from the authorities. Until the Black Lives Matter movement, only their families, volunteers with the Change the Record campaign, a few journalists and a very small number of people holding vigils have brought these matters to our attention. These deaths are the tip of the iceberg. Most others have passed without any public attention or anything like justice.

Aboriginal women are also being increasingly arrested, held in remand and imprisoned and are dying in custody. There are too many cases of Aboriginal women who have died in police custody to recount here. Their lives were cut short by violence compounded by what seems to be a contempt for Aboriginal women that can pass for normal and acceptable across all classes and cultures in Australia.

There have been several harrowing cases in recent times, and among them the death of Tanya Day in a police cell in Victoria is notable because while there was no justice for her family, their campaign for the decriminalisation of public drunkenness was successful, thirty years after the Royal Commission into Aboriginal Deaths in Custody made this recommendation.[152] Among the coroner's findings, summarised by the Human Rights Law Centre, were these:

> *The Coroner found that the decision-making process of the V/Line train conductor – who formed the view that Ms Day was 'unruly' and organised for the police to attend the train station – was influenced by Ms Day's Aboriginality and the train conductor's unconscious bias. This was in part because Ms Day was the first sleeping passenger ever removed from a train by that V/Line train conductor.*
>
> *The Coroner found that the decision of the police to arrest Ms Day was not influenced by her Aboriginality ... The findings of the Coroner did, however, detail a 'culture of complacency regarding intoxicated detainees' within Victoria Police and found that there is a systemic failure to recognise the medical dangers of intoxication and comply with the mandatory terms of the governing policy and procedures regarding the management of persons in care or custody. This shows 'the power of stereotype and its resistance to correction'.*

Traditional clapsticks held high during a NAIDOC March on the steps of Parliament House, Naarm/Melbourne (photo Wayne Quilliam)

The Coroner also found that the physical checks conducted by the police on Ms Day were 'illusory' and that the police officers did not take proper care of Ms Day's safety, security, health and welfare as required by the Victoria Police Manual and the Standard Operating Procedures.

The Coroner notes that if the physical checks had been done by the police in accordance with the relevant requirements, Ms Day would have been checked 10 minutes after her fall.

The Leading Senior Constable was found by the Coroner not to be a credible witness and the findings noted that the accuracy of his custody module entries (regarding the observation and monitoring of Ms Day) are concerning.

The Victorian Charter of Human Rights and Responsibilities Act 2006 *is relevant to how police carry out their duties, including 'ensuring appropriate monitoring and supervision of people in detention and providing appropriate medical care'. The Coroner made a finding that Ms Day was 'not treated with humanity and respect for the inherent dignity of a human person as required by the Charter'.*

This is why the Black Lives Matter movement is important. That Aboriginal and Torres Strait Islander people should be 'treated with humanity and respect for the inherent dignity of a human person' by police and the criminal justice system needs to be stated repeatedly to remind the authorities that their actions that lead to the deaths of our people are not acceptable. The Human Rights Law Centre also reports that 'the Coroner did find that the totality of the evidence supported a belief that an indictable offence may have been committed. Accordingly, the Coroner directed that the Director of Public Prosecutions be notified.'[153] The Director of Public Prosecutions, however, decided not to prosecute the two police officers and did not provide any reasons for this decision.

> Throughout the inquest, the Day family had submitted that an offence of negligent manslaughter may have been committed by the Sergeant and Leading Senior Constable involved in Ms Day's death, who the Coroner found failed to monitor and observe Ms Day in accordance with the relevant guidelines.[154]

This is a rare case of a coronial inquiry into a death in custody resulting in an acknowledgement of our humanity and right to be treated with dignity and in accordance with the laws of this country.

At the very least, the recommendations of the Royal Commission tabled in the federal Parliament thirty years ago should be implemented to avoid deaths such as Ms Tanya Day's.

That Governments must ensure that:

> Police Services, Corrective Services, and authorities in charge of juvenile centres recognise that they owe a legal duty of care to persons in their custody;
>
> That the standing instructions to the officers of these authorities specify that each officer involved in the arrest, incarceration or supervision of a person in custody has a legal duty of care to that person, and may be held legally responsible for the death or injury of the person caused or contributed to by a breach of that duty; and
>
> That these authorities ensure that such officers are aware of their responsibilities and trained appropriately to meet them, both on recruitment and during their service.[155]

There are many ways of coming to an understanding of Aboriginal and Torres Strait Islander cultures and histories. This book presents just a few. The understanding might one day lead to justice – justice for the First Peoples whose polities have been suppressed and whose right to exist and be acknowledged is one of the outstanding challenges that Australians must eventually face.

Conclusion

This conclusion has been written as I consider my role in the Week of Action for the campaign to convince Australians to vote yes in the referendum on the Indigenous Voice. In this year of 2023, like most Indigenous Australians I am counting on my fellow Australians to think about the facts of Australian history and its impacts on our lives. We cannot hope to close the gaps in the many disadvantages without having a say in the policies – almost all designed by non-Indigenous Australians – that affect our lives, and almost always in a detrimental way. When we say that we want a Voice – a guaranteed constitutional right to a Voice to advise Parliament and the Government – we do so with a profound understanding of how so many Indigenous people, most of them children, came to be living in such disastrous circumstances. The long history of conflict and racism accounts for much of the statistical picture of inequity and disadvantage paraded each year in the parliamentary reports on Closing the Gap.[156]

Indigenous people have a fundamental right to self-determination and this means that we have a right to choose the way in which our lives are shaped by the nation state that has encapsulated us. Since Federation was established in 1901, we have been excluded. Our right to have a say in the way that the national Parliament treats us can be recognised in the Australian Constitution, putting an end to the paternalistic history of making policy and laws about us, and yet, almost always without us. Constitutional recognition of an Indigenous Voice to work with the Parliament and governments to ensure our ideas and views are heard in policy and decision-making is a practical way to overcome our historical disempowerment and powerless status as a tiny minority in the Australian population.

It is my hope that this book appeals to the better angels of the readers, those who want to know how to treat Indigenous people with dignity, avoid unwitting racism, and work for inclusive public places, workplaces, classrooms and meeting rooms where our cultural and historical differences are acknowledged respectfully. I hope that this book makes a positive contribution to all who read it, empowering them to improve their encounters across the cultural and historical divide. Sometimes, acknowledging that non-Indigenous people are unsure or hesitant to play a role in improving the lives of the Indigenous people is as simple as giving them permission and guidance to do so. If, after reading this book, a police officer hesitates before jumping to the tired old conclusions in policing that have contributed to world-record and shameful incarceration rates, I will have done my job of providing a form of cultural awareness to make the lives of all Australians better. If a teacher reads this book and encourages the Aboriginal children in her classroom rather than unwittingly marginalising them with tired old assumptions about their learning ability, I will have done my job. The lives of our children are shaped by these encounters and their chances of living a full and satisfying life, free from discrimination and suffering, improve if their experiences are positive, not denigrating and painful. If the Indigenous representative of a community organisation feels welcome at the table when government officials are discussing policies and laws and is able to contribute in a meaningful way and is listened to with respect and acknowledgement, I will have done my job.

There is much in this book and the works that I have referred to – whether written, artistic or embedded in the landscapes we inherited from our ancestors – that can be used in public places, workplaces and classrooms to complete the task of ending the discrimination and exclusion that began in the eighteenth century and became more elaborate as colonisation and postcolonial administrations took control of our lives. Great work has been done, such as the work of Reconciliation Australia and many other organisations, companies and institutions that acknowledge the ancestral country and its people where they are located. The change of place names to their original Indigenous names, and the flying of the Aboriginal and Torres Strait Islander flags because they are official flags of Australia, making an effort to enrol Indigenous children in school, Indigenous youth in universities and colleges, and employing Indigenous people, all of these initiatives and others have brought down the walls of habitual exclusion and increased the participation of Indigenous people in all walks of life. It has taken decades to make these changes and the Indigenous disparities continue, some at life-threatening scales.

We can eliminate the entrenched disadvantages that have captured hundreds of thousands of our people in permanent poverty and failure to thrive by having an informed approach to our encounters. Did we consider the right of Indigenous people to determine their place in the arrangements being made? Did we observe basic human rights in providing access to services? Did we treat Indigenous people with dignity? Do we understand the long history of Indigenous occupation of this continent and the destruction of Indigenous societies by the colonial invasion? Do we understand this history? What can we do to overcome these historical burdens? The history I have touched on in this book gives us many examples of the suffering of Indigenous people and also many examples of events that have changed the attitudes and treatment of us in radical and life-giving ways.

We can do more together if we have an accurate understanding of our history and a vision of our nation built on principles of human dignity and equality that also accommodate cultural and historical differences. Many young Australians envisage this Australia in which all are welcome and treated with respect in beautiful and exciting ways. They have left behind the old Australia of the White Australia Policy. None of this is difficult. But it will need all of us to do our part.

Glossary

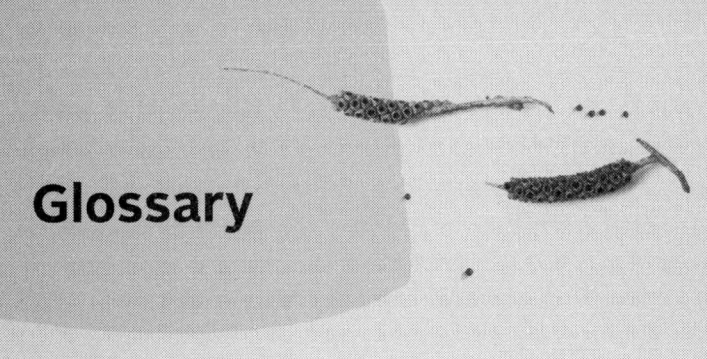

A comprehensive glossary of terms that apply to Australian Indigenous people, events, laws and practices is available online at the Agreements, Treaties and Negotiated Settlements Project website (atns.net.au).

AIATSIS map

A tool often used for teaching about Aboriginal and Torres Strait Islander languages is the Australian Institute of Aboriginal and Torres Strait Islander Studies (AIATSIS) map of Indigenous Australia (see Appendix C in the colour insert). The map will give you an idea of the many languages that are spoken in Australia, although, for some of the language names on the map, the spellings now widely adopted do vary. As the AIATSIS website notes:

> The map is an attempt to represent all the language, tribal or nation groups of the Indigenous peoples of Australia. Aboriginal and Torres Strait Islander groups were included on the map based on the published resources available between 1988 and 1994 which determine the cultural, language and trade boundaries and relationships between groups.

The map was created by David Horton and is based on data collected by AIATSIS, Aboriginal Studies Press and others.

The team at AIATSIS also produced *The Encyclopaedia of Aboriginal Australia: Aboriginal and Torres Strait Islander history, society and culture*. I recommend it as a resource if you want to read more about Aboriginal Australia.

You can hear one of our First languages being spoken through various online language resources. One such resource is the Eastern and Central Arrernte Learners' List (arrernte-angkentye.online/ECALL.html?v=1.3).

Another important language resource is the online compilation of language varieties by First Languages Australia (gambay.com.au). This is a living archive with an interactive map to which language speakers regularly contribute new materials in many formats, including audio and video. One that I follow is the 50 Words project of the Research Unit for Indigenous Languages at the University of Melbourne (50words.online). This is a resource for students and teachers to learn 50 words in the local languages, and for the general public to discover the diversity of languages around Australia.

AUSTLANG

The AIATSIS website also provides AUSTLANG. AUSTLANG is an online, interactive language resource developed at AIATSIS. On the website, it is explained:

> AUSTLANG provides a vocabulary of persistent identifiers, a thesaurus of languages and peoples and information about Aboriginal and Torres Strait Islander languages which has been assembled from referenced sources.
>
> The alpha-numeric codes function as persistent identifiers, followed by a 'string of changeable text'. This allows changes to the name or spelling of a language variety, according to community preference. In cases where there is more than one preference, two or three versions of the name are included, e.g. E6: Dhanggati / Dunghutti^.
>
> This vocabulary of persistent identifiers supports archives, libraries, galleries and other agencies to identify materials or projects in or about Indigenous Australian languages and peoples, without the confusion of a multitude of language names and spellings. The codes maintain an identity if a change is made to the spelling or the name.
>
> AUSTLANG can be searched with language names (including a range of spellings); the codes, for example E6: (note inclusion of the colon); placenames and via the map. AUSTLANG has links to MURA the AIATSIS catalogue and other online resources.

Pathways

AIATSIS also provides a search engine called the Pathways thesauri for Australian place names, Indigenous language groups and subject relating to Aboriginal and Torres Strait Islander studies.

TERMS FOR ABORIGINAL AND TORRES STRAIT ISLANDER PEOPLE

Aboriginal

People who have cultural and ancestral lineage from mainland Australia (including Tasmania) preceding colonisation by the British.

Also defined, for legal and technical reasons, as a person 'who is a member of the Aboriginal race of Australia, identifies as an Aboriginal and is accepted by their identified Aboriginal community as Aboriginal'.

Aboriginal people, Torres Strait Islander people, Indigenous people, First Australians, First Nations People, First Peoples

These terms are all generally acceptable when referring to Australia's original inhabitants. In international law, the term 'indigenous' refers to those peoples who predate colonising peoples. While the term 'Indigenous' is widely accepted in Australia, some would prefer, for personal reasons, that other terms are used.

Aboriginal Tent Embassy

The Aboriginal Tent Embassy was established in 1972 in front of Parliament House in Ngambri/Ngunnawal/Canberra as part of the land rights protest movement. It is still established as a permanent protest site.

Acknowledgement of Country
Any person – Indigenous and non-Indigenous – can acknowledge the Traditional Owners of the land at the start of a speech or an event. This is considered to be a sign of respect.

ancestors
For Indigenous people, the term 'ancestors' has two meanings. Firstly, it can refer to the ancestral beings who created every aspect of the landscape, and the laws by which people still live (see 'Dreaming').

Secondly, it can also refer to any deceased person(s) from whom an individual or group is descended. In Aboriginal culture, it is expected that ancestors are treated with reverence, just as Elders are revered.

ancestral
When a place, natural phenomena, spiritual being, word or thing is regarded as being made by or inherited from an ancestor or ancestors. See also 'songlines', 'Tjukurrpa' and 'Dreaming'.

anthropologist
A person who studies human behaviour and social structures. Historically, some anthropologists in Australia, the colonial anthropologists and some in the twentieth century, misrepresented Aboriginal cultures, people and communities in ways that have caused immense harm and contributed to racist beliefs about Aboriginal people.

A.P. Elkin's contribution to eugenicist and assimilationist policies, building on the work of physical anthropologists such as Norman B. Tindale, is a case in point. Most Australian anthropologists today are bound by ethical guidelines if they work at universities or receive research funding and engage with the communities they study in an ethical way.

assimilation
A policy implemented by the Australian state and territory governments between the 1920s and late 1960s that aimed to integrate Aboriginal people into white Australia, by removing children from their families and confining people considered to be 'full blood' to Aboriginal reserves or under the control of 'native superintendents' in order to achieve 'racial purity', and with the intention of eradicating Aboriginal people and culture in the belief that the 'race' was 'dying out'. The policy was described at the time as 'smoothing the pillow of the dying race'.[157] This policy was couched in terms of concern for Aboriginal people's welfare. See also 'Stolen Generations'.

cleverman
A Kriol term meaning traditional healer, doctor or spiritual healer. See also 'Kriol', 'marrngitj' and 'ngangkari'.

Country

'Country' is an Aboriginal Kriol (Creole) term that refers to the traditional estate of an Aboriginal group or clan. This may mean a specific area inherited from ancestors and belonging to a descent-based group of people, or a larger, more general region from which that person's ancestors originate. It may also be referred to as 'place'. See also 'Kriol'.

culture

The term 'culture' is used in many different ways. In the context of Indigenous people, it refers to the collective social, economic and artistic manifestations of the society, and encompasses their ideas, customs, languages and the distinctive material expressions of their society.

Dreaming

'Dreaming' (also 'dreamtime') is a term devised by anthropologists Francis Gillen and Baldwin Spencer to describe the religio-cultural worldview of the Central Australian Aboriginal people they studied. 'Dreaming' is not a direct translation of an Aboriginal word. The English language does not have an equivalent to express these complex Aboriginal spiritual concepts.

The term 'Dreaming' has become popular in the English language for a key religious concept, but there are others and they vary across the continent among the hundreds of Aboriginal and Torres Strait Islander societies. There are many different words across Australia that describe Aboriginal spirituality and beliefs, such as 'altjeringa' (Arrernte People, Central Australia), 'waŋarr' (north-east Arnhem Land) and 'bugari' (Broome, northern Western Australia).

In *The Aranda's Pepa*, Anna Kenny describes 'Dreaming' as a body of sacred laws and narratives that reveal 'how the landscape was created and imbued with meaning by ancestral beings' and how 'this landscape represents ancestral connections to the land and the mythical beings that created it'. The stories of these ancestral beings are passed down through singing, dancing, painting and teaching songlines. See also 'Tjukurrpa' and 'songlines'.

Elder

Elders are Indigenous people who are held in high esteem and have a position of authority within their community. In Aboriginal society, generally the older a person is, the more respect and authority they have because knowledge is passed down to each generation in a gradual way, often at ceremonies. As a sign of respect, Elders are usually addressed as 'Uncle' or 'Aunty'. Elders don't necessarily have to be old, but they must have earned that title as a result of their knowledge of culture and/or contribution to their community.

freehold title

This is the most complete form of property ownership in Australia. The land holder (owner) owns the land in perpetuity. It allows the land holder to deal with the land including selling, leasing, licensing or mortgaging the land, subject to compliance with applicable laws such as planning and environment laws. Freehold title is referred to as Torrens title by lawyers. Torrens is the mechanism used in all Australian states and territories to record who owns which land.

gurruṯu
A concept at the heart of the Yolŋu social system and system of governance. It can be described as the complex networks of kinship that link individuals and groups to each other.

indentured
An 'indenture' is a legal contract that binds someone to another person in order to pay a debt or purchase obligation. An indentured servant or indentured labourer is a worker within a system of exploitative (often forced) labour. The worker is bound by a signed or forced contract to work for a fixed time.

Indigenous Australian
In the 1980s the Commonwealth Department of Aboriginal Affairs defined an Indigenous Australian as 'a person of Aboriginal or Torres Strait Islander descent who identifies as Aboriginal or Torres Strait Islander and is accepted as such by the community in which he or she lives'. The capital 'I' specifically refers to Aboriginal and Torres Strait Islander people from Australia, as opposed to indigenous people of other nations.

Indigenous Land Use Agreement
According to the National Native Title Tribunal website, an ILUA 'is a voluntary agreement between a native title group and others about the use of land and waters. These agreements allow people to negotiate flexible, pragmatic agreements to suit their particular circumstances.'

kinship
Indigenous kinship systems are complex social systems that determine how people relate to each other, and determine their roles, responsibilities and obligations in relation to one another and Country. This feature of social organisation and family relationships exists in various forms across Australia. See also 'moiety', 'totem' and 'skin name'.

knowledge
Aboriginal and Torres Strait Islander knowledge systems are among thousands of indigenous knowledge systems in the world. They share common characteristics and are protected under international law in the Convention on Biological Diversity at Article 8 (j). UNESCO provides a useful description of indigenous knowledge systems:

> *Local and indigenous knowledge refers to the understandings, skills and philosophies developed by societies with long histories of interaction with their natural surroundings. For rural and indigenous peoples, local knowledge informs decision-making about fundamental aspects of day-to-day life. This knowledge is integral to a cultural complex that also encompasses language, systems of classification, resource use practices, social interactions, ritual and spirituality.*

Often, the term 'knowledges' is used to reflect this great diversity and an initial capital is used in technical terms such as Traditional Ecological Knowledge (TEK) and Traditional Environmental Knowledge (TEK).

Kriol
Kriol is a modern, post-contact Aboriginal language, spoken widely across northern Australia. Linguists class Kriol as a 'creole' language, which is a language typically born out of colonisation. Creole languages are largely derived from the dominant language (such as French, English, Portuguese or Spanish), but speakers of creole languages adapt and innovate upon the dominant language to such an extent that they create a separate dialect. Kriol is the second most common language in the Northern Territory.

land rights and native title
These are legal concepts that developed with the advent of human rights law in Australia. They mean different things in law, but both refer to legal recognition of Aboriginal rights to land. Land rights laws usually grant title to Aboriginal groups to be held in trust. See also 'native title'.

Indigenous languages
Estimates differ, but the consensus is that before colonisation there were between 250 and 500 Indigenous languages in Australia. These languages are often based on connections to Country, with specific words to describe weather patterns in the particular region (see also 'seasons'). Unfortunately, Australia can also lay claim to being a nation with one of the highest number of lost languages. Today, only about 120 languages are still spoken and often only by a handful of people that may include non-Indigenous linguists.

language group
A 'language group' is the community of speakers of a language. The primary members speak the language as a 'mother tongue' or home language. Many speakers of Indigenous languages are multilingual, that is, speaking more than one Aboriginal and/or Torres Strait Islander language.

lore
The term 'lore' is an Aboriginal Kriol term that stands in place of expressions in Indigenous languages that cannot be properly explained in English. Lore encompasses the religious, spiritual and practical laws that Indigenous people observe in their own cultures. See also 'Tjukurrpa'.

makarrata
A Yolŋu word meaning a coming together after a struggle, facing the facts of wrongs and negotiating peace. The term has been used as an alternative name for a treaty process in Australia, notably in the Uluru Statement from the Heart.

manikay
A Yolŋu word meaning 'songs', in particular, public clan songs accompanied by clapsticks and yidaki.

marrŋgitj
The Yolŋu word for doctor. 'Marrŋgitj' are traditional healers who diagnose and treat complaints, and advise on physical and spiritual wellbeing. Marrŋgitj have a deep knowledge of Yolŋu medicines based mainly on native plants and ancient techniques. See also 'ngangkari'.

midden
Shell middens are places where the debris from eating shellfish and other food has accumulated over time. Shell middens are studied by archaeologists to find out about Indigenous activities in the past.

missionary/mission
A 'missionary' is a person who is sent to another place, usually to 'spread the word of God' or convert people to the Christian religion ('mission' relates to the vocation or calling of a religious organisation). In Australia, when First Peoples were forcibly removed from their land, they were often sent to missions which had been established in cooperation with the government. Missions were also notoriously often brutal places for Indigenous people, who were often punished for practising their culture or speaking their languages.

moiety
A Latin word meaning one of two equal parts. The term is used to describe how the Indigenous kinship system is organised into groupings. The word has been used in Australia by anthropologists to describe the first level of the Aboriginal kinship system, which divides everything including people, plants, animals and the environment into two halves. Each half is a mirror of the other, and to understand the whole universe these two halves must come together. Each Aboriginal nation has its own term for their moiety. For example, the Yolŋu moieties in north-east Arnhem Land are called Dhuwa and Yirritja. See also 'kinship'.

NAIDOC
An acronym for the National Aborigines and Islanders Day Observance Committee. NAIDOC Week celebrations are held across Australia each year between the first Sunday in July until the following Sunday. NAIDOC Week celebrates the history, culture and achievements of Aboriginal and Torres Strait Islander Peoples.

native title
Native title is the legal doctrine that includes the recognition of Aboriginal and Torres Strait Islander rights to land and water. The *Native Title Act 1993* (Cth) requires these rights to be based on proof of an Indigenous group's traditions of owning specific land before colonisation, and for this land custodianship to have been inherited from forebears according to local descent principles. Native title rights have been recognised in limited circumstances, such as when no other title has been issued by an Australian government or colony.

ngangkari
The Pitjantjatjara word for doctor. The 'ngangkari' are traditional healers who,

according to the Ngaanyatjarra Pitjantjatjara Yankunytjatjara Women's Council, for thousands of years 'have nurtured the physical, emotional and social wellbeing of their people. These traditional healers are esteemed for their unique ability to protect and heal both individuals and communities from harm'. See also 'marrŋgitj'.

non-Indigenous
By definition, non-Indigenous Australians are those people who cannot be defined as Aboriginal or Torres Strait Islander because they are not descended from an Aboriginal or Torres Strait Islander ancestor.

Old People
A creole term for 'ancestors' generally referring to First Peoples who lived in traditional ways prior to colonisation. See also 'Kriol'.

oral histories
Oral traditions and oral histories in Aboriginal and Torres Strait Islander families and communities are the records of their peoples, and they should be regarded as a significant part of Australian history.

Reconciliation Place
An urban landscape located in Canberra that contains a number of public artworks. This symbolic area recognises the importance of understanding the shared history of Indigenous and non-Indigenous Australians.

referendum
A direct vote in which an entire electorate is invited to vote on a particular proposal. The Australian Constitution can only be changed by referendum. Section 128 of the Constitution sets out certain rules that must be followed in order for a change to be approved. There have been forty-four referendums held since 1901 and only eight of these have been successful.

republican
In the Australian context, this term refers to a person who supports constitutional change to remove the British monarchy as Australia's head of state.

seasons
Seasonal calendars and seasons vary in different Aboriginal and Torres Strait Islander communities due to the specific land and weather patterns in the region. Most Indigenous seasonal calendars have three large seasons with two or three sub-seasons, or six seasons.

segregation
This word generally refers to racial segregation – the formal or informal separation of a population on the basis of race and/or skin colour. It is usually just one part of a system of racial oppression. It is well known that this occurred in the US; however, Australia's 'White Australia Policy' that led to the Stolen Generations is also an example of segregation. Charlie Perkins famously campaigned against this in his 1965 Freedom Ride.

skin name
Indigenous people are given 'skin names' that determine where they fit within the kinship system. See also 'kinship'.

social order
Social order is a concept used in anthropology and sociology that refers to the way various social structures or behaviours create or maintain a society.

song series or songlines
A 'song series' is a body of songs that are sung sequentially or in repetitive groups, or in repetition by authorised Indigenous singers. These songs are intended to convey a sacred narrative. The term 'songlines' comes from the title of the popular travelogue by British writer Bruce Chatwin.

Stolen Generations
Refers to Indigenous children who, under various Australian federal and state government policies, were forcibly removed from their families. These policies were implemented between approximately 1905 and 1967, but continued illegally into the 1970s. These policies were justified by the now discredited pseudo-science of eugenics, which assumed the superiority of white people over all other races. It was believed that children referred to as 'half-caste', 'quarter-caste' and 'quadroon' had enough European lineage to be assimilated into white Australian society, thus 'breeding out' Indigenous people from Australia. On 13 February 2008, then prime minister Kevin Rudd issued a formal apology to the Stolen Generations.

terra nullius
A Latin term which translates literally as 'land belonging to nobody'. When Captain Arthur Phillip claimed the continent of Australia for the British Crown in 1788, he did so on the basis of this doctrine. This act was a denial of the (approximately) one million Indigenous people who inhabited the continent, as well as their cultures, customs and tenure of the land. Terra nullius was used for over 200 years to justify the dispossession of Indigenous people. In 1993, the High Court of Australia overturned the doctrine of terra nullius in the case of *Mabo (No. 2)*, which granted the people of Meriam Island (in the Torres Strait) rights 'as against the whole world to possession, occupation, use and enjoyment of the lands of the Murray Islands'. This decision paved the way for the *Native Title Act* to be passed.

Tjukurrpa
The Pitjantjatjara word which describes their sacred narratives and law. Tjukurrpa refers to a way of seeing and understanding the world in which Country, places, objects, songs and stories embody sacred power and knowledge. Most Australians would know this as the 'Dreaming', but that term was invented by British explorers and does not properly capture the Aboriginal religio-cultural worldview.

Torres Strait Islander
People who have cultural and ancestral lineage from the Torres Strait Islands preceding colonisation by the British. Torres Strait Islanders were often defined in

the same terms as 'Aboriginal' people and included under the legal definitions of 'Aboriginal', even though they comprise a different cultural, linguistic and ethnic group.

totem

In the Australian Indigenous context, many people use this term to refer to those revered spiritual ancestors that manifest themselves in non-human forms.

Depicted in sacred traditional designs, they are the emblems of particular clans or other social forms. Totems often appear in contemporary visual art, although traditionally they were depicted in rock art and ceremonial body painting and objects. The word is a version of 'doodem' borrowed from Ojibwa, an Algonquian language spoken by a native American people from the regions around Lake Superior. Anthropologists use the term to refer to the sacred emblems in 'animistic' societies, but the common use by Indigenous people worldwide refers to ancestral spiritual beings.

traditional

In Aboriginal and Torres Strait Islander cultures, traditional practices have been passed down through generations and form an important part of their identity. Traditions are adapted to changing circumstances in all societies, and Aboriginal and Torres Strait Islander people also adapt their traditions to ensure their survival in the modern world.

Traditional Owner(s)

Indigenous people or persons who, as a result of their ancestral heritage, cultural ties and/or customary laws, have authority and custodial obligations over a particular area of land and/or clan group.

Waŋarr

The Yolŋu term for 'Dreaming'. It refers to both the ancestral past as well the ancestral beings themselves.

Wanjina/Wandjina

To Aboriginal people in the Kimberly region, 'Wanjina' is the supreme creator and a symbol of fertility and rain. Aboriginal people in the Kimberly have been painting Wanjina (also spelled 'Wandjina') in rock-art sites for millennia.

Welcome to Country

This is a custom among many Indigenous groups to ensure the safe passage of visitors through their Country. It is now extended to include Traditional Owners giving a welcome at the start of a speech or an event.

yidaki

The Yolŋu word for the long wooden wind instrument more commonly known as the 'didgeridoo'. The word 'didgeridoo' is thought to be an onomatopoetic word invented by English settlers, describing the instrument's unique resonances. There are numerous names for the instrument among the First Peoples of northern Australia. Yolŋu customs require that only men play the yidaki.

Endnotes

1. Australian Bureau of Statistics: https://www.abs.gov.au/media-centre/media-releases/aboriginal-and-torres-strait-islander-population-approaching-1-million; accessed 3 February 2023.
2. See, for instance, Nancy Williams 1982, *A Boundary is to Cross*, Routledge; Nancy Williams 1988, *Intellectual Property and Aboriginal Environmental Knowledge*, Centre for Indigenous Natural and Cultural Resource Management; Nancy Williams 1986, *The Yolŋu and Their Land*, Stanford University Press; Nancy Williams 1987, *Two Laws*, Australian Institute of Aboriginal Studies; Nancy Williams and Eugene Hunn 1982, *Resource Managers*, Westview Press; Nancy Williams and Graham Baines 1993, *Traditional Ecological Knowledge*, Centre for Resource and Environmental Studies, ANU; Janice Reid 1983, *Sorcerers and Healing Spirits*, ANU Press.
3. Damien Finch et al. 2021, 'Ages for Australia's Oldest Rock Paintings', *Nature Human Behaviour* 5, 310–18.
4. Joint Standing Committee on Northern Australia, *Never Again*, Commonwealth of Australia, December 2020: https://www.aph.gov.au/Parliamentary_Business/Committees/Joint/Former_Committees/Northern_Australia_46P/CavesatJuukanGorge/Interim_Report
5. Bill Gammage 2011, *The Biggest Estate on Earth*, Allen & Unwin, Sydney.
6. Patrick Nunn & Nicholas Reid 2015, 'Aboriginal memories of inundation of the Australian coast dating from more than 7000 years ago', *Australian Geographer*, 47:1, 11–47.
7. ibid.
8. UNESCO 2019, World Heritage List, 'Budj Bim Cultural Landscape: Description': whc.unesco.org/en/ list/1577/
9. Colin Barras 2020, 'Is an Aboriginal tale of an ancient volcano the oldest story ever told?' *Science*, 11 February: www.sciencemag.org/news/2020/02/aboriginal-tale-ancient-volcano-oldest-story-ever-told
10. Gunditj Mirring Traditional Owners Corporation, *Budj Bim Master Plan*: gunditjmirring.com/budj-bim-master-plan
11. Ian J. McNiven 2017, 'The detective work behind the Budj Bim eels traps World Heritage Bid', *The Conversation*, 8 February: theconversation.com/the-detective-work-behind-the-budj-bim-eel-traps-world-heritage-bid-71800
12. ibid.
13. Rosita Holmes and Leah Umbagai, 'Wandjinas, ochre and the art of Mowanjum people', *Japingka Aboriginal Art*: japingkaaboriginalart.com/articles/wandjinas-ochre-and-the-art-of-mowanjum-people/
14. Tasmanian Department of Primary Industries, Parks, Water and Environment, *Tasmanian Coastal Works Manual*, chapter 5: dpipwe.tas.gov.au/Documents/Tasmanian_Coastal_Works_Manual_Chapter_5_Aboriginal_Heritage_Management.pdf

15   Letitia Murgha 2012, 'Indigenous science: shell middens and fish traps', *Queensland Museum*, 8 October: qmtalksscience.wordpress.com/2012/10/08/indigenous-science-shell- middens-and-fish-traps/

16   Australian Government. Australian Electoral Commission, Fact Sheet No. 2: https://www.aec.gov.au/about_aec/Publications/Fact_Sheets/fact_sheets/fact2.pdf; accessed 30 October 2022.

17   Julianne Schultz 2021, 'Facing Foundational Wrongs' *Griffith Review* 73: Hey Utopia!

18   Alfred Deakin 1901, 'Immigration Restriction Bill', House of Representatives, *Debates*, 12 September, pp. 4805–4806, as cited in Timothy Kendall, Chapter One: Federation and the Geographies of Whiteness, in *Within China's Orbit? China through the eyes of the Australian Parliament*: https://www.aph.gov.au/About_Parliament/Parliamentary_departments/Parliamentary_Library/pubs/APF/monographs/Within_Chinas_Orbit/Chapterone; see also, National Museum of Australia. *Defining Moments. White Australia Policy*: https://www.nma.gov.au/defining-moments/resources/white-australia-policy/, accessed 30 October 2022.

19   Lyndall Ryan et al. 2023, as this project appears to be ongoing 'Colonial Frontier Massacres in Australia, 1788–1930', The Centre for 21st Century Humanities, The University of Newcastle: c21ch.newcastle.edu.au/colonialmassacres/

20   ibid.

21   See Colonial Massacres project at: https://c21ch.newcastle.edu.au/colonialmassacres/introduction.php; and https://c21ch.newcastle.edu.au/colonialmassacres/statistics.php; accessed on 3 February 2023. See also the map timeline at: https://c21ch.newcastle.edu.au/colonialmassacres/map.php; and the group massacres at: https://c21ch.newcastle.edu.au/colonialmassacres/groups.php

22   National Museum of Australia, Indigenous Cultures and History Timeline: https://www.nma.gov.au/learn/encounters-education/timeline; Australian Museum, Aboriginal and Torres Strait Islander Collection Timeline: https://australian.museum/learn/cultures/atsi-collection/timeline/; ABC Timeline: Recognition of Australia's Indigenous people: https://www.abc.net.au/news/2015-07-06/indigenous-recognition-timeline-of-australian-history/6586176; Australian Human Rights Commission: Historical context – ancient history: https://bth.humanrights.gov.au/significance/historical-context-ancient-history

23   Charles Dunford Rowley 1978, *A Matter of Justice*, Australian National University Press.

24   Human Rights and Equal Opportunity Commission 1997, *The CDEP Scheme and Racial Discrimination, A Report by the Race Discrimination Commissioner*, December.

25   Matthew Thomas 2017, 'The 1967 referendum', Parliament of Australia, 25 May: www.aph.gov.au/About_Parliament/Parliamentary_Departments/Parliamentary_Library/FlagPost/2017/May/The_1967_Referendum

26   Megan Davis 2016, 'Seeking a settlement', *The Monthly*, July.

27   *The Australian Wars*, SBS TV: https://www.sbs.com.au/ondemand/tv-series/the-australian-wars

28   https://ulurustatement.org/the-statement/view-the-statement/

29   Thomas Mayo 2019, *Finding the Heart of the Nation: The Journey of the Uluru Statement towards Voice, Treaty and Truth*, Hardie Grant Travel.

30   NAIDOC, '2019 theme': www.naidoc.org.au/get-involved/2019-theme

31   Australian Parliamentary Library 2019, 'Deakin's Letters to the *Morning Post*': https://trove.nla.gov.au/work/237566498/version/274535479?keyword=deakin%27s%20letters

32   Further information can be found in the history and timeline of the gay rights movement by Arisa White, 'From midnight raids to same-sex marriage: what's changed in the 50 years since Stonewall': refinery29.com/en-us/lgbt-gay-rights-movement-history-timeline; and Erika W. Smith, 'From Stonewall to Pride 50: the history of the Pride Parade': refinery29.com/en-us/when-was-first-gay-pride-parade-origin

33   To find out more, see: mardigras.org.au, and especially see the AGM and annual report at mardigras.org.au/agm; further history of the Evolution of the Mardi Gras can be read in the

2018 annual report of Sydney Gay and Lesbian Mardi Gras Ltd, which also celebrates the 40th anniversary: https://www.mardigras.org.au/wp-content/uploads/2022/04/MG_2018_Annual_Report.pdf

34 Sydney Gay and Lesbian Mardi Gras [@sydneymardigras], (2019, October 20), *A quick message from Graham from First Nations Rainbow and Team Sydney as we celebrate bringing WorldPride to Gadigal land! #SydneyWorldPride2023* [Tweet], Twitter: https://twitter.com/sydneymardigras/status/1185857309479710720

35 State Library of Queensland 2023, 'Aboriginal and Torres Strait Islander languages': www.slq.qld.gov.au/discover/aboriginal-and-torres-strait-islander-cultures-and-stories/languages

36 Ngaanyatjarra Pitjantjatjara Yankunytjatjara Women's Council, 'Ngangkari – Traditional Healers': www.npywc.org.au/what-we-do/ngangkari-traditional-healers/

37 Aaron Corn & Joseph N. Gumbula 2006, 'Rom and the academy repositioned: binary models in Yolŋu intellectual traditions and their application to wider inter-cultural dialogues' in L Russell (ed.), *Boundary Writing*, University of Hawai'i Press, pp. 170–179.

38 Aaron Corn 2003, 'Dreamtime wisdom, modern-time vision,' PhD thesis, The University of Melbourne, vol. I, p. 219.

39 Aaron Corn, 'Dreamtime wisdom,' vol. II, pp. 148–50.

40 Bill Gammage 2011, *The Biggest Estate on Earth*, Allen & Unwin, Sydney.

41 Bruce Pascoe 2014, *Dark Emu*, Magabala Books.

42 ibid.

43 Ian Keen 2021, 'Foragers or farmers: Dark Emu and the controversy over Aboriginal agriculture', *Anthropological Forum*, 31:1, 106–28.

44 James Boyce 2021, *Imperial Mud: The Fight for the Fens*, Icon Books.

45 The map is available at: naturaldisaster.royalcommission.gov.au/submissions/summary-submissions

46 John C. Z. Woinarski, et al. 2015, 'Ongoing unraveling of a continental fauna: Decline and extinction of Australian mammals since European settlement', in *Proceedings of the National Academy of Sciences*, 112(15), April, 4531–4540: https://www.pnas.org/doi/epdf/10.1073/pnas.1417301112

47 ibid.

48 ibid.

49 Submission to the Royal Commission into National Natural Disaster Arrangements by a collective of Indigenous and non-Indigenous academics primarily from the University of Melbourne, but also from Deakin University and Griffith University: https://indigenousknowledge.unimelb.edu.au/__data/assets/pdf_file/0012/3385578/RC_FULL-VERSION.pdf

50 James Boyce 2012, '"The Biggest Estate on Earth" by Bill Gammage', *The Monthly*, January: www.themonthly.com.au/issue/2011/december/1322699456/james-boyce/biggest-estate-earth-how-aborigines-made-australia-bill-g

51 Victor Steffensen 2020, *Fire Country*, Hardie Grant Explore.

52 ibid.

53 Australian Government, *National Indigenous Australians Agency:* https://www.niaa.gov.au/indigenous-affairs/environment/indigenous-ranger-programs; accessed 3 February 2023.

54 D. W. Hamacher, et al. 2020, 'Solstice and solar position observations in Australian Aboriginal and Torres Strait Islander traditions', *Journal of Astronomical History and Heritage*, 23(1), 89–99.

55 ibid.

56 ibid.

57 Janice Reid (ed.) 1982, *Body, Land and Spirit*, UQP.

58 J. Bach 1966, 'Dampier, William (1651–1715)', *Australian Dictionary of Biography*: https://adb.anu.edu.au/biography/dampier-william-1951

59 *Buku-Larrŋgay Mulka Centre 1999, Saltwater: Yirrkala Bark Paintings of Sea Country: Recognising Indigenous Sea Rights*, Jennifer Isaacs Publishing.

60 Kate Hagan 2007, 'And this is the Libertos, who thought they'd get away with it', *The Age*, 3 November: www.theage.com.au/national/and-this-is-the-libertos-who-thought-theyd-get-away-with-it-20071103-ge67mm.html

61 Terri Janke and Maiko Sentina 2018, *Indigenous Knowledge: Issues for Protection and Management*, IP Australia, Commonwealth of Australia.

62 See Brook Andrew's website biography: brookandrew.com/ngadhi/me

63 ANKA, 'How to buy ethically': www.anka.org.au/art-centres/buy-ethically/

64 Indigenous Art Code, 'How to buy ethically': indigenousartcode.org/how-to-buy-ethically/

65 The Importance of Torres Strait Island Singing and Dancing, Australian Institute of Aboriginal Studies, 1979, Canberra ACT

66 'Garma Statement on Indigenous Music and Performance,' archived by the National Recording Project for Indigenous Performance in Australia: https://msa.org.au/nrpipa/#vision; accessed 3 February 2023.

67 See Aaron Corn 2009, *Reflections and Voices: Exploring the Music of Yothu Yindi with Mandawuy Yunupiŋu*, Sydney University Press.

68 See Victorian State Government description of the State Memorial Service at: https://www.vic.gov.au/state-memorial-service-uncle-archie-roach-am; accessed 5 February 2023.

69 Declan Byrne 2020, 'Bars behind bars: how jail and motherhood forced rising rapper Barkaa to turn life around', *triple j*, 10 November: www.abc.net.au/triplej/news/musicnews/bars-behind-bars:-how-having-a-child-in-jail-forced-rising-rapp/12866456

70 Al Newstead 2021, 'Ziggy Ramo's update of a Paul Kelly classic is a history lesson every Australian should hear', *triple j*, 31 May: www.abc.net.au/triplej/news/musicnews/ziggy-ramo-paul-kelly-little-things-every-australian-should-hear/13366924

71 Stephen Page is quoted in Fiona Magowan 2000, 'Dancing with a difference: reconfiguring the poetic politics of Aboriginal Ritual as a national spectacle', *The Australian Journal of Anthropology*, 11:3, 1–14.

72 Nathan Sentance 2018, 'My ancestors are in our memory institutions, but their voices are missing', *IndigenousX* in *The Guardian*, 6 March: www.theguardian.com/commentisfree/2018/mar/06/my-ancestors-are-in-our-memory-institutions-but-their-voices-are-missing

73 Billy Griffiths 2016, 'Reading Australia: "Legendary Tales of the Australian Aborigines" by David Unaipon', *Australian Book Review*, 31 August: www.australianbookreview.com.au/reading-australia/legendary-tales-of-the-australian-aborigines-by-david-unaipon

74 *The Yield* by Tara June Winch teachers' resources: static.booktopia.com.au/pdf/9780143785750-1.pdf

75 Maxine Beneba Clarke 2018, 'Author Melissa Lucashenko aims for the heart', *The Saturday Paper*, No. 235, 15–21 December.

76 Eve Vincent 2013, 'Country matters: *Mullumbimby* by Melissa Lucashenko', *Sydney Review of Books*, 17 May: sydneyreviewofbooks.com/review/country-matters/

77 Declan Fry 2020, 'Fire Front: First Nations Poetry and Power Today, edited by Alison Whittaker', *Australian Book Review*, no. 423, August.

78 The Wheeler Centre, 'Fire Front: First Nations Poetry and Power Today' event: wheelercentre.com/events/fire-front-first-nations-poetry-and-power-today/

79 Art Gallery of New South Wales, 'Winner: Archibald Packing Room Prize 2020', accessed 5 March 2021: artgallery.nsw.gov.au/prizes/archibald/2020/302

80 Griffin Theatre Company, '*City of Gold* by Meyne Wyatt, 26 July – 31 August 2019': griffintheatre.com.au/whats-on/city-of-gold/

81 Victorian Premier's Literary Awards, 'City of Gold': wheelercentre.com/projects/victorian-premier-s-literary-awards-2020/city-of-gold (site inactive March 2023)
82 ibid.
83 Meyne Wyatt 2020, 'Monologue from City of Gold', *Q&A*, 9 June: youtube.com/watch?v=ys2FTUmOnIg
84 Chelsea Watego 2018, 'The irony of the Aboriginal Academic', *IndigenousX*, 20 May: indigenousx.com.au/chelsea-bond-the-irony-of-the-aboriginal-academic/
85 Belinda Quinn 2021, '"High Ground" producer Witiyana Marika: "I would like to show Australia to the world",' *NME*, 27 January: www.nme.com/en_au/features/film-features/high-ground-movie-producer-witiyana-marika-yothu-yindi-australia-interview-2865665
86 Xan Brooks 2020, '*The Furnace* review – brutish western is tough as old leather and good as gold', *The Guardian*, 5 September: www.theguardian.com/film/2020/sep/04/the-furnace-review-brutish-western-roderick-mackay
87 *Screenwest* 2020, 'Acclaimed WA film *The Furnace* premieres at Perth Festival', 11 November: www.screenwest.com.au/news/latest-news/acclaimed-wa-film-furnace-premieres-perth-festival/
88 *La Biennale di Venezia* accessed 20 March 2023, 'The Furnace': www.labiennale.org/en/cinema/2020/orizzonti/furnace
89 *Northern Territory v Mr A. Griffiths (deceased) and Lorraine Jones on behalf of the Ngaliwurru and Nungali Peoples* [2019] HCA 7.
90 Human Rights and Equal Opportunity Commission, *Bringing them home: Report of the National Inquiry into the Separation of Aboriginal and Torres Strait Islander Children from Their Families*, Commonwealth of Australia, 1997: humanrights.gov.au/sites/default/files/content/pdf/social_justice/bringing_them_home_report.pdf
91 Australian Government 2008, 'Apology to Australia's Indigenous Peoples', 13 February: indigenous.gov.au/reconciliation/apology-australias-indigenous-peoples
92 Monument Australia, 'Stolen Generations Memorial': monumentaustralia.org.au/themes/culture/indigenous/display/23125-stolen-generations-memorial
93 Monument Australia, 'Stolen Generations Memorial': monumentaustralia.org.au/themes/culture/indigenous/display/80245-stolen-generations-memorial
94 Monument Australia, 'Stolen Generations Memorial': monumentaustralia.org.au/themes/culture/indigenous/display/20437-stolen-generations-memorial
95 See Lyndall Ryan et al. 2023, 'Colonial Frontier Massacres in Eastern Australia 1788–1872': The Centre for 21st Century Humanities, The University of Newcastle: c21ch.newcastle.edu.au/colonialmassacres/
96 RRR Project Team 2021, 'Why were ancestral remains taken?', *Return, Reconcile, Renew*: returnreconcilerenew.info/ohrm/biogs/E002083b.htm
97 Dr Stan Florek 2016, 'Fortieth anniversary of returning to Truganini land (and water)', *Australian Museum*, Published on 20 July 2016: australian.museum/blog-archive/science/our-global-neighbours-remembering-truganini/
98 Paul Turnbull 2016, 'Managing and mapping the history of collecting Indigenous human remains', *Australian Library Journal*, 65:3, 203–12. See also Ros Langford 1983, 'Our heritage—your playground', *Australian Archaeology*, 16, 1–6.
99 RRR Project Team 2021, 'Why were ancestral remains taken?': returnreconcilerenew.info/ohrm/biogs/E002083b.htm
100 Victorian Aboriginal Heritage Council 2020, 'An historical overview of the desecration of Aboriginal burial places and repatriation of Ancestors back to Country': aboriginalheritagecouncil.vic.gov.au/historical-overview © Copyright State Government of Victoria
101 Display of human remains for memorial purposes is sensitive in many cultures. See the debate about human remains displayed at Choeung Ek Killing Fields in Brigitte Sion 2011,

'Conflicting sites of memory in post-genocide Cambodia', *Humanity: An International Journal of Human Rights, Humanitarianism, and Development*, 2:1, 8; the debate about displaying human hair in the US Holocaust Memorial Museum in Timothy Ryback 1993, 'Evidence of evil', *New Yorker*, 15 November.

102 Rob McWilliams 2016, 'Resting places: a history of Australian Indigenous ancestral remains at Museum Victoria', *Museums Victoria*, 25 August: museumsvictoria.com.au/media/4273/resting_places__history_of_ancestral_remains_25_aug_2016.docx

103 ibid.

104 B. Andrew, M. Langton, J. Neath, 'Making visible the Frontier Wars and comparative memorialization', in J. Barrett, A. Alba and D. Moses (eds), *The Holocaust, Human Rights, and the Museum*, University of Pennsylvania Press, 2021.

105 Report of the Joint Select Committee on Constitutional Recognition relating to Aboriginal and Torres Strait Islander Peoples, List of Recommendations: aph.gov.au/Parliamentary_Business/Committees/Joint/Former_Committees/Constitutional_Recognition_2018/ConstRecognition/Final_Report/section?id=committees%2freportjnt%2f024213%2f26813

106 Brook Andrew 2018, 'Representation, Remembrance and the Memorial (RRM) – Forum 2018': rr.memorial/forum

107 Brook Andrew 2018, 'Representation, Remembrance and the Memorial (RRM) – Introduction', accessed 28 January 2020: rr.memorial/introduction

108 For informed discussion of the concept, instances of and laws relating to genocide, see Donald Bloxham and A. Dirk Moses (eds) 2010, *The Oxford Handbook of Genocide Studies*, Oxford University Press.

109 R. Nielsen et al. 2017, 'Tracing the peopling of the world through genomics', *Nature* 541, 302–10.

110 ibid.

111 See the University of Melbourne 2021, 'Indigenous business booming: new data reveals sector's success', 30 April: about.unimelb.edu.au/newsroom/news/2021/april/indigenous-business-booming-new-data-reveals-sectors-success

112 Henry Reynolds 2004, *Fate of a Free People: The Classic Account of the Tasmanian Wars*, Penguin; Lyndall Ryan 1981, *The Aboriginal Tasmanians*, UQP.

113 N.J.B. Plomley 1988, 'The sealers of Bass Strait and the Cape Barren Island Community', *Tasmanian Historical Research Association*.

114 Paul Daley 2021, 'A statue of a Tasmanian colonist has been covered up. Should it ever return?' in *The Guardian*, 16 September: theguardian.com/culture/2021/sep/16/a-statue-of-a-tasmanian-colonist-has-been-covered-up-should-it-ever-return; accessed 3 February 2023.

115 Yothu Yindi Foundation, 'Garma event info: protocols and conduct': yyf.com.au/garma-festival/protocols-and-conduct/

116 Parks Australia 2017, 'Uluṟu climb closure - Words from the Chair', November: parksaustralia.gov.au/uluru/pub/uktnp-climb-closure-words-from-chair-nov-2017.pdf

117 Parks Australia, 'Uluru climb to close in 2019': parksaustralia.gov.au/uluru/news/uluru-climb-to-close/

118 Chelsea Heaney and Samantha Jonscher 2019, 'Uluru climb closed permanently as hundreds scale sacred site on final day', *ABC News*, 25 October: abc.net.au/news/2019-10-25/uluru-climb-closed-permanently-by-traditional-owners/11639248

119 Race, human, in Britannica: britannica.com/topic/race-human; accessed 13 November, 2022.

120 Carey, J., 2012. The Racial Imperatives of Sex: birth control and eugenics in Britain, the United States and Australia in the interwar years. *Women's History Review* 21, 733–752. https://doi.org/10.1080/09612025.2012.658180

121 The Biological State, Nazi Racial Hygiene 1933-1939, in 'Introduction to the Holocaust,' *Holocaust Encyclopedia*: encyclopedia.ushmm.org/content/en/article/introduction-to-the-holocaust, accessed on 13 November 2022.

122 See Jennie Carter 1998, h-anzau Discussion Logs by month, HNet (Humanities and Social Sciences Online): https://lists.h-net.org/cgi-bin/logbrowse.pl?trx=vx&list=h-anzau&month=9801&week=b&msg=6C6XT8j04zXGWrpNnAysdA&user=&pw=

123 As cited by Jennie Carter 1998, A.P. Elkin, *The Australian Aborigines*, (5th edition), 1973, p.366.

124 As cited by Jennie Carter from Charles Rowley 1998, *The Destruction of Aboriginal Society*, Canberra: ANU Press, 1972, p.103; open source file: https://openresearch-repository.anu.edu.au/bitstream/1885/114963/2/b12160490.pdf

125 As cited by Jennie Carter from Anna Haebich 1998, *For their own good. Aborigines and Government in the South West of Western Australia*, Nedlands, W.A. Published by the University of Western Australia Press for the Charles and Joy Staples South West Region Publications Fund, 1992, p.54.

126 *Cairns Post* 1926, May 5, Trove search, 13 November, 2022, https://trove.nla.gov.au/newspaper/article/40497593; the Trove entry states May 5 for this article but the image of the newspaper column states May 6.

127 ibid.

128 Curated by Roslyn Poignant ; community consultation coordinators: Walter Palm Island, Manbarra ; Josephine Geia, Palm Island ; and Ernest Grant, Girringun, Education Services, Public Programs, National Library of Australia, *Captive lives: looking for Tambo and his companions*, A travelling exhibition of the National Library of Australia, exhibition background information kit, Canberra: National Library of Australia, 1998; Mungall Tours, Captive Lives Story: https://www.mungallaaboriginaltours.com.au/about/captive-lives; accessed 14 November, 2022; see also, Katherine Gregory, The Human Zoo: Documentary sheds light on stolen Aboriginal people 'treated as animals', *ABC online*: https://www.abc.net.au/news/2017-01-28/the-human-zoo-documentary-aboriginal-people-forced-exhibits/8219116

129 ibid.

130 Gilles Boëtsch and Yann Ardagna 2008, *Human Zoos : the "Savage" and the anthropologist*.

131 Mary Frances O'Dowd 2020, 'Explainer: what is systemic racism and institutional racism?', *The Conversation*, February 5: https://theconversation.com/explainer-what-is-systemic-racism-and-institutional-racism-131152

132 Presidential Committee on Harvard & the Legacy of Slavery 2022, 'Report of the Presidential Committee on Harvard & the Legacy of Slavery': legacyofslavery.harvard.edu/report; see also Ayana Archie, 'Harvard releases report detailing its ties to slavery, plans to issue reparations', *National Public Radio*, April 27: www.npr.org/2022/04/27/1094971897/harvard-university-report-slavery-slave-trade-reparations-students#:~:text=The%20committee%20found%20that%20Harvard,Harvard's%20presidents%2C%20professors%20and%20students; accessed 13 November, 2022.

133 ibid.

134 Julianne Schultz 2022, *The Idea of Australia, A search for the soul of the nation*, Allen & Unwin

135 Commonwealth of Australia Constitution Act: https://www.legislation.gov.au/Details/C2013Q00005, accessed 30 October 2022. The Commonwealth Constitution maps out the distribution of power in the federation with the states and territories allocated particular powers, while, usually, the Commonwealth retains only those with national significance. Other important constitutional legislation includes the *Statute of Westminster Adoption Act 1942* which established Australia as an independent Commonwealth nation, and the *Australia*

Act 1986 which completed the process of independence from the UK. States and territories have their own constitutions.

136   Heidi Norman and Anne Maree Pyne 2022, 'In The Australian Wars, Rachel Perkins dispenses with the myth Aboriginal people didn't fight back', *The Conversation*, September 21: https://theconversation.com/in-the-australian-wars-rachel-perkins-dispenses-with-the-myth-aboriginal-people-didnt-fight-back-190967; accessed 29 October 2022.
137   ibid.
138   ibid.
139   American Anthropological Association 1998, 'AAA Statement on Racism': https://www.americananthro.org/ConnectWithAAA/Content.aspx?ItemNumber=2583; The statement was 'adopted by the Executive Board of the American Anthropological Association on May 17, 1998, acting on a draft prepared by a committee of representative American anthropologists. It does not reflect a consensus of all members of the AAA, as individuals vary in their approaches to the study of 'race.' We believe that it represents generally the contemporary thinking and scholarly positions of a majority of anthropologists.' I note that no such statement on racism has been made by Australian anthropologists, and certainly not the Australian Anthropological Society.
140   Stephen Jay Gould 1981, *The Mismeasure of Man*, New York: Norton.
141   The Go Foundation: https://www.gofoundation.org.au/; accessed 14 November 2022.
142   Mary Frances O'Dowd 2020, 'Explainer: what is systemic racism and institutional racism?', *The Conversation*, February 5: https://theconversation.com/explainer-what-is-systemic-racism-and-institutional-racism-131152
143   ibid.
144   ibid.
145   ibid.
146   Yin Paradies 2006, *International Journal of Epidemiology*, Volume 35, Issue 4, August, Pages 888–901: https://doi.org/10.1093/ije/dyl056
147   Mark McKenna 2018, 'Moment of truth: history and Australia's future', *Quarterly Essay*, 69, March.
148   Stan Grant 2019, *Australia Day*, HarperCollins.
149   Noel Pearson 2018, 'A rightful place: race, recognition and a more complete commonwealth', *Quarterly Essay*, 55, September.
150   ibid.
151   The research and reporting on Aboriginal deaths in custody by *The Guardian* and *Guardian Australia* have been exemplary. See, for instance, Lorena Allam, Calla Wahlquist and Nick Evershed 2020, 'Aboriginal Deaths in Custody: 434 have died since 1991, new data shows', *The Guardian*, 6 June: theguardian.com/Australia-news/2020/jun/06/aboriginal-deaths-in-custody-434-have-died-since-1991-new-data-shows; 'Deaths Inside, Indigenous Australian Deaths in Custody 2020' is an interactive database, researched and published by *Guardian Australia*: theguardian.com/australia-news/ng-interactive/2018/aug/28/deaths-inside-indigenous-australian-deaths-in-custody
152   The Human Rights Law Centre in Melbourne represented the family of Yorta Yorta woman, Ms Tanya Day, in the coronial inquest into her death, and the website provides information and a chronology of events: hrlc.org.au/tanya-day-overview
153   Human Rights Law Centre 2020, 'Tanya Day inquest: summary of findings', 9 April: https://www.hrlc.org.au/human-rights-case-summaries/2020/9/8/tanya-day-inquest-summary-of-findings#:~:text=The%20Victorian%20Government%20decriminalise%20the,Custody%20had%20recommended%20its%20abolition.

154 Coroners Court of Victoria 2020, 'Finding of the inquest into the death of Tanya Louise Day', 9 April: www.coronerscourt.vic.gov.au/sites/default/files/2020-04/Finding%20-%20Tanya%20Day-%20COR%202017%206424%20-%20AMENDED%2017042020.pdf

155 For an explanation and analysis of these recommendations, see Chris Charles 2011, 'The Royal Commission into Aboriginal Deaths in Custody and the duty of care owed to prisoners in South Australia', *Australian Indigenous Law Review*, 15:1, 110–16.

156 Dr John Gardiner-Garden access date as 20 March 2023, *Closing the Gap, Parliament Of Australia*, at URL: https://www.aph.gov.au/About_Parliament/Parliamentary_Departments/Parliamentary_Library/pubs/BriefingBook44p/ClosingGap

157 See, for instance, The Cairns Post 1925, 'Our Aboriginals. Smoothing the pillow of dying race. Missionary's efforts', 6 May: trove.nla.gov.au/newspaper/article/40497593

Image credits
(left to right, top to bottom where more than one image appears on a page)

Cover artwork: Antara © Betty Kuntiwa Pumani / Licensed by Copyright Agency, 2023. Image courtesy the artists, Mimili Maku Arts and Alcaston Gallery
Page: 2, 3, 9, 14, 22, 35, 36, 42, 54, 68, 71, 75, 78, 79, 103, 111, 134, 136, 138, 146, 147, 181, 184, 190, 191, 203, 204, 205, 217, 230, 234, 241, 246, 247, 252, 254a Wayne Quilliam; 5, 206 Rainforestation Nature Park; 8 Peter Randolph/Western Australian Museum/Wunambal Gaambera Aboriginal Corporation; 18 Wunambal Gaambera Aboriginal Corporation; 21 Melinda Sawers; 28a, 85, 120, 176 National Archives of Australia; 28b Australian News & Information Bureau/John Tanner/National Archives of Australia; 32 W Pedersen/National Archives of Australia; 38 Courtesy of AIATSIS, Jean Horner Collection, item HORNER2.J01.BW-N04612_12; 39 Courtesy of AIATSIS, Department of Aboriginal Affairs (DAA) Collection, item DAA.003.BWN04528; 43 Mark Metcalfe/City of Sydney; 58 courtesy of the NT AIDS & Hepatitis Council; 61 Joseph Mayers/Miss First Nation Australia; 66 Courtesy of AIATSIS, Barbara Wentworth Collection, item WENTWORTH.B03.CS-000168946; 73a Illustrator: Katelyn Griffin/NPY Women's Council; 73b NPY Women's Council; 74 Illustrator: Joshua Santospirito/NPY Women's Council; 83 Aaron Corn 2003 'Dreamtime Wisdom, Modern-Time Vision,' Vol. I, p. 219, PhD thesis, The University of Melbourne; 88 Department of Agriculture, Water and the Environment (DAWE); 91 Courtesy of AIATSIS, Sylvie Poirier Collection, item POIRIER.S09.CS-000115846; 93 courtesy of Victor Steffensen; 98 Mirima Dawang Woorlab-gerring Language and Culture Centre (MDWg); 101a Image modified from Google Earth; 101b Andrew Smith; 108 Courtesy of AIATSIS, Aldo Massola Collection, item MASSOLA.A01.BW-N02450_11; 112 Rohan Thompson; 114 Dreamtime Kullilla-Art/Greg Dries; 115, 122, 125 Buku-Larrŋgay Mulka Centre; 117 Australian News & Information Bureau/National Archives of Australia; 123 House of Representatives/Commonwealth Parliament of Australia; 128 Vincent Namatjira/Iwantja Arts/THIS IS NO FANTASY/Art Gallery of NSW; 130 LuGu Productions; 142 www.missionsongsproject.com; 149 Courtesy of Short Black Opera; 154 Richard McDowell/Alamy Stock Photo; 177 Trevor Graham Yarra Bank Films Pty Ltd/National Archives of Australia; 179 Courtesy of AIATSIS, Aboriginal and Torres Strait Islander Commission (ATSIC) Collection, photographer Peter Smith, item ATSIC.006.CN-E00011_03; 196 Courtesy of AIATSIS, Royal Commonwealth Society of Tasmania Collection, item RCS.001.BW-N00701_07; 212 Russell Ord/Koomal Dreaming; 214 Melanie Faith Dove/Yothu Yindi Foundation; 218 Nura Gunyu; 221 Michele and Tom Grimm/Alamy Stock Photo; 222 Jeff Greenberg/Contributor/Getty Images; 225 Wim Wiskerke/Alamy Stock Photo

Index

Abdulla, Ian 128
Aboriginal 260
Aboriginal and Torres Strait Islander Commission (ATSIC) 43
Aboriginal and Torres Strait Islander Peoples
  collaborations with scientists 6, 12
  colonial impressions 107–9
  in custody 29, 106, 251–5
  and federal Parliament law-making powers 37–8, 44
  and frontier wars 17, 23, 25–6, 108, 150, 175, 234–5
  importance of better understanding of 251
  inclusion in national census 37, 38–9
  institutional control 31–2
  as low-paid labour force 32
  move from rural to urban areas 3–4, 34
  population 4
  recognition in Australian Constitution 24, 27, 37–9, 233
  rightful place 36–53
  war service 40–1
  see also Indigenous *headings*; Traditional Owner(s)
Aboriginal art 110–32, 163–4
  advice on buying authentic art 128–32
  bark paintings 116–17
  central to Aboriginal life, identity and culture 113
  collecting 115
  and Country 121–4
  ethical dealings 124–6
  in galleries and exhibitions 110–11, 119, 121–2, 127–8, 130
  in the global market 126–8
  meaning within 112–13
  Pintupi art movement 117–19
  rock art *see* rock art
  styles 110, 118–20
  themes 116, 118, 119
  Warlpiri art 119–21
  Yolŋu art traditions 116–17, 121–2, 123–4
Aboriginal artefacts 19–20, 21
Aboriginal Arts Board of the Australia Council 121
Aboriginal deaths in custody 29, 106, 251–5
Aboriginal English 67–8
Aboriginal fire management practices 91–7
  fire in Country 93–4, 95–7
  to build resistance to natural disasters 91–3
Aboriginal flag 41, 257
Aboriginal Land Commission 33
Aboriginal land management practices 3, 10–11, 85, 86–9
Aboriginal land rights 3, 28–9, 121, 123, 180, 264
  see also native title
Aboriginal Land Rights (Northern Territory) Act 1976 29, 123, 224
Aboriginal Languages Act 2017 (NSW) 66–7
Aboriginal medicine and healing 72–3, 103–5
Aboriginal or Torres Strait Islander person, current legal definition 57
Aboriginal pastoralists 33–4
Aboriginal People(s) 1, 260
  dehumanising 231
  occupied and cared for continent for over 65,000 years 1, 7, 22, 44, 53, 64, 84, 86, 92, 126, 143, 201
Aboriginal populations, diversity 7–8
Aboriginal 'race' 23–4, 32, 229–31, 234, 236
Aboriginal Reconnaissance Unit in Arnhem Land 40
Aboriginal rights 34, 37, 42, 158
  and 1967 referendum 24, 37–9
  strong support for 39
Aboriginal Tent Embassy 42, 260–1
Aboriginal women in custody 243–5
Aboriginal words in Australian English 76
acknowledgement of Country 261
AFL, racism within 239–41
agribusinesses 34
agricultural practices vs hunter-gatherer debate 10–11, 86–9, 157
AIATSIS map 259
Albanese, Anthony/Albanese Government 50, 251
Alberts, Jada 166–7
alcohol/alcoholism 108, 253
ancestors 10, 22, 55, 56, 70, 261
  stories from 11–12
  see also spiritual ancestors
ancestral 261
ancestral beings/events 56, 146, 147
ancestral remains 195–200, 210–11
  collecting and display 199
  National Resting Place 200
  reasons institutions kept 197–8, 239
  repatriation 195–7, 198–200, 239
  as sacred objects 199
ancestral spirits 104, 225
Andrew, Brook Garru 127, 200
Ang-Gnarra Aboriginal Corporation 148
ANKA (Arnhem, Northern and Kimberley Artists) Aboriginal Corporation 129
anthropologists 55, 67, 80, 89, 112, 239, 261
Anu, Christine 136, 137
APY Women's Collaborative 112
aquaculture system (Budj Bim) 13–17
Araluen, Alexis, Melissa and Evelyn 152
archaeological evidence 10
  middens 19–21, 265
  rock art 10, 17–18
  vegetation patterns and land management 10–11, 85–9
archaeological methods 9, 15
archaeologists 1, 7, 8, 10, 15, 17
Archibald Prize 126, 163–4
art *see* Aboriginal art
Arthur, Governor Sir George 209
assimilation period/policies 29, 32, 36, 142, 189, 216, 261
Association of Northern Kimberley and Arnhem Aboriginal Artists 125
astronomy 99–103
  solar points 100–2
  star maps 102–3
AUSTLANG 260
Australia Day (January 26) 27, 245–7
  suggested change to January 1 246
Australia Post, recognition of traditional names for mail delivery 65
Australian citizens 24–5, 27, 233
Australian colonies 23, 27
Australian Constitution 27
  and 1967 Referendum 24, 27, 37–9
  Aboriginal and Torres Strait Islander peoples not citizens under 27, 233
  difficulties to change 37, 52
  drafted during the Australian Wars 234–5
  recognition of Voice for First Nations peoples in 45–53, 250, 256
  right for the Yolŋu clan to exist and be recognised in 250
Australian Declaration Towards Reconciliation 45
Australian Indigenous Minority Supplier Council (AIMSC) 204

Australian Institute of Aboriginal and Torres Strait
  Islander Studies (AIATSIS) 199, 239, 259
Australian Museum 29, 152
Australian values 30
Australian War Memorial 40–1
Australian Wars, The (documentary series) 234–5
authenticity of Aboriginal art 128–32

Bacow, Lawrence 232
Baker, Danzal (Baker Boy) 73, 138, 143
Balanggarra Traditional Owners 17
Bangarra Dance Theatre 147, 148
Bani, Ephraim 136
Banks, Joseph 232
bäpurru 122
Bardon, Geoffrey 117–18
Bardon, James 118–19
bark paintings 116–17
Barkaa 143
Barns, Greg 248
Barunga Festival 55
Barunga Statement 139
Beautiful, Talented & Deadly 62
Beautiful One Day (play) 167
becoming Australia 23–30
Behrendt, Larissa 161–2
Bell, Diane 57
Bennelong 107, 108
Bennett, Lou 144–5
Berg, Uncle Jim (Gunditjmara Elder) 198, 199
Berndt, Ronald and Catherine 116
bicentennial celebrations (1988) 245
biodiversity of Country, protecting 3, 6, 14, 90, 94
Birch, Tony 159
Bird, Michael I. 8
Birrarung Marr 4
Birritjama, Dawidi 117
Black Johnny 116
Black Lives Matter movement 143, 251–5
Black Olive, The 212
Black Rainbow 62
Black Summer (2019–2020) 89–92
Black Wars (Tasmania) 209–11
Blackburn, Justice 121, 187–8
Blackfulla Bookclub 169
Blake, Andrew 124
Blue Mud Bay High Court sea rights claim 121–2
body paint 2, 147
Boon Wurrung People 62
Bora grounds 148
Bosun, David 100–1, 102
Bourke, Chris 59
Boyce, James 88–9, 94
'Bradshaws' 116
Briggs, Adam 144
Briggs, Tony 173
Bringing Them Home report 29, 32–3, 190
British
  claim possession of east coast of continent 23, 233–4
  establish penal colony at Port Jackson 23, 234
British invasion of Australia 23
  force Indigenous people from their land 17, 28, 37, 179
  and frontier wars 17, 23, 25–6, 108, 150, 175, 209–10, 234–5
Budj Bim Cultural Landscape (south-west Victoria) 9, 12–17, 89
Buku-Larrŋgay Mulka Centre 115
buŋgul (dance and performances) 122
Burney, Linda 50
business *see* Indigenous businesses

Calma, Tom 49, 71, 72
capital cities, traditional names 65, 68, 257
carbon credits 95

Carter, Jennie 230
Central Desert art 118
ceremonies
  body painting 147
  dance as part of 146–7
  funeral 146
  sunset 75–6
  Welcome to Country 30, 55, 56, 268
Chant of Jimmie Blacksmith, The (Keneally) 247
Charter of Human Rights and Responsibilities Act 2006 (Vic) 254
Chatwin, Bruce 55
Cheetham Fraillon, Deborah 149–50
children's literature 167–8
City of Gold (play) 164, 165
clan system 54, 81–2
clapsticks 138, 254
Clarkson, Chris 7
Cleverman (TV series) 173
clevermen 104, 261
climate change 89, 99
Closing the Gap 193, 256
Cochrane Smith, Fanny 133–4
Code Certificates 131
Code of Practice of the National Association for the Visual Arts 129
Cole, Malcolm 60
Coleman, Claire G. 158–9
colonists
  encounters with First Peoples 107–9
  and frontier wars 17, 23, 25–6, 108, 150, 175, 234–5
Coloured Stone (band) 245
Commonwealth of Australia Constitution Act 1900 27, 234
Commonwealth Government, Indigenous procurement policy 202, 205
Commonwealth Parliament
  opening of first 24
  white Australia policy 23–6, 233
  see also Voice to Parliament for First Nations peoples, constitutional recognition of
Community Development Program (CDP) 205
Conciliation and Arbitration Commission 33
Connolly, Michael J. 114
Convention on the Elimination of All Forms of Racial Discrimination 239
Cook, Captain James 23, 76, 233
cool burns 94
Corn, Aaron 81, 139, 140, 141
Council for Aboriginal Reconciliation 29, 45
Council for Aboriginal Reconciliation Act 1991 248–9
Country 262
  and art 121–4
  biodiversity of 6, 14, 53, 90, 94
  fire in 93–4, 95–7
  Indigenous rangers Working on Country Program 3, 97–8
  and kinship 77–83
  and language 65–76
  listening to 22
  living on, and knowledge 5, 84
  spiritual beliefs connection to 55–6, 187–8
  and star maps 102–3
  and tourism 2–3
Coutts, Pete 15
COVID-19 pandemic and restrictions 59, 127, 129–30, 206, 213, 251
Creoles 67–8
criminal justice system 29, 106, 251–5
Crispin, Judith 119–20
Crown lands 179
Crowther, William 210–11
culinary tourism 212–13
cultural awareness for visitors 216–26

Index 279

language rules 220
photographs and videos 221
questions which may not be welcome 219
signs and published cultural rules and protocols 221–6
speaking a few words of a First language 217
when to use names of people and places and when not to 219–20
cultural burning 91–7
cultural diversity and resilience 54–64
   gender identities 57–64
   identity 56–7
   religious life and rituals 55–6
   traditions and cultures deserve respect 64
cultural heritage 9
   destruction of 9–10
culture 4–5, 262
   definition 29–30
   as a pillar 29–30
   storytelling is 174
   see also dance; music
Cummeragunga Mission walk-off 149, 150
Curtis, Roy Jupurrula 120

Daley, Paul 210–11
Dambimangari Traditional Owners 17
Dampier, William 107
Dan, Uncle Seaman 137
dance 122, 134, 135
   adornment and body painting 147
   ceremonial performances 146
   contemporary 147
   festivals 2, 3, 54, 147–8
   Indigenous dance traditions 135, 145–9
   movement and gestures 146
Dark Emu (Pascoe) and debate 11, 86–9, 105, 157
Davis, Megan 39
Day, Aunty Tanya 253–4
Deakin, Alfred 24
deceased persons, use of substitute names for 56, 219–20
Desart 125, 129
Dhungala Children's Choir 150
Dhuwa (crow) 81, 82, 122
Dickson, Greg 68
digital writing 168–9
dinner camps 19–21
disempowering racism 242
Djab Wurrung People 215
Djatpaŋarri 140
Djawa, Tom 117
Dodson, Mick 190
Dodson, Patrick 50
Donovan, Clayton 213
Donovan, Emma 144
'the Dreaming' (the Dreamtime) 55, 75, 113, 118, 120, 139, 262
Dreamtime Divas (drag duo) 63
Dreyfus, Mark 50
Drover's Wife: The Legend of Molly Johnson (play and film) 159, 169
Dunaman, Lasey (TJay) 63, 64
'dying race' 23–4, 229–31, 235

Eades, Diane 67
East Journey 141
Eckermann, Ali Cobby 152
eel traps (at Budj Bim) 14, 15–16
Elders 22, 55–6, 79, 108, 262
Elkin, A. P. 230
employment 32, 33
   see also indentured labour
endemic mammal extinctions 90–1
equal pay 33–4
Erub dialect 269
Eseli, Peter 101

ethical dealings in Aboriginal art 124–6
Eumeralla Wars 17, 150

fairness 30
family life 36, 54
Farmers or Hunter-Gatherers? The Dark Emu Debate (Sutton and Walshe) 88, 89
farming practices vs hunter-gatherers debate 86–9, 157
Faulkhead, Shannon 199
Federal Council for the Advancement of Aborigines (FCAA) 37
Federal Council for the Advancement of Aborigines and Torres Strait Islanders (FCAATSI) 37
Federation Movement 27
festivals 2, 3, 22, 27, 54, 147–8, 213, 245–6
film and television storytellers 75, 169–74
Final Quarter, The (documentary) 143, 240
fire *see* Aboriginal fire management practices
fire extent map, July 2019 to May 2020 88, 89–90
'firestick farming' 94
First Australians 260
First Languages Australia 71–2
First Nations National Constitutional Convention 46, 47–8, 250
First Nations People 260
First Nations Rainbow 60
First Nations Voice to Parliament 45–53, 250, 256
First Peoples 260
First World War, Aboriginal men enlist in 40
Fisk Jubilee Singers 134–5
Forrest, Andrew 205
Fortescue Metals Group 204
fraudulent art 125–6, 131, 132
Frazier, Franklin 237
freehold title 123, 178, 262
frontier wars 17, 23, 25–6, 108, 150, 175, 209–10, 234–5
   see also genocide; massacres
Fuller, Robert 102–3
funeral ceremonies 146
Furnace, The (film) 169, 170–1
future for Indigenous Australia 245–55
   Black Lives Matter 251–5
   improving cultural awareness and avoiding racism 256–8
   January 26 as date of protest or celebration 27, 245–8
   reconciliation 248–9
   treating Indigenous people with dignity 256, 258
   see also Voice to Parliament for First Nations peoples, constitutional recognition of

Gammage, Bill
   on Aboriginal peoples use of fire 94
The Biggest Estate on Earth: How Aborigines Made Australia 10–11, 86
Ganalbiŋu language 75
Garimara, Doris Pilkington 174
Gariwerd Grampians National Park 214–15
Garma Festival 55, 131, 213–14
   protocols and conduct 221–3, 224
'Garma Statement on Indigenous Music and Dance' 137
Garrett, Peter 13
gay and lesbian people *see* Indigenous LGBTQIA+
Gayarra Wanjina Aarwarrndju 18
gender identities 57–64
gender roles 57–8
genocide 190, 195, 200, 209, 210, 235
George, Tommy 95
Ghillar, Uncle (Euahlayi Elder) 102–3
Gina, Nova (Dallas) 63
Giro Giro 116
glossary 259–68
Goodes, Adam 126, 143, 160, 227, 239–40, 244

Gould, Stephen Jay 238–9
gourmet food 212–13
government administered settlements 28, 31, 36
  see also missions/missionaries; reserves
governments
  assimilation policies 32, 36, 94, 142, 229, 261
  control of Aboriginal 'race' 32
  forceful removal of 'half-caste' children *see* Stolen Generations
  investment in Indigenous communities 34
  'protection and segregation' era 35, 94, 229, 266
  removal of 'full-bloods' to reserves 32, 189
Grant, Stan 57, 161, 240, 246–7
graphic novels 168
Griffen, Ryan 173
Griffiths, Billy 153
'gulag archipelago' 31–2
Gulpilil, David 75, 174
Gumatj clan/tongue 75, 76
Gumbala, Joe 81
Gunditj Mirring Corporation 16
Gunditjmara People 12–17, 150, 198
Gungaletta People 179
Gunyu, Nura 218
gurrutu 263
gutharra–märi (daughter's child–mother's mother link) 81, 122
Gwion Gwion 7, 116

Haddon, Alfred C. 135, 177
Haebich, Anna 231
Hamacher, Duana 99, 100
Hawke, Robert 139
healers 104
Healing Foundation 193
Heiss, Anita 160–1
High Court of Australia
  Mabo case 3, 175–80, 182, 188
  Timber Creek case 187
  Wik case 181
  Yanner v Eaton 178
  Yorta Yorta case 180–1, 185
High Ground (film) 169–70
Hohnen, Michael 145
Holmes, Rosita 18–19
Holt, Harold 24
homophobia 63
Honey Art Dreaming mural 118
Horman, Heidi 235
Howard, John/Howard Government 43, 45, 181, 191
human evolution 239
Human Rights and Equal Opportunity Commission 29, 32–3, 189
Human Rights Law Centre 253–4, 255
hunter-gatherers vs farming practices debate 10–11, 86–9, 157
Hurley, General David 41

Ice Age 8, 12, 84, 201
identity *see* Indigenous identity
Ilan style of music 136–7
Immigration Restriction Act 1901 24
incarceration rates of Aboriginal people 29, 251–3, 257
incipient agriculture 89
indentured labour 77, 84, 171, 189, 263
Indigenous Art Code (IartC) 129, 130–2
Indigenous Australian 263
Indigenous Business Australia (IBA) 208
Indigenous businesses 34, 202, 204–6
Indigenous communities 34–5
  on ancestral lands 35
  in urban areas 4, 34–5
Indigenous identity 56–7
  gender identities 57–64

Indigenous Land Use Agreements 9–10, 182, 187, 263
Indigenous languages 65–76, 216–17, 264
  Aboriginal English 67–8
  Aboriginal words in Australian English 76
  and Country 65–76
  in film and music 75–6
  Kimberley region 18
  language work of ngangkari to heal 72–3
  in New South Wales schools 66–7
  preservation strategies 71–2
  right to speak mother tongue 67, 70–1
  role 43–4, 65–6
  as sacred 70
  social relations of 70
  speaking 66
  Torres Strait Islander languages 68–9
Indigenous laws and customs 29, 180
Indigenous LGBTQIA+
  accept and empower brothers and sisters 63–4
  cultural life 58–60
  culture and lifestyle 61–2
  Melbourne's LGBTQIA+ MIDSUMMA Festival 62
Indigenous people 260
Indigenous rangers 217
  working on Country 3, 97–8
Indigenous sportspeople, racism towards 239–41
Indigenous tourism 1–3, 4–5, 201–2, 206–15
  COVID-19 restrictions 206
  cultural awareness for visitors 216–26
  domestic and international demand 207–8
  gourmet food and culinary tourism 212–13
  immersive cultural experiences 213–14
  and information about Indigenous culture and history 209–11
  landscapes of Indigenous Australia 214–15
  what if your guide is not Indigenous? 208–12
Indigenous Tourism Champions Program 208
Indigenous Voice *see* Voice to Parliament for First Nations peoples, constitutional recognition of
IndigenousX Pty Ltd. 154, 168, 169
institutional control 31–2
institutional racism 243
interpersonal racism 239–41

Janke, John Paul 44
Janke, Terri 126
Jannawi Dance Clan 43
January 26 protests and festivals 27, 245–8
Jardwadjali People 215
Johnson, Crystal 58
Johnson, Patricia 44
Juukan Gorge caves, blasting of 9

Kaberry, Phyllis M. 57
Kahau, Mahealani 208
Kala Lagaw Ya (language) 68, 69
Kalaw Kawaw Ya dialect 69
Karntawarra, Walangari 130
Kawrareg dialect 69
Keating, Paul 187
Kelly, Paul 139, 143
Kimberley rock art 9, 17–19, 114–15
kinship systems 54–5, 122, 263
  Aboriginal 77–83
  complex systems and nomenclature 78–9
  and Country 77–83
  and identity 57
  Kimberley region 18–19
  skin names 77, 80–1, 82–3, 267
  Torres Strait Islander 77
  Yolŋu People 81–3, 122
knowledge 5, 11–12, 84–109, 126, 263–4
  Aboriginal fire management practices 91–7
  astronomy 99–103

hunter-gatherer vs farming practices debate 11, 86–9, 157
Indigenous rangers: working on Country 3, 97–8, 217
Indigenous sorcerers 106
seasons and weather knowledge 98–9
stories handed down from ancestors 11–12
taught through living on Country 5, 84
Traditional Aboriginal medicine and healing 72–3, 103–5
Koomal Dreaming 213
Koorie Heritage Trust 4
Kow Swamp ancestral remains 7, 198–9
Kriol 76–8, 264
Kulgalgau Ya dialect 69
Kupka, Karel 116–17

Lake Condah 12, 14, 15
Lake Mungo burials 7
Land Bilong Islanders (documentary) 177
land rights *see* Aboriginal land rights
Langton, Marcia 286
Langton-Batty, Ruby 63–4
language *see* Indigenous languages
language groups 65, 264
language rules (for visitors) 220
Lanne (husband of Truganini) 210–11
Laura Dance Festival 2, 3, 54, 147–8
Liberto, Pamela Yvonne and Ivan 125
listening to Country 22
Lloyd, Jessie 61–2, 138, 142
Loos, Noel 175
lore 264
Love-Johnson, Crystal 63
Lowe, Doug 195, 196
Lucashenko, Melissa 152, 156–7
Lui, Nakkiah 165–6

Mabo, Eddie Koiki 175, 177
Mabo case 3, 175–80, 182, 188
Mabuyag dialect 69
McCarthy, Malarndirri 50
McGuire, Eddie 227, 240
McKay, Roger 59
McKenna, Brenton 168
McLeod, Michael 204
McNiven, Ian 15
McNiven, Liz 135
makarrata 46, 264
Makarrata Commission 46, 48, 250
Mangolamara, Sylvester 8
Manikay 75, 122, 141, 264
Marawili, Baluka 115
Marawili, Djambawa 121, 122, 124
Marawili, Noŋgirrŋa Marawili 115
Mari Nawi (Big Canoe) 4
marriage rules 32, 79, 82
marrŋgitj (traditional healers) 104, 265
Martin, Anne 43, 44
massacres
of First Peoples 23, 25–6, 108, 195, 197, 200, 229, 231, 235
memorialisation 200
Mayo, Thomas 46, 48
medicine and healing, Traditional 72–3, 103–5
Meggitt, Mervyn 121
Melbourne, Indigenous tourism 4
Melbourne's LGBTQIA+ MIDSUMMA Festival 62
Mer dialect 69
Mer Island (Murray Island), Torres Strait 69, 135, 175
recognition of native title 175–80
Meriam Mir (language) 68–9
Meyne (self-portrait by Meyne Wyatt) 163–4
middens 19–21, 265

MIDSUMMA Festival 62
migration routes to Australia 7–8, 201
Miles Franklin Award 152, 154
Milirrpum v Nabalco 123, 187–8
mining companies
and business opportunities for Indigenous people 204–5
and native title 184–5
Miriwoong seasonal calendar 98, 99
'miscegenation' 189
Miss First Nation pageant 63–4
Mission Songs Project 142
missions/missionaries 31, 32, 34, 35, 36, 109, 122, 149, 150, 265
Mitchell, Ben 43, 44
Moffatt, Tracey 127
moieties 78, 81, 265
Mongagu, Ashley 237
Morrison, Scott 49
'mosaic' burns 94
Mother Country, Australians clinging to 248
Mowanjum Art and Cultural Centre 18
Muecke, Stephen 153
Mununggurr, Barayuwa 125
Murgha, Letitia 20
Murray Black Collection 199
Museum of Victoria 198
museums
and ancestral remains 198, 199
as 'memory institutions' 152
Musgrave, George 95
music 133, 245
first recorded Aboriginal songs 133–5
in Indigenous languages 75
Indigenous music and innovation today 141–5
Mission Songs Project 142
new anthem ('Treaty') 139–40
protecting traditional styles 137–8
Torres Strait Islander 136–7
Yolŋu musical tradition 75
see also song series or songlines
Myers, Fred 118

NAIDOC/NAIDOC Committee 41, 43, 48–9, 62, 265
NAIDOC Week
and burden of Australia's political history 41–4
celebrations 41–2
themes 42, 43–4
'Voice Treaty Truth' (2019 theme) 44, 46, 48–9
Namatjira, Albert 126
Namatjira, Vincent 126–7, 128
Narragunnawali 249
Ŋarritj 80–1
National Aboriginal and Torres Strait Islander Music Awards 76, 143
National Gallery of Australia 125
National Gallery of Victoria 128
National Inquiry into the Separation of Aboriginal and Torres Strait Island Children from their Families 189
National Museum of Australia 29
National Native Title Tribunal 186
National Reconciliation Convention 29
National Recording Project for Indigenous Performance in Australia 137
National Resting Place 200
National Sorry Day 191, 193
native title 9–10, 121, 174–88, 250, 264, 265
'bundle of rights' 178
claim process 182
consent determinations 185–6
extinguishment 179, 185, 188
'future acts' 183–5, 188
Mabo case 175–80, 182, 188
and mining companies 184–5

'past acts' 182–3
and property law 178–9
and the 'Ten Point Plan' 181, 182
Timber Creek case 187
and Traditional Owners ongoing connection with their land 179–80, 187–8
and Traditional Owners rights to negotiate 183–8
Wik decision 181
Yanner v Eaton 178, 179
Yorta Yorta case 180–1, 185
Native Title Act 1993 (Cth) 9, 178, 180–8
amendments 181–2, 186–7
and Indigenous Land Use Agreements 9–10, 182, 187, 263
Neath, Jessica 200
Needham, Rev. J. S. 231
Nelson, Paddy Jupurrula 120
Never Again 10
Ngaliwurru People 187
ngangkari (traditional healers) 104, 105, 265–6
language work to heal 72–4
Ngarinyin People 19
'Ngarra Burra Ferra' (song) 134–5
Ngarrindjeri People 153
Nichols, Roy 195, 196
Nielsen, Rasmus 201
No Fixed Address (band) 141, 245
Noongar Country seasonal calendar 99, 213
Norris, Ray 100
NPY Women's Council 72, 73
Nungali People 187
Nunn, Patrick 11

O'Dowd, Mary Frances 243
'Old People' (spiritual ancestors/ancestral remains) 55–6, 198–9, 200, 266
Olive, Mark 212, 213
Oliver, Steven 63
Olkolo People 184
on survival 31–5
oral histories 136, 168, 266
Ottoson, Åse 58
'out-of-Africa' thesis of migration 7, 201
OutBlack 62

Page, Stephen 147, 148
palawa People 195, 209–11
Pamagirri Dancers 5
Papunya art/Papunya Tula Artists Pty Ltd 117–19
Paradies, Yin 243
Parkes, Henry 27
Pascoe, Bruce 88, 157
Dark Emu: Black Seeds: Agriculture or Accident? and debate 11, 86–9, 105, 157
Loving Country: A Guide to Sacred Australia 157
Salt 157
pastoral stations/pastoral industry 31, 33–4
Pathways (search engine) 260
Payne, Anne Maree 235
Pearson, Luke 60–1, 154, 168
Pearson, Noel 30, 46, 244, 251
Pecan Summer (opera) 149–50
Pemulwuy 108
performance 133–50
and festivals 2, 3, 22, 37, 54, 147–8
opera 149–50
protecting traditional styles 137–8
see also dance; music
Perkins, Rachel 40, 171–2, 234, 235
Phillip, Governor Arthur 23, 107, 108, 179
photographs and videos 221
Pinikura People 9
Pintupi art movement 117–19
place names, change to original Indigenous names 65, 68, 257

plagiarism 153
poetry 160–1, 162–3
Polina, Mikka 62
Pratten, Anne 59
pre-colonial history 7–22
Pride marches 58, 59, 60
primary students, Wiradjuri language lessons 67
property law, and native title 178–9
public drunkenness, decriminalisation 253
Purcell, Leah 159–60, 169
Puutu Kunti Kurrama People 9
Pybus, Cassandra 210, 211

Queen's Birthday holidays 248
Queensland Coast Islands Declaratory Act 1985 176
questions which may not be welcome 219
Quilliam, Wayne 111
Quinkan rock-art galleries 2

Rabbit-Proof Fence (film) 84, 174
'race'
definition 228
meaning of 235–9
in national polity and politics 236–7
and what it means to be Australian 24–5, 27, 233
see also Aboriginal 'race'
race theory 237, 238–9
Racial Discrimination Act 1975 24, 176, 188, 229
racial hygiene 189, 229
racism/racial discrimination 24, 32–3, 37, 40, 44, 49, 208–9, 227–44
and Australia's dangerous fiction of race 233–4
can Australians overcome racism? 244
disempowering racism 242
and the 'dying race' 23–4, 229–31, 235
interpersonal racism 239–41
racism definition 228–9
racism in everyday life 241–2
stereotypes of Indigenous people and their origins 4, 5, 30, 106–9
systemic or institutional racism 243
and 'white privilege' 232–3
Rainbow KINection (radio program) 62
Ramo, Ziggy 143
rappers 144
ration system 28, 31, 36
reconciliation 29, 36, 45, 209, 248–9
Reconciliation Action Plans (RAP) 202–3, 249
Reconciliation Australia 30, 45, 202–3, 249, 257
Reconciliation Place 266
Red Room Poetry 163
Reece, Nicholas 248
referendum 266
1967 referendum 24, 27, 37–9
Voice to Parliament 49, 50–1, 250–1
Reid, Janice
Body, Land and Spirit: Health and Healing in Aboriginal Society 105, 106
Sorcerers and Healing Spirits: Continuity and Change in an Aboriginal Medical System 105
Reid, Nicholas 11
religious life *see* spiritual beliefs and rituals
Representation, Remembrance and the Memorial (RRM) 200
republicans 248, 266
reserves 31, 32, 34, 35, 36–7
Reynolds, Henry 175, 211, 234–5
Ridgeway, Aden 43
rightful place 36–53
rituals *see* spiritual beliefs and rituals
Roach, Archie 141, 145
Roadmap for Reconciliation 45
Roberts, Rhoda 202
rock art 2, 8, 10, 113–16, 148, 215, 220
Kimberley region 9, 17–19, 114–15

Roelands Village 213
Rowley, Charles 31, 230
Royal Commission into Aboriginal Deaths in Custody 29, 53, 106, 248, 252, 255
Royal Commission into National Natural Disaster Arrangements 88, 89–92
Rubuntja, Wenten 139
Rudd, Kevin 45, 174, 191, 192–3, 250
Ruhanen, Lisa 207, 208
Russell, Dug 204
Ryan, Lyndall 25, 211

sacred ancestral entities 17, 82
sacred designs 118
sacred objects and rituals 122, 198, 199
sacred paintings 122
sacred sites/places 17, 121, 225
　destruction 9–10
sacred world 55
safety signs 225–6
saltwater crocodiles 225, 226
Sapphires, The (film and song) 135, 173
Sawers, Melinda 240
Sayers, Andrew 116
'scientific racism' 109
scientists, Indigenous Australians collaborations with 6, 12
Scott, Kim 152, 155–6
sea country 121–2, 123–4
sea-level rising 11, 12
seasonal calendars and seasons 98–9, 213, 215, 266
segregation 35, 42, 202, 229, 246, 266
self-esteem of younger Indigenous Australians 4–5
Sentance, Nathan 152
Sentina, Maiko 126
shell middens 19–21, 265
Shoemaker, Adam 151–2, 153
Shukuroglou, Vicky 157
Sims, Paddy Japaljarri 120
'Sistergirls' 58, 62, 63
'skin names' 77, 80–1, 82–3, 267
slavery 232, 236
smallpox epidemic 108
Smith, William Ramsay 153
smoking rituals 56, 62
Social Darwinism 229
social order 267
social security benefits, exclusion from 33
Soft Sands 141
solar points 100–2
Soldier Settlement Scheme 40
Solis, Gabriel 134, 135
song series or 'songlines' 11, 55, 102, 267
sorcerers, Indigenous 106
South Australian Museum 120
species extinction 90–1
Spencer, Larry Jungarrayi 120
spiritual ancestors 55–6, 268
spiritual beliefs and rituals 55–6
　connection to Country 55–6, 187–8
　depicted in art 118
　fire and symbols of fire in 93–4
　in kinship relationships 81, 82, 122
　recorded in rock art, songs and ceremonies 55
　spiritual Old People 55, 56
　use of body paint in 147
Standard English 67
star maps 102–3
Steffensen, Victor
　Fire Country: How Indigenous Fire Management Could Help Save Australia 95
　learns about cultural burning from Awu-Laya Elders 95–7
Stella Award for women writers 152

Stewart, Dean 4
Stewart, Paddy Japaljarri 120
Stolen Generations 32, 36, 54, 174, 189–200, 213, 267
　apology as grounds for compensation 192
　and *Bringing Them Home* report 29, 190
　Howard rejects national apology to 45, 191
　Kevin Rudd's apology to 29, 45–6, 174, 191, 192–3
　significance of apology 193
　songs about 141
　as special instance of genocide 190–1
Stolen Generations Memorials 193–5
　Beinda Street, Bomaderry, NSW 194–5
　Phillip Creek Native Settlement, Manga Marda Waterhole Tennant Creek, NT 194
　Reilly Lane, Sydenham Green, Sydney, NSW 194
stories from ancestors 11–12
storytelling 151–74
　children's literature 167–8
　digital writing 168–9
　film and television storytellers 169–74
　graphic novels 168
　is culture 174
　poetry 162–3
　theatre, scriptwriting, plays and stage production 163–7
　writers 153–62
Sultan, Dan 143
sunset 75–6
Supply Nation 204–5
Sutton, Peter and Walshe, Kerryn, *Farmers or Hunter-Gatherers? The Dark Emu Debate* 88, 89
Sydney Gay and Lesbian Mardi Gras 59–61
Sydney Harbour
　bicentennial celebrations (1988) 245
　cultural cruises 4
　January 26 protests 245–6
systemic racism 243

taboos 56
Tapsell, Miranda 62
Tasmanian Aboriginal People 195–7, 209–11
Tasmanian Aboriginal songs 133–4
Ten Canoes (film) 75
terra nullius 121, 175–6, 177, 187, 267
theatre, scriptwriting, plays and stage production 159–60, 164–7
Thomson, Donald 40
Thornton, Warwick 172–3
3 Rivers Festival 22
Tieman, Petina 203
Timber Creek case 187
Tjakamarra, Long Jack Phillipus 118
Tjapaltjarri, Billy Stockman 117
Tjukurrpa 55, 267
Torres Strait Creole 68, 69
Torres Strait Islander flag 41, 257
Torres Strait Islander people 1, 260, 267–8
　astronomical and traditional knowledge 100–2
　dance, songs and music 135–7
　kinship systems 77
　languages 68–9
totems 11, 268
tourism *see* Indigenous tourism
trackers 84, 85
traditional 268
traditional Indigenous knowledge, importance of learning 11–12
Traditional medicine and healing 103–5
　books about 105
　language work of ngankari to heal 72–4
Traditional Owner(s) 1, 3, 56, 62, 91, 95, 126, 175, 179, 215, 268

archaeologists working with 10
forced off their land 17, 28, 37, 179
and Indigenous Land Use Agreements 9–10, 182, 187, 263
ongoing connection with their land and native title 179–80, 187–8
rights and protocols over activities on their land 221–6
rights to negotiate over native title 183–8
stories from ancestors 11–12
to maintain natural and cultural heritage 12, 17
'Treaty' (new anthem) 139–40
treaty and treaty rights 42, 44, 45, 49, 139, 249–50
Trevorrow, Bruce 192
Trials (rapper) 144
Truganini (Neunonne woman) 195–7, 210
'truth-telling about our history' (to acknowledge Australia's treatment of First Peoples) 46, 48, 250

'Uluṟu Statement from the Heart' 46, 47–8, 53, 139, 249, 250
Uluṟu–Kata Tjuta National Park Board of Management 223
ban on climbing Uluṟu 223–4
Umbagai, Leah 18
UN education program to reduce race prejudice 237–8
Unaipon, David 153–4
UNESCO World Heritage Listing 12, 13, 14
United Nations Declaration on the Rights of Indigenous Peoples 67, 70–1
University of Melbourne 198, 199
'urban' Indigenous people 4, 34–5
Us Mob (band) 141, 245
Uti Kulintjaku Project 73, 74

van Neerven, Ellen 160
vegetation patterns and land management 10–11, 85–9
Veth, Peter 17
Victorian Aboriginal Heritage Council 198, 199, 239
Voice to Parliament for First Nations peoples, constitutional recognition of 45–53, 250, 256
Design Principles for a Voice to Parliament 51–2
importance of 48
and NAIDOC Committee's 'Voice Treaty Truth' 48–9
outcome of a No vote 52
outcome of a Yes vote 52–3
proposed addition to Constitution 51
proposed referendum question 51
referendum 49, 50–1, 250–1
Referendum groups 50–1
Senior Advisory Group report on 'Voice to Government' 49–50
to create conditions to end racism 244
and 'Uluṟu Statement from the Heart' 46–8, 53, 250
'Voice Treaty Truth' 44, 46, 48–9, 143, 249
von Guérard, Eugene 16

Walk for Reconciliation 191
Wallace, Allen 195
Waŋarr 268
Wanjina/Wandjina 17–19, 114–15, 268
war service 40–1
Warlpiri People
art style 119–20
skin systems 82
Warlukurlangu Artists (co-operative) 119, 121
Warumpi Band 141
Watego, Chelsea 168–9
water blessing rituals 56

'We Have Survived' Festival (26 January) 245
weather and seasons knowledge 98–9, 100
Welcome to Country (online site) 202
'Welcome to Country' ceremonies 30, 55, 56, 268
Wentworth, William (Bill) 66
West, Aunty Ida 195–6
Western Desert acrylic art movement 118
white Australia policy 23–6, 233
white corella of Galiwin'ku 80
'white privilege' 232–3
Whiteland, Josh 'Koomal' 212, 213
Whitlam, Gough 24, 28–9
Wik case 181
Wilson, Sir Ronald 189, 190
Wilson, Sammy 223
Winch, Tara June 162–3
Windham Campbell Prize for poetry 152
Wiradjuri language 67
Woodward, Justice Edward 29, 121
workforce 32, 33
see also indentured labour
World War II, Indigenous Australians service during 40, 41
WorldPride 60
Worrorra people 19
Wright, Alexis 152, 158
Wunambal Gaambera people 8, 19
Wyatt, Ken 49, 250–1
Wyatt, Meyne 163–5

Yabun Festival 27, 245–6
Yagun Gulinj Wiinj (How Man Found Fire) (video) 93
yidaki (didgeridoo) 125, 138, 268
Yirritja (saltwater crocodile) 81, 82, 122
Yirrkala Bark Petitions 123
Yirrkala missionaries 122
Yolŋu matha languages 75, 138, 143, 145
Yolŋu People
art and Country 121–4
art and law 123–4
art traditions 116–17, 121–2
bush medicine 105
clan groupings 81–2
Dhuwa and Yirritja 81, 82, 122
Garma Festival 55, 131, 213–14, 221–3, 224
gurrutu (kinship) 81–3
kinship system 81–3, 122
land and sea rights 121–2, 123–4
musical tradition 75
native title case 121
right to exist and be recognised in the Constitution 250
Yorta Yorta case 179, 180–1, 185
Yorta Yorta People 149, 150, 180, 181
Yothu Yindi (band) 75, 139, 141
yothu–yindi (child–mother link) 81, 82–3, 122
Yothu Yindi Foundation (YYF) 214
Yuendumu school, art painted on doors 119–20
Yunupiŋu, Galarrwuy 250
Yunupiŋu, Gurrumul, tribute to 144–5
Yunupiŋu, Dr Mandawuy 76, 139, 140

About the author

Professor Marcia Langton AO PhD Macq U, BA (Hons) ANU, FASSA is one of Australia's most important voices for Indigenous Australia. As an anthropologist and geographer, she has made a significant contribution to government and non-government policy as well as to Indigenous studies, native title and resource management, art and culture, and women's rights. Professor Langton has held the Foundation Chair of Australian Indigenous Studies at the University of Melbourne since February 2000. In 2016, she was honoured as a Redmand Barry Distinguished Professor, and was then appointed as the first Associate Provost at the University of Melbourne in 2017. She has received many other accolades, including the Officer of the Order of Australia award in 2020.

Much of the content in this publication was published *Marcia Langton: Welcome to Country 2nd ed* (2021), where full acknowledgements for individual contributions appear.

This edition published in 2023 by Hardie Grant Explore, an imprint of Hardie Grant Publishing.

Hardie Grant Explore (Melbourne)
Wurundjeri Country
Building 1, 658 Church Street
Richmond, Victoria 3121

Hardie Grant Explore (Sydney)
Gadigal Country
Level 7, 45 Jones Street
Ultimo, NSW 2007

www.hardiegrant.com/au/explore

All rights reserved. No part of this publication may be reproduced, stored in a retrieval system or transmitted in any form by any means, electronic, mechanical, photocopying, recording or otherwise, without the prior written permission of the publishers and copyright holders.

The moral rights of the author have been asserted.

Copyright text © Marcia Langton 2023
Copyright concept and design © Hardie Grant Publishing 2023

 A catalogue record for this book is available from the National Library of Australia

Hardie Grant acknowledges the Traditional Owners of the Country on which we work, the Wurundjeri People of the Kulin Nation and the Gadigal People of the Eora Nation, and recognises their continuing connection to the land, waters and culture. We pay our respects to their Elders past and present.

For all relevant publications, Hardie Grant Explore commissions a First Nations consultant to review relevant content and provide feedback to ensure suitable language and information is included in the final book. Hardie Grant Explore also includes traditional place names and acknowledges Traditional Owners, where possible, in both the text and mapping for their publications.

Traditional place names are included in *palawa kani*, the language of Tasmanian Aboriginal People, with thanks to the Tasmanian Aboriginal Centre.

The Welcome to Country Handbook
ISBN 9781741178227

10 9 8 7 6 5 4

Publisher
Melissa Kayser
Project editor
Amanda Louey
Editor
Julianne Schultz
Proofreader
Rosanna Dutson
Design
Pfisterer + Freeman

Typesetting
Kerry Cooke
Mike Kuszla
Index
Max McMaster
Production coordinator
Simone Wall

Colour reproduction by Splitting Image Colour Studio

Cover artwork: *Antara* © Betty Kuntiwa Pumani / Licensed by Copyright Agency, 2023. Image courtesy the artists, Mimili Maku Arts and Alcaston Gallery

Betty Kuntiwa Pumani paints at Mimili Maku Arts, an Anangu-owned contemporary art centre on the Anangu Pitjantjatjara Yankunytjatjara (APY) Lands. Betty's mother was one of the founding members of the art centre, and today Betty is an award-winning artist who works in the Mimili studio alongside her daughter.

Printed in Australia by Opus Group Pty Ltd, an Accredited ISO AS/NZS 14001 Environmental Management System printer.

 The paper this book is printed on is certified against the Forest Stewardship Council® Standards. Griffin Press – a member of the Opus Group – holds chain of custody certification SCS-COC-001185. FSC® promotes environmentally responsible, socially beneficial and economically viable management of the world's forests.